Living on a Hill

by

Lewis Lawrence Houde

PublishAmerica
Baltimore

© 2005 by Lewis Lawrence Houde.
All rights reserved. No part of this book may be reproduced, stored in a retrieval system or transmitted in any form or by any means without the prior written permission of the publishers, except by a reviewer who may quote brief passages in a review to be printed in a newspaper, magazine or journal.

At the specific preference of the author, PublishAmerica allowed this work to remain exactly as the author intended, verbatim, without editorial input.

First printing

ISBN: 1-4137-7317-6
PUBLISHED BY PUBLISHAMERICA, LLLP
www.publishamerica.com
Baltimore

Printed in the United States of America

This book is dedicated to my parents,
Joseph and Delma Houde

Acknowledgements

I would like to express my thanks to all the old timers and neighbors who played a part in molding my life.

I thank my wife for putting up with me while I tried to learn to type and for her patience while I put this story into words.

Without the skills of my son, Ed and his wife Sharon, this book would not have been possible and to them I owe my sincere thanks. I also thank my friend, Albert Stark for his photographic skills.

And most of all I thank the Lord for letting me live this story.

Joe Houde in His Cowboy Years

Chapter 1
Born of the Land

The tears freeze on my cheeks as I look down at the snow-covered trees in the Valley below. *How will I ever be able to leave this place that I love with all my heart?*

I have to pick up all the traps that I set a month ago. I find it very hard to concentrate on the job at hand. Why did they have to come home and tell me that we have to leave? The pain in my chest is almost more than I can stand. Maybe I'll be lucky and have a heart attack. Right now it would be the most merciful thing that could happen to me. *Jesus take me right now and get this pain over with.*

Why do we have to move? It's something that I simply cannot comprehend. I keep thinking that there must be some gross mistake, some terrible joke that my folks are playing on me. Maybe I'm sleeping and all this is just a bad dream. I hope that I wake up soon. This whole crazy thing is killing me.

Yesterday, Ma and Pa came home with the news that we have to leave this old homestead and move into town. Pa said that they already sold the cattle and that the guy would be coming to get them in a few days. Then they said that we would move in two weeks if everything goes right. How can anything this wrong, go right?

As I pick up my traps, I remember all the good times that I've had at this old place. With blurred vision, I look at all the places where I've spent all of my life. Places where I've had the happiest times of my life. Dusk settles in ever darkening layers as I pick up my last trap. Snow falls silently as day gives way to night. I sit on a snow-covered log and as if in slow motion, memories of my life here flood my mind.

The silence is broken by the gliding sound of near silent wings. Like a ghost, a large snowy owl swoops through the trees and helps himself to a snowshoe rabbit, that I hadn't even seen sitting in the snow. I don't feel the cold creeping in on me as I watch this event of nature unfold and I reflect on the past. I wonder how I could ever explain to someone how I feel about this place that has captured my very soul. This is the homestead where I was born and have lived and loved all the twelve short years of my life.

For me, life began here November 15, 1933. It was 2:00 a.m. when Ma shook my Pa awake. "Joe, wake up, the baby is coming."

"It can't be, it's a month too soon," Pa said as he rubbed his eyes.

"Tell that to the baby, but in the meantime get Alf to go and get Mrs. Gammon."

Alfred was the eldest son and Pa got him out of his nice warm bed. He dressed warmly and set out on foot the six-mile trip to Gammon's. Not a nice trip in the pitch dark with a blizzard blowing and the mercury at 30 degrees below zero. It sure wasn't something he was happy about.

The little log cabin was doing a good job of keeping the storm out and everyone inside warm and cozy, so in this quiet environment, I was introduced to this world. My Pa ushered me in and kept passing out. He spent most of the time sitting on the floor. With a short easy labor, my mother was able to handle most of it herself with Pa helping, when he wasn't passed out. My sister Helen heard me crying in the night and asked Ma if the cat was all right.

"Everything is fine, go back to sleep," Ma told her.

When morning arrived both Helen and my other brother, Francis, were quite thrilled and surprised to find that they had a new five-pound baby brother. Helen thought that I was so sweet that she bit my toe. I'll bet that she wouldn't want to do that now. My poor brother had braved the elements and arrived with Mrs. Gammon around six in the morning. Gammons had a team of horses and a sleigh so the trip back was a little easier than the trip there and the storm had blown itself out but the temperature was still 30 below.

Mrs. Gammon stayed with Ma for a couple of days to help her out with the house and me. Once she was sure Ma was fine and could look after me Mrs. Gammon headed home again.

The depression was at its worst and the last thing that my parents needed was another mouth to feed and another bare butt to cover. We were six, seven when Uncle Fred was home. There was Joe and Delma, my parents, my two brothers, Alfred and Francis, my sister, Helen and me. They named me Lewis, after my grandfather on my Ma's side of the family. Uncle Fred was Pa's bachelor brother who seemed to follow Pa around. I guess Pa's family was his family and we all loved him.

My family moved to this homestead in northern Alberta in the spring of 1930. They came here from Dryden, Ontario because of Francis. He had developed serious lung problems and the doctor said that they had to get to a drier climate and away from the fumes of the pulp mill. They liked what they had heard of the Peace River country, so in the spring of that year they took what they could and moved. There could be a book written about that adventure alone, but that's another story.

Shortly before they left Dryden, Francis had been very sick. The Priest actually came to give him the last rites and the doctor said that it was just a matter of hours. Ma was very religious and she knelt down and prayed for him. They had already lost their oldest son, Henry, to pneumonia and now they were faced with losing another. As Ma prayed the priest placed the host on Francis's tongue. "This is the body of Christ," the Priest told him.

"I can't see him," Francis whispered.

The priest left and Ma covered his little body. "Go to sleep now son." Ma said through the tears. About an hour later he woke up and he had a funny feeling in his chest.

"Sit me up, Ma," he called, and as she helped him up he heaved out a huge bunch of greenish black stuff. It flew halfway across the room. He breathed deeply, something that he hadn't been able to do in years. Ma laid him down again and cleaned up the mess. She didn't know what to think of this. An hour later he wanted food. Ma fed him and he wanted more. For the next few days she could hardly fill him up. He was feeling much better and was getting stronger. Their move was already set up, so they went ahead with it hoping that the dry fresh air of Alberta would help him to recover and it did. Is it any wonder that Francis believes in miracles and prayer?

Homesteading was not new to my parents. My father was born and raised on a logged-over old farm close to the little town of Turtle Lake, Wisconsin. Pa called it a stump ranch. When he was fifteen, he went with a neighbor, a man named Timothy Landeau, to Saskatchewan. The Canadian prairies had been open to homesteaders and Mr. Landeau took some land not far from Swift Current. Railroad regulations stated that every boxcar of livestock required someone to ride with it so Pa went with a boxcar full of cattle.

Pa liked it there and so he took a homestead close to Mr. Landeau. There was a big ranch close by named the Matador Ranch. Pa got a job there working as a cowboy. The ranch covered a large area and had over five thousand head of cattle. While he worked there he was one of the cowboys that rounded up over four hundred head of buffalo. They were the few stragglers left from the millions of buffalo that once roamed the plains and they were the forefathers of all the buffalo in the world today.

At about the same time, my mother's folks, Delma and Louis Mingo, and their family moved to the same area. They were from St. Cloud, Minnesota. Grandpa Mingo was a fairly well off farmer for those days. He bought a big steam tractor and a twelve-bottom plow and started plowing up the prairie. In the fall of the second year he bought a threshing outfit and Pa got a job as fireman on the steamer.

This was where Pa met my mother. He started courting her and escorted her to dances when her parents would allow it, she was only fifteen. Ma liked to tell a story about when Pa was courting her. He had a great little saddle horse named Cheyenne. One day as he was leaving he wanted to show off a little. With a little tug on the reins, Cheyenne would rear up on his hind feet in quite a dramatic fashion. Cheyenne was feeling his oats that day and had a little bucking fit. Pa hit the ground rather hard and, a little more than red faced, he caught his horse and went home.

In 1913 they were married, Pa was twenty and Ma had just turned sixteen. They went to live in Minneapolis for a while where Pa got a job as a motorman on the streetcars. He soon found a gym where the boxers trained and as he always liked a good fight, he spent a lot of his spare time there. He got to know some of them and before long he was in the ring as a sparring partner. This was evening work and I don't know if he was paid anything at all, but he loved it. Ma didn't love it at all, staying home alone while he sparred and drank a little beer. Ma wanted to go back home and by the time that they did, Pa was a pretty tough guy to tangle with.

Their first child, Henry, was born in 1915 and died of pneumonia at eighteen months old. They were broken hearted. Their second child, Alfred, was born shortly after, in 1917. Francis came along in 1922 and they moved to Dryden, Ontario where Helen was born in 1924. They lived in Dryden until 1930 when they moved to the Peace River country. And that's where they had me!

Our homestead is really out in the woods. It's three miles from the Alberta / B.C. border, on the Alberta side. Our nearest store and post office is at Tupper Creek, B.C., four miles as the crow flies and across Swan Lake. If the crow has to walk around the lake, it's seven miles.

Like all the homesteaders in the area, we are only one jump ahead of starvation most of the time. There is no work and no money, the only way to get money is by trapping and fur prices are at an all time low. Besides that, the man that owns the store is also the fur buyer. He raises the prices of his store goods and pays people half of what their fur is worth. Nearly every homesteader in the area owes him money for a grocery bill. With him exploiting them, they would never catch up.

He also owns a ranch at the south end of the lake. In the spring of 1935, our family moved to the ranch to work off the grocery bill. Ma cooked and Pa and Alfred worked on the ranch. This was where my memories begin. There was a terrible flood that spring and all the low areas around the lake were covered with water. As the water rose, the ranch house and barns became deep in water. I can remember sitting on the table in the kitchen as the water splashed up on it. Someone came with a boat and took us to safety.

As we rowed away we went right over a bridge where a creek ran into the lake. We could see the railing just barely sticking out of the water. A sow pig with about ten little piglets swam towards higher ground. As they swam across where the creek was they got caught in an undercurrent and they all disappeared under the water. A minute or so later, they all popped up like corks on the other side of the bridge, all still swimming.

Chapter 2
Cabin in the Pines

In 1936, the homesteaders all got together and built a log schoolhouse in Independent Valley. The valley had been settled quite well and there were enough children for a school. There had to be at least twelve children before the school board would send in a teacher. The only trouble for our family was that we didn't live in that valley. There was a big hill between the valley where we live and the one where the school was built. It was just too far for the kids to go.

The solution to the problem was to move closer to the school. Alf was old enough to register for a homestead, which he did, right on top of the hill. There was a nice stand of pine and that was where they built our new log cabin. It was winter when we moved there, and the snow was deep. We had an old gray mare called "Bird." I think that she was called that because she was so flighty. When you were riding her, the slightest rustle in the bush would cause her to jump straight sideways, leaving you sitting where she had been.

They made a few trips with Bird and a stone boat to move our belongings. A stone boat is like a small sleigh and we use it for hauling things around in the summer months. On the final trip Ma and I went along. I was scared as hell. They put the kitchen table upside down on the stone boat and, wrapped up in a quilt, I sat in the middle of it. When you're my size and you sit that low down behind a horse, they look really big. *What if she should step back, she would step right on top of me*, I thought. She didn't step back and we arrived in about an hour.

It is in this new cabin on the hill that my story really begins. This was where I was old enough to start clearly remembering things. Right from the start, this little cabin became home. It was only about sixteen feet wide by twenty-four feet long, but to me it was a castle. I have never felt so safe or so at home anywhere I have been since.

I have to lay a little groundwork for this story so that it makes some sense. Most of the things that happen to me are not from trying to be bad but are caused by three things. Number one is that I have an insatiable curiosity; I just have to know what will happen. Number two is that I have ignorant innocence meaning I believe everything that I see and hear. This causes me no end of problems. Number three is I have just too much ambition. I believe that I should be able to do or make anything. I just have to find out how and failures never discourage me, I just try again. I have come to understand that these three attributes could get a kid killed.

Nearly all the kids at this time and place were trained to exist in the woods. We all carried matches and knew how to make a fire in case we got lost or too cold. We were taught to get dry branches, in close under a spruce tree and how to get the thin paper bark from a birch tree to use to start a fire. These things were normal for five-year-old kids. I hunted grouse, rabbits and squirrels with a little .22 rifle at that age.

One of my friends, Jimmy Gunter, shot a big coyote when he was only six. The coyote was sneaking up on their sheep and Jimmy saw it. He quietly went to the house and got the rifle. That coyote became part of somebody's coat somewhere. Of course Jimmy was the talk of the area and the envy of the rest of us for a while.

I had my fifteen minutes of fame with the help of a big chicken hawk. Hawks were always after our chickens so the rifle was always kept loaded and close to the door. One evening as we were eating supper we heard the hens putting up a ruckus. I was the first one out the door with the rifle to find a big hawk with a nice fat hen in his talons trying to take off with her. I planted a little piece of lead right in his butt. He dropped the hen and crashed headfirst into the side of the barn. The hen was a little ruffled but not seriously hurt and walked away rather indignantly. Shooting that hawk in the air made me a hero for a couple of days but then it was history.

Helen and Francis were going to the new school and I wanted to go with them, but I was too little. Ma taught me the ABCs and how to count. I looked at Helen's reader and it had some good pictures in it. One picture got me really excited. It was a picture of Puss 'n Boots. The way that cat could walk across oceans in those seven league boots was awesome. I wanted a pair of boots like that.

I was after Ma and Pa for a pair of rubber boots for weeks and lo and behold, they came home one day with a little pair of boots. They were beautiful, shiny black with red soles with little bumps all over them. It was early spring and there were puddles all over the yard so I put on my new boots and ran outside. Everyone was watching to see me jump in the puddles and have a lot of fun. However I had bigger plans for those babies. I was going to give them the ultimate test.

Last fall they started to dig a new well and it was about four feet square and six feet deep and, of course, it was plumb full of water. My plan was to test those boots out by walking across the well. Well, it turned out those damn boots were no good at all and I sunk like a stone. Luckily for me, Alf was watching, he ran out and as I came up for the third time he grabbed me by the collar and fished me out. He carried me to the house at arms length. I was soaking wet and really mad.

As Ma dried me off and changed my clothes she chewed me out real good. "You silly little twit, what are you trying to do, drown yourself?"

"But it's the boots, Ma, they are no good, you have to take them back."

"What do you mean, they're no good," Ma asked.

They just didn't understand. I ran and got Helen's reader and showed them the pictures of the cat and the boots. "See, he can walk on water with his boots, mine must be no good!"

"That's just a story," Ma said, "its not a true story, it's like Little Red Riding Hood."

"That's not true either? Why do they write all this stuff if it's a lie?" I just didn't understand it.

"It's just a story," Ma told me "there aren't any boots you can walk on water with." Well, that was a fine time to tell me after I bloody near drowned myself!

Later in the spring Alf went to work for a farmer named Charlie Weaver down by Grande Prairie. The pay wasn't much but every little bit helped. After he was there a few days he discovered that the root cellar was still half full of potatoes. We hadn't had any potatoes at home for months. Alf told Mr. Weaver that we had no potatoes at home and asked if he could buy a couple of bags. Mr. Weaver gave him two bags and advanced him the two dollars that it cost to send them on the train.

Alf wrote a letter home to tell Pa when the potatoes would arrive. As there was no station agent, Pa had to meet the train to pick them up. If he didn't it was a sure bet that somebody else would. So on the scheduled day Pa took old Bird to meet the train. Sure enough, the potatoes were there. He tied them on Bird, a bag on each side and headed for home. Of course he had to walk and lead her because the spuds were already quite a load for her.

When he came to the bridge where the Pouce Coupe River runs out of Swan Lake he came upon an Indian camp. They were snaring big black suckerfish as they went up river to spawn. Pa stopped and talked to them and they wanted to know what he had in the bags. When he told them that he had potatoes their eyes lit up. "Would you trade some potatoes for some fish?" We hadn't had fish for a long time either so it sounded like a good trade. Pa traded about twenty pounds of potatoes for a sack full of fish. Pa arrived home around three that afternoon with his precious cargo.

Ma said that we couldn't wait any longer to have a good meal. She peeled a big pot of potatoes and the rest of us cleaned some fish. Oh what a feast we had! Fluffy white potatoes, a platter of golden brown fried fish and as a special treat Ma made a bread pudding with nutmeg and a little brown sugar. How great it was to have a wonderful meal like that. We always seem to have enough to eat but the variety is not always the best. No one ever complains about the meals though, we're all just glad to have a bellyful.

Pa and my brothers cleared a little piece of land and planted it in wheat. The seed was broadcast by hand after the ground was plowed. When the wheat was ripe, Pa cut it with a scythe. They raked it up with a homemade rake and then they flailed it out on a tarp. After it was all flailed out they winnowed it to separate the grain from the chaff. This was our porridge. Ma had to wash some of the wheat and then soak it for a day to soften it up. After a couple hours of boiling it was ready for breakfast.

One afternoon Ma and I walked over to Sullivan's place. It's about a two-mile walk and Ma wanted to see Mrs. Sullivan about something. They visited for a while but soon it was time to go home. As we were getting ready to go I whispered to Ma, "I'm hungry." Ma gave me the look. You know the one that makes you shrink down to nothing. I had been told before we got there, not to ask for anything to eat. But there were big loaves of fresh baked bread on the cupboard and I'd risk getting a licking for a piece of it. Of course I whispered loud enough for Mrs. Sullivan to hear me, at least I hoped that I had.

She was a nice kind little woman and they are as poor as we are but sharing is a given in these days. "Oh yes, wait and I'll get the lad a piece of bread." She cut a big thick slice and put a good smear of lard on it. Then came the treat, she sprinkled a pinch of sugar on it! I thanked her and munched happily on my bread half of the way home. The crust was burned a quarter of an inch thick and the bread itself was heavy but it was the best piece of bread that I've ever had. Thank you Mrs. Sullivan!

Chapter 3
Mounties and Hard Work

It was early summer and Alf was home from working at Weavers. However Mr. Weaver couldn't pay him until after harvest time and he sold some grain. So Alf caught a ride to Tupper from Grande Prairie in Ed Anderson's freight truck.

Another mouth to feed and no money! Pa told Alf that we were out of meat and that there were no shells for the rifle. "How about asking for some on credit at the store?" Alf asked Pa.

"No damn way," Pa said, "I don't want to be beholding to that guy anymore."

"Why don't you go for relief like everyone else does," Ma interjected.

"God, I don't want to go asking for a handout," Pa told her.

"Well how about swallowing your pride before we all starve to death," said Ma.

"Okay, I'll go to Hythe tomorrow and ask the Mounties about some shells."

Pa left early the next day and walked through the bush to where the railroad went through a rock cut. The freight goes pretty slow there and Pa caught one to take him the thirty miles to Hythe.

Sergeant Rivers was the Mountie in charge of government assistance. "What do you want?" he asked Pa. Pa told him that we were out of meat and we needed a little help. "You should be ashamed of yourself, a healthy man like you begging for help. Why don't you go shoot a moose to feed your family instead of bothering me?"

Pa lost it right there. "It's because I don't have any bullets, you smart ass son of a bitch. Take off that goddamn hat and jacket and I'll knock your frigging head off!"

"Oh, don't have a shit fit," the Sergeant told Pa, "Jesus, you guys are really touchy." He handed Pa a slip of paper and told him to take it to Oakford's store and they would give him some shells. "Don't let me see you around here again," he told Pa.

"You sure as hell won't," Pa replied as he went for the shells.

It was dark and late when Pa got home and put the shells on the table. "How did it go?" Ma wanted to know.

"I won't ever ask any man for help again, it's just too damn humiliating." So, tired, hungry and dejected, Pa had a cup of tea and went to bed. In the morning over breakfast, Pa told his story to us all. Ma had tears in her eyes because she knew how hard it had been for him to ask for help. Alf sat there and shook his head, "I'd sure like to find that bastard in a fix sometime, maybe he wouldn't feel so damn superior." Ma said to just forgive him because he didn't know any better.

That night Pa and Alf went to the moose lick. That's a place where there's a spring and the water trickles out on the salt and mineral encrusted ground. The moose come at night to drink and lick the ground. They came home in the morning with a fresh moose liver and high spirits. After breakfast they took old Bird and the stone boat and went to get the rest of the meat. Oh what a feed of fried liver we had for supper that night!

The weather was warm and the meat wouldn't keep very long so Alf went to the neighbors to see if they needed meat. They did, and they came over and got some. They were glad as well because it had been a while since they had meat. The rest had to be taken care of quickly. Some was cut up and salted down in a twenty-five-gallon barrel, some was cut into strips and smoked for jerky. The rest was sliced thin, fried and put into any clean can or jar we could find and covered with melted tallow. When it's put in a cool place it will keep for a long time like that.

It was a busy summer. There was a barn to be built along with a lot of other buildings. There was no money but the logs were free for the cutting.

Pa had made a deal with Mr. Finlay for some little chicks.

The Finlays are nice, hard working religious people. They have a son named Tom about the same age as Francis. They too are very poor but they have an incubator. It is quite an old primitive device that hatches four dozen chicks at a time. The temperature is somehow, controlled by a kerosene lamp.

So Pa built a little chicken coop and soon we were nursemaids to a bunch of fuzzy baby chicks. I thought that they were just the neatest little things that I had ever seen, but I soon found out that they are quite fragile and that you cannot pick them up by the necks. When you put them down they seem to be dead! After I looked at two of them, I was not allowed to pick them up any more.

The next log structure they built was an icehouse. We didn't have any good drinking water close to home and it had to be hauled from a spring a couple of miles away. The icehouse would be filled with ice cut from the lake in the middle of winter. It would then be covered with a layer of snow and about two feet of sawdust. This way we not only would have drinking water all year long but it would be quite cold in the building as well and it would serve as a cold storage unit.

Fall had arrived, the buildings were built and the winter wood was cut and stacked. The blueberries, raspberries and Saskatoon berries were ripe and ready for picking. We picked all we could and Ma canned them. There was no sugar so she canned them without, hoping that there would be some when the time came to eat them. Sometimes we had sugar and sometimes we didn't, but we ate them anyway. They cleared and spaded up a garden spot for next year. New soil isn't very good for a garden but when it's spaded up the winter frost breaks it up and it sort of composts itself. It wouldn't be great next year but it would be better than no garden at all.

Pa and Alf went down to Grande Prairie for harvesting. In a good fall they would bring home about thirty dollars each. That would help buy the winters essentials: tea, coffee, salt, sugar and flour. If there was enough money left maybe they would buy a pail of Rogers Golden Syrup. What a treat that was! *Thick as molasses and as golden as its name suggests.* Of course after a little taste it was diluted down two to one with water. That made it go a lot farther.

Fall and Indian summer were wonderful times of the year. The birch and poplar trees made a yellow background for the bright red cranberry bushes. The sky was as blue as the water in the creek that was so still in little pools. The reflection of the clouds made it look like the clouds themselves were floating on the water. The leaves had fallen off the low bush blueberries, but the berries stuck to the bushes as if they didn't want to let go. I liked it like that because it made the berries easy to pick. The partridges liked them that way too, and we liked the partridges, they tasted very good fried up nice and brown. They made a nice addition to our diet.

Ma saved a lot of tallow and it was time to make some soap. I liked it when she did this and sometimes I helped a little. She took an old pail with holes in the bottom and filled it with ashes. Then she poured water on the ashes until it came out the holes in the bottom. Lye water then leached out of the ashes. She made a fire outside and put a big kettle over it. She put the tallow and the lye water in the kettle and boiled it for a long time. When it was done boiling she poured it in a shallow box and let it cool. After it cooled she marked it into squares with a knife. I wanted to do this but she said that I was too little. Then she cut it deeper and soon she took it out in bars. This was the laundry soap that she rubbed on the clothes as she scrubbed them on the scrub board. Ma and us kids picked a big bunch of petals from the wild roses and she soaked them in water. She strained off the water and it smelled just like roses. She made another batch of soap with less lye in it and added the rose water. It made a nice-smelling hand and face soap.

The nights got colder and the days got shorter. Long Vs of ducks and geese were heading south and the cold north wind blew the few remaining leaves from the trees. We saw a few rabbits and they had already started to change color from brown to white. They looked kind of funny that way, sort of half and half. In the morning there was a skiff of ice on the creek and the fire in the cook stove felt good. It was cold on the bare feet and it soon would be time to get the moccasins out. Ma had made me a pair from an old pair of Pa's.

I was playing in the yard one day and our old dog started to bark. I went around the corner of the cabin and saw five Indians coming on horseback. They came galloping into the yard and they scared the hell out of me. They were wearing black hats with feathers in the brims. It was pretty cold and they had blankets around their shoulders. They had Winchester rifles in their scabbards and the back stock on some of them were decorated with shiny brass tacks. They looked pretty fierce and noble sitting up on those horses.

Ma came out to talk to them and I was quite surprised to find that they were friendly. They told her that they were looking for moose hides that they could tan and their women could sew into moccasins and jackets. Ma asked them if they were cold and would like to have a cup of tea. The one who did all the talking told her "No, we go now." They spun their horses around and in an instant they disappeared into the bush.

Pa and Alf returned from harvesting and the money was soon spent on some badly needed supplies for winter. It was good to have them home again. After a couple of days of rest they started preparing for a season of trapping. They got the traps out and checked them all over. Then they made a fire with spruce branches and held the traps over the smoke. It made them all shiny-looking and Pa said that it took the smell of people off of them. He said not to touch them with your bare hands, only with mitts on to keep the scent off.

They got out the bait that they made last summer and checked it out. Boy did it ever smell bad! I wondered why any animal would want to eat that stuff. They put their traps in a gunnysack and set out on the trap line, setting them in the best places to catch animals.

I sometimes wonder if it is a nice thing to do, catching these animals just for the fur. I asked Pa about it once and he said that he didn't know but that we had to do it if we wanted to eat. Somehow it doesn't seem so bad when he puts it that way. I guess that it is our way of life.

Chapter 4
Trapping and Switches

The air got colder and the big purple-gray clouds came rolling down from the north. We woke in the morning to a world covered in a thick blanket of cold white snow. I couldn't wait until after breakfast to get out and play in it. I didn't have much for winter clothes but Ma fixed me up with some hand-me-downs and I went out to play. Helen and Francis went off to school and Pa and Alf did the chores and headed out on their trap line. Winter had set in early and the cold weather had helped the animals' fur to prime up early as well.

Pa and Alf had a trap line and Helen and Francis had a little trap line of their own on the way to school. I was the only one without a trap line. Well, every log cabin had mice and we had mousetraps so I decided to make a trap line of my own. I had a little jack knife and every time I caught a mouse I skinned him out and stretched the skin on a stick. Mice are pretty hard to skin because they are so small but if you're careful it all works out. I had gotten my trap line and I was pretty happy until Ma found out about it.

"My God, what are you doing?" Ma asked.

"Skinning a mouse, Ma."

"Don't play with those dirty things. You could catch some sort of disease."

"They aren't dirty Ma, I seen one washing his hands and face just yesterday."

"Throw them dirty things in the stove right now!" Ma sounded like she was getting mad.

"Can I keep these skins that I've got stretched"?

"No!" she said and she was getting louder, "you could get sick playing with those dirty things."

"I don't think so Ma, if mice were sick they would all die and there wouldn't be so many."

"In the stove, now!" she really meant it so when she opened the door I threw them in. I hated to but if I didn't she was gonna skin me!

"How many mouse skins would it take to make a coat, Ma?"

"Probably a million," she said.

"Is that a lot more than ten, Ma?"

"A whole lot more, besides who would want a mouse skin coat anyway."

"I think lots of people would, the skins are nice and soft, aren't they Ma?" She put some warm water in the basin and told me to wash my filthy little hands. She said that they were covered with blood and dirty mouse stuff.

"How come you call one mouse, a mouse and more than one, mice," I asked Ma.

"Mice is a plural," she told me.

"A what?"

"A plural, it means more than one."

"How many more?" I asked.

"It doesn't matter, any amount more than one."

"How about moose, Ma?"

"It doesn't matter how many there are they still say moose."

"Is there no plural for moose?"

"I don't know." Ma said and she looked up at the ceiling. I looked up but I didn't see anything.

Ma sat down with the last cup of coffee from the pot. She looked out the window and I could see there were tears in her eyes. "Are you crying Ma? Is it because I skinned those mice?" She shook her head no. "You miss grandma and your family in Ontario?" She nodded her head yes and the tears ran down her cheeks. It made me cry to see my mother cry. I went over to her and crawled up on her knee. "You still got me," I tell her. She hugged me tight to her. "I love you Ma. I know I'm not good like Henry was, he was real good, wasn't he?"

She nodded again and looked up at his picture on the wall. He was her first born and died at a year and a half old. I don't think that she ever got over it. She always said how good he was and when he played outside how the birds would come and sit on his hands. Kind of like the holy pictures of Jesus, I thought. I wanted so badly to be good like that but it just never seemed to work out. Once I had a whiskey jack sit on my hand and take a piece of bread but it just doesn't seem the same. I wanted her to love me as much as she loved Henry but he was a hard act to follow.

After a while she seemed better. She said that she had work to do and for me to go and play. I was a little confused about all this and I decided to go and think about it for a while. I went to the bedroom and got Timmy, my old yellow tiger cat out of the sock box under the bed. We lay on the bed together and I hugged him, he was big and warm and he made me feel better.

I was thinking about being the last kid in the family. It was really hard. Alf was too old to play but when he had time he sometimes did things with me. When I was too small to play, Helen and Francis would play together and wouldn't play with me. Then when I was bigger, they didn't want to play any more. They wanted to do other stuff. It was hard to just be myself, I wanted to be tough like my Pa but I was too small. I wanted to be like Alf big and strong and he never seemed to be afraid of anything. I tried to be like that but most of the time I was scared as hell. I wanted to be like Francis, he was talented and an inventor, he could make nearly anything. I tried to make things but most of the time they didn't turn out. I wanted to be like Ma and Helen they were loving and caring. Most of all I wanted to be like Henry, but I didn't want to be dead. As I hugged old Tim, I realized that I would never be like any of them I would just be like me. So feeling kind of sad I fell asleep.

The trapping was going pretty good, everybody was bringing in fur and stretching it, combing it out and getting it ready to sell. Since my mouse trapping was cut short I didn't have a trap line at all. I had a little red and brown plush toy dog. I'd had it as long as I could remember. I thought, maybe I could pretend that it was a fox, and pretend to catch him in a trap. He was pretty easy to catch. I hit him on the head a couple times with a kindling stick to make sure that he was dead. Time for skinning. I got out my jack knife and started to split him down the hind legs and up the belly. *Boy, this plush stuff is tough!* I finally got the cuts made and tried to get the skin off. He was packed solid with some kind of wood shavings and it was hard to get out. By the time I got it all out I had a pile nearly two feet high.

Then I had to stretch his hide out on a stick. I was by the wood box trying to pull his skin over a piece of firewood when Ma saw me. "Now what are you doing?"

"I'm stretching my fox skin, Ma."

"What is that? Let me see. My God! You skinned your toy dog. What's the matter with you anyhow?"

"You wouldn't let me skin mice Ma, and that's all that I had."

"One toy is all you have and now you ruined it, now what will you play with?"

"I was playing with it now Ma."

"Where's the stuffing?"

"It's in by the bed."

"Oh, blessed Mother, look at the mess, you really did it this time, whatever is going to become of you? Take that little knife you're so handy with and go cut a switch."

"Ah, please Ma, don't make me go cut a switch right now, its cold outside. Ma, I need a coat."

"No coat, now go." Damn, if I had a coat on I could have stay outside for a while and let her cool off a little but I had to hurry and do it before I froze. There were a lot of long red willows just east of the house. During my childhood I must have cleared about an acre of them. They were frozen hard and it was hard to cut one. I finally got one cut but I was half frozen so I had to go in.

Ma took the switch and said, "It's froze too stiff to use now, we'll have to wait until it thaws out."

She put it up on the warming oven on the old cook stove. If I gave her a little more time maybe she'd forget about it and I wouldn't get my little arse switched after all. I went and played quietly with Tim in the bedroom praying that she might forget.

What a memory she had! "Lewis, come out here now, it's time for your switching."

"Ah Ma, do you really have to switch me, I'll be good from now on and I promise that I'll never skin anything again in my whole life." I was really begging.

"You've been building up to this for quite a while and now we have to do it."

Jeez, it was like walking to the gallows. She held me up by my left arm until I was on my tiptoes, pulled my pants down and commenced to put some color in my little cheeks. After the first swat, I was doing the Irish jig and hollering like a wounded goose. After ten or twelve good welts she let me go. "Go to bed for a while and ask Jesus to help you be a good boy."

I headed for the bed, still doing the jig and holding my arse with both hands, letting out a whoop every couple of jumps.

I lay face down on the bed feeling sorry for myself. Somehow I didn't feel like talking to Jesus just then, so wallowing in self-pity, I fell asleep. Ma woke me up, "Come for supper now," she said.

"Please don't tell Pa, please Ma. I don't want him to give me another whipping."

"No, I won't tell him, I'm fixing up your dog and don't you ever skin it again."

"Oh, I promise Ma, I promise."

We had supper and after we eat I like to lay on the floor by the stove. The floor was warm and my belly was full. The grown ups were talking and Tim came and lay down beside me. My whipping was over and I was at peace with the world once more.

Chapter 5
Better Times

The fur supply had been abundant that year and there was a good bunch of skins ready to be sold. "I was talking to a guy at the store the other day." Pa said. "He told me that a store in Hythe is buying fur and paying twice what Watson is paying. Soon as it warms up a little I'm loading up the pack board and going to find out."

"It's a long way, Joe." Ma replied.

"I'll go through the bush to Demmitt and catch a ride or jump a freight. I'm tired of giving our hard caught fur away to Watson."

A few days later Pa came in and said, "There's a Chinook arch in the sky, it should be here by tomorrow." Pa got the pack board loaded up and had everything ready for morning. Sure enough, in the morning the Chinook had blown in and the temperature was up to 40 degrees. Ma made him some roast moose sandwiches and a sealer of tea. Pa left early. "I don't know when I'll be back, two or three days at the most." He kissed Ma goodbye and headed off through the bush for Demmitt. It would take him a while because the pack was heavy and it was about eight miles. Ma was a worrier and she started to worry as soon as Pa was out of sight, and she would keep worrying until he walked through the door again.

The weather held warm and around bedtime on the second night, Pa staggered through the door. He was worn out but he was smiling. Alf jumped up to help him take the pack board off. "My God, what have you got in there, it must be well over a hundred pounds!"

"Lots of stuff. Make me a cup of tea and let me rest up a bit." Pa took his boots and coat off and let out a long sigh as he lowered himself into his chair.

"Are you hungry?" Ma asked.

"No, I'm too damn tired to eat right now."

"How did the fur sale go?" Alf wanted to know.

"You won't believe it. More than double what Watson pays. Open the pack and see what I bought. The price of the groceries is way cheaper than Watson's is too."

Everybody was excited and wanted to know more about the prices.

"What did we get for the big coyote, Pa?"

"Twelve bucks and fourteen for that cross fox."

"That's great!" Alf said "How about the squirrels?"

"Ten cents each, double what Watson pays." Francis and Helen wanted to know how much they got for their weasels. "Up to two bucks for the really big one." Pa told them.

Ma unpacked the pack board, "My goodness, look at all this." There was tea and coffee, sugar, salt and baking powder. Pa also bought some medicine, Buckley's, Vicks and mustard for mustard plasters. There were aspirins, a few Christmas candies and a little ham. Ma said that we hadn't had ham for years. I had never had ham, and was not quite sure what it was but if Ma said that it was good, then it must be. Pa said that the ham was for Christmas dinner. There was also a half dozen pork chops for supper the next night. Everyone wanted to hear everything that happened but Pa made us wait until morning because he was really tired and needed to go to bed.

Morning came, and over breakfast the conversation from the night before continued. "What did we get all told for the fur?" Alf wanted to know.

"A hundred and sixty two bucks," Pa replied. "There's three dollars each for Helen and Francis." He took out his wallet to give them their money. They smiled and went to put it away for safekeeping. They both had things that they had been saving for. Pa gave the rest of the money to Ma, "Count it and see how much is left."

"Ninety two dollars," Ma said.

"Well, I feel kind of guilty," Pa confessed, "I spent a couple of dollars in Hythe and forty-five cents for a train ticket back to Tupper."

"Tell us how it went," Alf asked.

"Well, I made it to Hythe around two in the afternoon and went straight to Flayton's store where the fur buyer is. He looked everything over carefully and told me how much he would pay. I told him that was good and he paid me.

Then I went to the hotel and was able to get a small room for fifty cents, most of the rooms were empty. I spent forty-five cents for a pork chop supper and twenty cents for two beers. Come morning, I had breakfast for a quarter and then I went back to Flayton's store where I bought all the groceries. When I was in the bar the night before, I was talking to a guy and he told me if you send a four dollar money order to Woodwards in Edmonton that they send you a twenty pound box of dried fruit. He said that it was a mixture of prunes, peaches, apricots, apples and figs, he said it was so fresh it was just like off the tree."

"We should send for some," Ma said.

"I already did, it should be in the mail in a couple of weeks." Since Pa could neither read or write, Ma wondered how he had done that. "I had to go to the post office to make out the money order and I had the lady there make the order out for me."

Ma was really happy because Pa also bought her some print material to make a new dress. "I just can't believe that you got so much stuff for so little money."

"How much do we owe Watson," Pa wanted to know.

"Around eighty dollars, I think," Ma replied.

"I'm going to town tomorrow and pay him off and we'll still have enough money for train fare for the next trip to Hythe. Damn, it's going to feel good not to owe him any more."

The next day Pa and Alf walked to Tupper. Pa asked Mr. Watson how much his grocery bill totaled. "Eighty two fifty," he told Pa, who counted out the money and laid it on the counter.

"Rob a bank?" Mr. Watson smiled.

"No, the robbing days are all over, thanks for the credit." Pa replied.

"Your credit is always good here Joe. Do you need more groceries now?"

"Nope, thanks, I'll remember that." Watson still wasn't satisfied, he couldn't figure out where Pa had gotten the money.

"You must have some fur to sell you haven't been in with any all winter."

Pa just smiled and said, "Nope." He was feeling good, for the first time in years he didn't owe anybody and he still had six and a half bucks left in his pocket. He and Alf picked up the mail and headed on home.

Christmas was good that year. Francis and Helen cut a tree and put it up in the corner. Ma opened the trunk and in the bottom were the treasures. We never dared open the trunk but stood in awe as she removed the few decorations. There were three paper bells that were folded flat but they opened up and made these beautiful and amazing bells. There were a dozen gold balls carefully wrapped in a box. We made chains of colored paper and icicles from tinfoil gathered from tobacco packages. We had a bit of popcorn that we strung on a thread. Francis made a star from something and put it on top. How beautiful the tree was! The light from the coal oil lamp sparkled on the gold balls and the tinsel so that I could hardly take my eyes off it.

Christmas Eve was magical. I looked out the window and the moon was bright, it made the snow look pale blue, sparkling with a thousand diamonds and shimmering with frost. I went to bed dreaming about Santa and wondering if he would come in the door or try to wedge himself down the stovepipe. *Well, that was his problem, just as long as he got here.*

Morning came to find Pa lighting a fire in the cook stove. It was still pitch dark outside. The moon that had been so bright when I went to bed seemed to have gone out.

"Did he come, Pa?"

"Yes son, but stay in bed for a while till it warms up in here."

"How long Pa," I was anxious to know.

"I'll tell you when," Pa said. He stood by the stove in his underwear and lit a smoke, he hadn't lit the lamp yet but the light from the fire draft put a dim light in the room. It was a picture that will be in my mind forever.

After what seemed like an eternity, Ma got up and Pa lit the lamp. "Okay kids, come and see what Santa brought."

I ran to my sock hanging on a nail on the wall. There was an orange, some nuts and a few candies. There was a wooden car that, I would find out later, Francis had made for me. I tried on a pair of freshly knit mitts that looked an awful lot like an old pair of socks that used to be in the sock box. Francis, Helen and Alf got home-knit socks, mitts and toques. I didn't know if there was any thing else for anyone because I was too busy playing.

Ma made us a special breakfast. After our porridge we had fresh baking powder biscuits with Rogers Golden Syrup. She also fried up a platter of griads, small thin strips of moose steaks. They even let me have a little bit of watered down coffee.

After breakfast dishes were cleared away Ma started making Christmas dinner. The ham was put in the oven along with some blueberry pies. My day was spent playing and the grown ups reminisced about the old days. They told stories about their childhood, friends and relatives and laughed a lot. It was a wonderful day!

Christmas dinner was truly a wondrous thing. Helen had set the table with the tablecloth from the trunk. The ham was sliced and the bowl of mashed potatoes looked so fluffy and white. There was onion gravy and low bush cranberry sauce. The carrots were a golden orange color and the steaming blueberry pie waited on the cupboard. We bowed our heads as Ma gave thanks to the Lord for our good fortune and then we ate. Such a meal I had never partaken of before.

As I went to bed that night I felt so contented. I said my prayers and thanked Jesus for this very special day. Old Tim crawled down to the foot of my bed, he felt nice and warm on my feet. As I did most every night, I rubbed his fur backwards in the darkness under the covers. The little blue sparks that flew through his fur always amazed me. It was nice to lie in the warmth of my bed and listen to the murmurs of the grown ups in the next room. So in total contentment I drifted off into a blissful sleep.

A couple of days after Christmas, Frank Sullivan came walking over to our place. He came in for a cup of tea and a smoke while he and Pa talked.

"The boys and I are going to be putting up ice starting the day after New Year's, I checked it out yesterday and it's at least two feet thick. If you and Alf want to help us, we'll help you put up yours and use my team and sleigh."

"That sounds good to me" Pa agreed "we'll see you at the lake on the morning of the second." Frank left for home and Pa smiled, "It's nice to have good neighbors like that. I was wondering how we would get our ice home."

Cutting ice is a dangerous job. After the snow is shoveled off the ice a hole is chipped through it with a spud, a three-inch wide chisel with a four-foot handle. A hole has to be chipped through the ice where every saw cut begins. After the first two long cuts are made, there are crosscuts made every two feet. The first block is hard to get out; it is heavy and has to be lifted straight up. Then the job becomes dangerous, as the blocks are pulled out with a pair of tongs you have to be very careful not to slip into the water. One slip in that frigid water and thirty below temperatures will freeze a person pretty fast.

As some of the men cut the ice, the others hauled it home and put it in the icehouse. They put a good layer of snow between the blocks to keep it from sticking together. When the icehouse was full they covered the ice with two feet of sawdust. It would keep for a long time. A few days later the job was finished and Pa was pleased. *Next summer we will have good ice water to drink.*

Chapter 6
Worse Times

For every action there is a complete and opposite reaction. This theory seemed to hold especially true that winter. For a while everything seemed to be going in the right direction, but then it all seemed to change. Helen had been complaining about a pain in her stomach for a few days. She came home from school one day and she was in major pain. That night it got worse and when Ma pressed on her stomach she hollered.

"I think she has bad appendicitis, we have to get her to a doctor." Early in the morning they wrapped her in a quilt and took her to Tupper with old Bird and the stone boat. Alf brought the horse home and Pa took Helen to Pouce Coupe on the train to see Doctor Hollis.

He examined her and told Pa, "They are really hot, they have to come out right away before they burst." Helen went to the hospital and Pa had to find a place to stay. Pa's money was almost all gone and the weather was cold. The man at the livery stable was nice and let Pa sleep there overnight.

In the morning he got toast and coffee at Songs Café and walked to the hospital to see how Helen was doing. The doctor had operated the night before and she was awake when Pa arrived. "Will I be all right, Pa?"

"You'll be fine you rest now and get better." Doctor Hollis told Pa that she was going to be fine and that he should come back and get her in two weeks.

"I'll miss you, Pa."

"I'll miss you too." Pa caught the train back to Tupper and walked the six miles home.

Of course, Ma was worried sick and was having one of the terrible migraines that she got a couple times a week. When Pa arrived home and told her that Helen was fine it made her feel a little better. "We have to go to Hythe and sell some fur; the money is nearly all gone."

"We don't have as much fur as last time," Alf said. "This last month of cold weather has kept most of the animals pretty quiet."

"We'll have to take what we have. The doctor's bill is thirty bucks and a dollar a day for the hospital. Doc says that I can pay him in a few payments but the hospital has to be paid right away."

"We've got ten days before we have to go to Hythe," Alf said "I'll hit the trap line hard and if we try for more squirrels maybe we will do all right."

So they worked the line real hard and even expanded it further east and south into new territory. When the time came for them to sell the fur they had a respectable amount. Pa made the trip again and returned with just a little over a hundred dollars. "This has to last a long time," Pa said "we won't get a lot more fur before spring. If we're lucky we might catch some muskrats, they bring in a fair dollar."

When the two weeks were up they went to get Helen. Alf stayed in Tupper with the horse while Pa took the train to Pouce Coupe. Helen was doing fine except that she was homesick and was really glad to be going home. Ma was so glad that Helen was home again.

Helen was tired after the trip and Ma put her to bed. She made her some tea and toast with a little jam and as Helen ate a bit Ma sat on the bed and they talked. Ma and Helen were always close, what with her being the only daughter.

I was excited too. I missed her real bad and I wanted to see the hole in her belly. She said that it was all bandaged up but she promised to show me sometime. Helen was weak from being in bed for two weeks and she had to get up and get some exercise. I went with her for little walks everyday and she soon got stronger.

I love my sister a lot. She is good to me and sometimes she played with me. She calls me "Cuck," little rooster in French. I call her "Gug," which didn't mean anything but it was the best I could think of.

Francis brought her schoolwork home so she wouldn't be too far behind when she could go back to school. I wanted to do schoolwork with her but I seemed to be more of a nuisance than a help. Finally after enough asking she showed me her incision.

"Yuck, oh ick, it's a big red thing, aren't you afraid your guts will fall out?"

"No it's healed up and the red will go away in time."

"It looks icky to me. I don't want to see it anymore." That was enough for me.

Pa was out on the trap line one day and he saw some deer on the hillside some five hundred yards away. Our meat supply was getting low so he took a good aim with the old Winchester rifle and dropped one. A deer was not a lot of meat so he tried for a second one. Pa was a good shot and the second one fell down. He was kind of surprised because that was a long shot for that old .32 special.

The snow was deep and powdery and even with snowshoes it was slow going to where the deer were. As soon as he left the main trail he sunk halfway to his knees. When he finally got there he had to dress them out. He took off his snowshoes and left them and the rifle by a tree. He waded through the snow to the first deer and cut its throat with his hunting knife. You have to do that to bleed them out. He went over to the next one. It was lying on its side in the snow. It must have been in shock or playing dead because when Pa started to cut its throat it went berserk. It reared up on its hind feet and started flailing Pa with its front legs. The knife blade broke and Pa was knocked down in the snow.

The shot had been low and instead of hitting the deer in the shoulder it broke both front legs at the knees. Pa was on his hands and knees in the deep snow and could hardly move. The big buck kept pounding him on the back until he couldn't breathe anymore. His wool mackinaw was in shreds and he knew that he had to do something soon or that deer would kill him. Mustering up all his strength he managed to push the deer over backwards and get away from it. Beaten half to death he lay in the snow trying to get his breath back. His back was raw and it felt like his ribs were broken. He crawled over to where he had left the rifle and finished off the deer. He still had to dress out both deer and with his hunting knife broken all he had was his jack knife. He managed to get them dressed out and get back to his snowshoes. He still had four miles to struggle home.

Around seven that evening the door opened and Pa stumbled in and collapsed on the floor. He was covered in frost and blood and his coat was cut to ribbons.

"Oh my god!" Ma screamed, "What happened to you, are you all right?" Pa just lay there and gasped for air. "Help me," Ma hollered to Helen and Francis.

They came running from the bedroom and helped sit him up. Ma got his tattered coat and hat off. His face was a bloody mess and he was half frozen.

Ma got down beside him with some warm water and gently washed his hands and face. They got him up and over to a chair by the stove. He hollered every time they touched his ribs. Ma got him a cup of hot tea and after a few sips he was able to talk. He slowly related the events that led to this disaster.

"Let's see your back and arms," Ma said. He slowly took his shirt off and his underwear top down. "Oh my god!" Ma cried. He was black and blue from the neck on down, his arms were all beat up and he had welts an inch high all over.

"Are your ribs broke?" Ma asked.

"I don't know, but it sure hurts to breathe."

Ma got him a bowl of soup. He said that he wasn't hungry, just tired. "Have some anyway it'll make you feel better." Pa ate a little soup and Ma got the bed ready. He was hurting so bad that he could hardly make it to bed. Ma put some Watkins ointment on his back and wrapped his ribs with a strip of cloth ripped from an old sheet. He was worn right out and fell asleep in minutes.

In the morning Pa was rested but stiff and sore all over. "You'll be staying close to that bed for a few days," Ma told him. Coffee and breakfast made him feel some better and he was dying for a smoke, which made him feel better still.

Alf asked Pa where this all took place. "Francis and I had better go and bring them home before the wolves get them." Pa told them where the deer were and they took old Bird and set off through the snow.

Pa had some more coffee and went back to bed. I sat on the bed and asked him to tell me about it again. Ma came in with a cup of coffee and Pa related the story to us again. "You're lucky that you weren't killed," Ma said. "Let me see your back again." She removed the bandages, "My lord, are you ever beat up, does the salve make it feel any better?"

"It seems to soothe it a bit."

"Do you think you have any broken ribs?"

"I don't think so" Pa replied "cracked maybe, but I don't think they are broke."

Alf and Francis had to make two trips for the meat. "You're lucky to be alive" Alf said, "It looks like a slaughter house down there where that buck had you down. I don't know how you survived."

"Just lucky I guess," Pa mumbled. Pa took it easy for a week or so and before long he was back to normal, but it would take quite awhile for the bruises to go away. His bruises were no longer black and blue. They had changed to green and yellow.

"How come they change color like that Pa?" I wanted to know. Pa said that they always do that.

Alf and Francis took care of the trap line and the cold weather hung on. Apart from the trap line there wasn't too much to do

Tim was my big old tiger cat, he wasn't really mine but I liked to think that he was. He was my best buddy and friend. I played with him, slept with him and talked to him. Sometimes I needed to talk about serious stuff and nobody else listened or understood. I didn't know if he understood but he always listened. I loved him more than anything. He was big and was a good hunter. Every night around eight o'clock he wanted out. It didn't matter how cold it was. He was always gone for at least an hour and he always brought back whatever he caught. He laid it on the step and meowed until somebody went out to tell him he was a good cat. As soon as he heard what a wonderful cat he was, he was ready to come in for the night.

One night he went out for his usual hunt, but by bedtime he wasn't back. I asked Ma, "How come Tim isn't back yet."

"I don't know," Ma said, "Sometimes cats stay out all night."

"Not Timmy Ma, there's got to be something wrong or he'd be home."

"Well, go to bed," Ma said, "he'll probably be home by morning."

I didn't sleep very well, worrying about Tim. In the morning I was up early with everybody else.

"Did Tim come home?" I asked.

"No," was all Pa said.

After breakfast Helen and Francis headed to school, Pa and Alf went out to make the rounds on the trap line.

"I've got to go look for Tim," I told Ma. She said no, I couldn't go because it was forty below outside and that I'd freeze. I was really worried about Tim and didn't know what to do.

About an hour later Alf came home, he was carrying Tim in his arms and he looked dead.

"Is he all right? What happened to him?" Ma asked.

"He was caught in a trap by the front foot, it's frozen solid and he's not much better, I don't know how come he's still alive but he is." They laid him on an old blanket by the stove. He was cold and stiff.

"Will he die Ma?" I asked.

"He might son. He may be frozen too much to recover."

"His toes are frozen nearly off," Alf said "they are just hanging on by the skin, I'd better cut them off before they thaw out, and they'll just fall off anyway." He took out his razor sharp jack knife and cut Tim's toes off. Tim didn't move. "All we can do now is wait and see if he thaws out, I've got to go catch up with Pa."

I went over and touched Tim. He felt cold and stiff. The tears streamed down my cheeks and I buried my face in his cold fur. "Don't die Timmy, don't die," I sobbed. It made his fur wet and he just lay there. "What can I do Ma, I can't let Timmy die."

"You can pray for him, I think that only God can save him now." I ran and knelt by my bed and prayed. I said some 'Our Fathers' and some 'Hail Mary's'. I ran back to see if Tim was better yet but he was still just lying there.

"It's not working Ma."

"What isn't working?"

"I prayed, Ma, but he's still not better."

"It doesn't work that way or that fast," Ma said.

Then it dawned on me, of course it didn't work, I didn't tell Jesus what I was praying for! Back to the bed I went and knelt down again. I didn't think that those first prayers that I said were right for a cat. "Please Jesus," I prayed, "Make Timmy better. Ma says that you brought some dead guy back to life and Tim isn't dead yet so it will be a lot easier, Ma says that you can do all things and love all things so please do it, Amen."

I ran back to where Tim was and looked down at him. "You know you don't have to go kneel by your bed to pray," Ma informed me.

"I don't?"

"No, you can pray anywhere, I pray when I do the housework."

"You mean that I could pray outside?"

"Yes, you can pray anywhere."

"How about in the barn?"

"Yes, you can pray there too."

Sometimes I think I didn't know anything.

"How come I'm such a dumb little bugger, Ma?"

"You're not dumb son, just little, when you get big you'll know more."

Sure, I think, and then I'll be big and dumb!

I sat on the dirt floor beside Tim's blanket. Our cabin didn't have a board floor. Pa said that the next summer we would get one. I held Tim's head on my knee, he was getting warmer and he didn't seem so stiff. As I pet his head, he opened his eyes a little bit. "He opened his eyes a little, Ma!" I hollered. He moved a little bit and I was getting really excited.

Ma had some meat boiling on the stove; she took some broth from it and blew on it to cool it down. She told me to dip my finger in it and put it on his nose and mouth. I tried and the broth ran down his chin. I tried again and he licked at my finger. "He's trying to eat, Ma." I gave him some more and he tried to sit up and drank a little from the dish.

He lay down again and started to shake. "I think the frost is coming out and he probably hurts real bad," Ma said. He held his leg out and the blood started to drip from where his toes used to be. He made painful meow sounds and I felt so sorry for him. I prayed some more.

"Please Jesus, make it so Timmy don't hurt so bad." After a little while he stopped shaking, Ma put some Lysol in a dish of warm water and she got the salve and a bandage. She carefully sponged off his leg and foot. He flinched but somehow he seemed to know that she was helping him. After it was washed she put the salve on and wrapped it up.

"That's all we can do, it's up to the Lord now." She took him a little bit of meat cut up small. He seemed hungry and ate quite a bit. He was more comfortable now and lay down to go back to sleep.

The days passed and Tim improved steadily. He hobbled around on three legs and seemed fine, except for his foot. Ma figured that it was time to look to see how it was healing. She unwrapped it, "It looks kind of infected, and I think we should leave it open for a while to air out." I looked at it. It looked kind of funny to me.

"If he gets that gangrene stuff in it will he die?"

"I'm afraid so, there's nothing you can do for it and it comes nearly every time with frost bite."

All of a sudden I had an idea that would fix it for sure. I ran to the bedroom and got the little bottle of holy water from the little table by Ma's bed. I ran back and poured some all over his foot. "Now what are you doing?" Ma asked.

"I put holy water on it. You said that bad stuff can't face up to holy water so that should fix it good!"

"My lord, you used it all up! I don't think that you should use it on a cat."

"But Ma, we can get the priest to bless some more the next time that he comes. Why not get him to bless the well and then we would never run out."

"You don't use it for everything, just to bless things and to baptize people."

"Have I been baptized, Ma?"

"Yes, you have to be so that you can get into heaven when you die."

"How come?"

"It takes away original sin and you can't go to heaven with a sin on your soul."

"How do you baptize someone, Ma?"

"You put holy water on their forehead and you say, 'I baptize thee in the name of the Father, and of the Son, and of the Holy Ghost, Amen'."

There were still a few drops of holy water left in the bottle so I poured it all on Tim's head and said the words that Ma had told me. "Now what are you doing?" Ma wanted to know.

"I just baptized Tim so that he can go to heaven."

"You don't baptize a cat!" She sounded kind of upset.

"Oh, we need cats in heaven Ma, so they can eat the mice."

"There are no mice in heaven," Ma said.

"There must be Ma. Pa says that you can't keep the little buggers out of anything."

"That's not a very nice word, don't say it anymore." Once again she looked up to the ceiling, *Help me Blessed Mother*, she seemed to plead. I looked up too but I still couldn't see anything.

Ma wrapped Tim's foot up again and she looked worried about it.

In a couple of days he seemed to want the bandage off so Ma removed it. She looked at it and seemed surprised. "It looks pretty good, there's some new pink skin and the infection seems to be gone." I was not surprised; after all I fixed it with the holy water, why shouldn't it be better? He licked it quite a bit and soon he was getting around like nothing had ever happened.

That night I knelt down and said my prayers and for once I didn't ask Jesus for something. That night I said, "Thank you Jesus for making Timmy better again because I really love him and I need him." Tim and I went to bed and I rubbed his fur backwards like I'd done a hundred times before and I thought, *he must be fine, he still sparked real good!*

Chapter 7
Uncle Fred Comes Home

The days were getting longer and the sun was warmer. The snow was gone from the roads but it was still deep in the bush. I liked to lie on the haystack and look up at the wind gently blowing in the tops of the pine trees. It was warm in the sun and it made me feel happy. Helen was all better and back to school. Pa was better and doing his work and Timmy was better and catching mice again. The chicks that we had gotten the summer before were full-grown and had started to lay a few eggs. This was something that I had hardly ever seen. Life was good!

It was just after supper when Old Ranger, our sled dog, started to bark. "There's a team and wagon coming," Pa said as he looked out the window "I wonder who that could be?" I ran to look and sure enough, there was a team of black and white horses hitched to a wagon. "Well I'll be damned, it's Fred!" Pa went out to meet him and we were all right behind him.

Uncle Fred pulled to a stop, "Whoa," he said and he got down from the wagon.

"Damn, you're a sight for sore eyes," Pa said as he shook hands with my uncle. Everyone exchanged hellos. Uncle hugged Ma and Helen and took a poke at me and made me laugh. Alf and Francis unhitched the horses and put them in the barn and Uncle went in the cabin and sat down. Ma got him some tea and stew and he ate like he hadn't eaten for days.

"Whose team and outfit have you got there?" Pa inquired.

"Ours, I've been working for Don Noyes down at Dimsdale for nearly a year and like everyone else he doesn't have any money. He's got more horses than he needs so I made him a deal for this old team and wagon. The old blue roan's name is Brian. He's a good old horse. The white one's name is Eagle and he's a knot head. Don't try to ride him! They say that he killed a guy at a rodeo down south. But all in all they make a pretty good team."

"Those horses are sure going to make things a lot easier around here," Pa told Uncle. Uncle warned that the harness was just made up of patched up pieces so not to use it too hard.

"I'm tired as hell," Uncle said, "I've been two long days on the road and I'm just about ready for some sleep."

"I'll bet you're tired," Pa responded, "That's a long old drive."

I had not seen Uncle for nearly a year and I was really excited to see him. I liked Uncle even though he teased me until I could hardly stand it.

"Bring that bag over to me," he told me. It was heavy but I managed to drag it over to him. He opened it up and took out a tobacco can and handed it to me. It was so heavy I nearly dropped it on the ground. I put it on a bench and opened it. It was full of shiny little blue shingle nails.

"Thanks Uncle, I'll be able to build all kinds of stuff."

"You do that." he said, "Delma, your cooking is even better than I remember it."

"It's just bread and stew, Fred."

"But it's your stew and your bread and it sure tastes good!" Uncle Fred always enjoyed a good meal and Ma's cooking was always delicious.

"Oh yes, I picked up the mail in Tupper." He looked in his pack again and took out the mail. He had a letter for Ma and a letter for Alf. Ma's letter was from Aunt Midrease and Alf's was from Charlie Weaver. Mr. Weaver wanted Alf to go work for him again and said that he could use him in a couple weeks. Uncle said that he had to go back in a week or so himself as the fields were drying up pretty good down by Grande Prairie.

The grown ups talked on into the night and Alf and Uncle set a date when they would both go together. Alf had to write a letter to Mr. Weaver telling him when to pick him up at the station in Grande Prairie. "We better pick up the traps and get the fur sold before you go," Pa told Alf. Alf agreed but he had to get that letter off first. I said my prayers and got ready for bed. I thanked Jesus for having Uncle come home and for how good it was to have everyone home at once again. They were still talking when Tim and I drifted off to sleep.

The next day was busy after Helen and Francis went off to school Pa, Uncle and Alf went to check out the horses. "I hope that you've got enough feed for them." Uncle said, "I've brought five bags of oats so they won't need too much hay until the grass comes up."

Pa told him that they still had some left that they cut for Bird and so they have enough. They watered the horses and gave them some hay and a little can of oats. Bird hadn't had oats in years and for her it was a real treat. She made that Na-Huh-Huh sound that horses make and she enjoyed every last oat. She seemed glad to see the other horses too, they nuzzled each other and rubbed noses and all seemed to be happy.

Pa shared with Uncle his plans to cut some logs and get them sawn into lumber for a floor in the cabin. "It would sure make things a lot easier for Delma," Uncle reasoned. They picked up the traps and got the fur ready to sell. This time it was Alf that took the fur to Hythe.

"Bring that new team and wagon and meet me at the train tomorrow," he told Pa and Uncle. "I'll buy some flour and groceries in Hythe where it's cheaper."

Pa and Uncle met the train and Alf had a lot of groceries. He had a hundred pound bag of Buffalo brand flour, salt, sugar and tea and all the other necessities, even a little can of popcorn. By the time they got home it was suppertime. After supper Alf gave the remaining money to Ma. She always looked after the money. "Take ten bucks with you, you might need something and we seem to be a little better off than last year," Pa told Alf. "We'll send ten dollars to the doctor for Helen's operation and then we'll only owe him ten more."

They spent the time till Uncle and Alf had to go by visiting and working on the old harness. They reinforced it with rawhide left over from making snowshoes.

At supper one evening Ma suggested that they subscribe to a newspaper. "I think that we can afford two dollars for the *Winnipeg Free Press*." Pa and Alf agreed that it would be a good idea.

"We've really lost track of what's going on in the world," Pa said. Pa can't read but Ma reads to him. Ma informed them that with a four dollar, two year subscription you get a free pocket watch as a premium. "I sure could use a watch," Pa said.

"Go for the two year deal and get Pa a watch, I think we can afford the four bucks," Alf chimed in. "I'll mail the letter when I go."

A couple days later Alf and Uncle left for spring work. As usual there were tears running down Ma's cheeks as they hugged her and said goodbye. I watched as they left and kept waving until they were out of sight. It suddenly seemed quiet and lonely with them gone.

Pa figured that he'd need about five hundred board feet of lumber for the floor and the same amount for the guy who saws it. It was usually cut on half and half shares. Pa and Francis figured it would take about fifty logs and that meant three trips with the team and wagon to haul the logs.

Bill Martin had a little sawmill at his home near Tupper and Pa made a deal with him to saw the logs. Pa took the wagon box off and loaded the logs on the bunks. The logs were heavy and just like he figured he had to make three trips. It took Pa most of a day to make each trip. Bill told Pa to come back in two weeks and it would be all ready.

A couple weeks passed and Pa was ready to go for his lumber. After a fair amount of begging he agreed to take me along. This was the first time that I'd seen Bill Martin. He was an awesome man, well over six feet tall, wide in the shoulders with a chest like a barrel. His sandy hair was in ringlets and hung down to his shoulders. He was a hulk of a man in his overalls with the legs torn off halfway between his ankles and his knees. His shirt had the sleeves torn off and he was barefoot. He was a cross between Wild Bill Hickock, Davey Crockett and a three hundred pound hillbilly. He just stood there as we drove up.

"Hello Bill, got my lumber ready?" Pa asked.

"Nope, I sold it."

"You what?"

"I sold it, a guy came along with some money and I needed the money so I sold it." Pa started to turn red.

"You son of a bitch, I drive all the way here and you tell me that you sold it?"

"Yes I did, what in hell are you gonna do about it?"

This was the first time that I have ever seen Pa really lose it. He jumped straight from the wagon and hit Bill square in the chest with both feet and knocked him flat on his back. Pa had him by the neck with his left hand and his right fist was cocked ready to unload on Bills jaw.

"How about this!" Pa roared, "What in hell are you planning to do about my lumber."

"Take it easy Joe, Christ sake I think you might a broke my ribs!"

"The lumber Bill, what about my lumber?"

"I'll get it next week for sure Joe, Jeez, don't get so riled up, how about you get off me, shit this ground is hard."

"Okay," Pa said, "One week from today I'll be back and if you ain't got my lumber I'll kick the shit out of you, you got that?"

"Yes, for sure, I'll get the logs and saw them up good. Okay?"

"Fine," Pa said, "One week from today." Pa climbed back up in the wagon and we headed home.

I was totally amazed by this encounter. I thought for sure that this big guy would beat Pa to a pulp. I mentioned this to Pa on the way home. He rolled himself a smoke and lit it, he looked over at me and grinned, "The bigger they are the harder they fall son." As it turned out Bill was a good guy, he was just used to doing things his way and because of his size no one ever stood up to him before. He had the full intention of getting Pa's lumber when he got around to it. He had a big family to feed and when a little money came his way he took it.

We stopped at the store on the way home and got the mail. There were a couple of letters and our first issue of the *Free Press*. "Ma's gonna be happy about the moose paper, right Pa?"

"I guess so," Pa kind of grinned. There was a little package in the mail as well. "Probably the watch," Pa said.

When we arrived home Ma came out to meet us, as she wiped her hands on her apron I told her, "We got the moose paper Ma!" She kind of laughed but didn't say anything. I guess that I didn't hear right or maybe it was because my whole world revolved around moose but that's what I thought it was called. I didn't know it was called a newspaper until I was big enough to read. Boy, did I feel stupid!

Ma asked where the lumber was and Pa filled her in on the happenings on the day. She said that she didn't blame Pa for being angry but he should try to control himself a little. He said that he did control himself a little. Ma was thrilled to have a newspaper to read and Pa was happy with his new watch. It was so nice and shiny. I thought that it was beautiful. Pa put a leather shoelace on it and put it in his overall pocket. "It's going to be nice to know what time it is for a change,"

After supper Ma read the paper to Pa. He said that it was nice to hear what was going on in the world. The *Free Press* is a great paper! There's something in it for everybody. Ma loves the 'Home Loving Hearts' a page of letters written in by housewives from all over Canada. Some of them have recipes and others just share events or ask for recipes or patterns. There's a kids' page with puzzles and things to do. Some kids write in asking for pen pals. Ma also likes the crossword puzzles and she sits up at night trying to figure them out. Then of course, there are the funnies, Little Orphan Annie, Sergeant King of the Mounties, Dagwood and a few others. Helen reads them to me if I don't tick her off too badly.

The only other paper that I've seen comes by airmail. There is a bush pilot that they call Wop May. He has an old bi-wing, open cockpit airplane and he flies up from Edmonton with a load of *Edmonton Journal* papers tied in nice round bundles. He buzzes a homestead or trapper's cabin until someone comes outside. Flying just over the treetops he circles the cabin and waves at everyone. We all wave back and then he drops a bundle of papers, wags his wings and he's gone. The papers are always a month old but are really appreciated never the less. They're also a welcome addition to the outhouse!

The other publications that are studied from cover to cover are the *Eaton's* and *Simpson's* catalogues. The women look at the clothes and dishes and the men check out the tools and guns. There are guns and trapping supplies, harnesses, saddles, fiddles and guitars. There's just no end of wonderful things that we cannot afford to buy. For kids there are toys and books and bikes, we all know the page number where our wished for item resides.

When the week was up Pa was ready to go for our lumber. Once more I convinced him to let me go along. This time our lumber was in a neat pile waiting for us. Bill apologized to Pa and they shook hands. I played in the sawdust pile while they loaded the lumber on the wagon. They shook hands one more time and Pa lifted me up on the load. He climbed up and we started for home, stopping at the store to get the mail. To my total surprise, Pa gave me a penny, which I promptly traded to the storekeeper for a butterscotch sucker.

The trip home was a high point in my short life. The sun was warm and the new pine lumber smelled good. The poplar trees were just leafing out, their shiny, sticky leaves unrolling from their buds. All in all it was the kind of day that just plain made you feel good.

Pa handed me the reins and said, "You drive for a while, I'm gonna roll me a smoke." The horses were taking their time plodding along. In reality, nobody had to drive. I felt so grown up though holding those reins. I thought that it was funny that the horses seemed to be taking turns farting. Pa laughed when I mentioned it to him. Oh, it was great, I was driving, Pa was smoking and I was really enjoying that sucker.

"Horses like to fart, huh Pa?"

"It seems so," he said.

"It feels good to fart when you have to, doesn't it Pa?"

He smiled, "Yes I guess so."

"You shouldn't fart in the house, should you pa?"

"No, and not around women either," he told me.

"What are farts, Pa?"

"It's gas, son."

"Like car gas, Pa?"

"No, it's an air kind of gas." I started laughing.

"What's so funny?" Pa asked.

"Oh, I was just thinking that if it was like car gas, wouldn't it look funny seeing everybody trying to fart into the gas tank?"

Pa burst out laughing, "I guess it really would."

"How come it makes a noise when you fart, Pa?"

"Maybe there's a little whistle in there," he kidded with me. That made me laugh again.

"Oh Pa, that would look real funny to see somebody trying to blow that whistle." What a great day it was! I didn't know how it could have been any better.

As we were riding along, I saw some horses out in a field. "Look Pa, what are those two horses doing?" One was rearing up with its front feet on the other's rump and they were making funny noises.

"Oh, I guess they're playing."

"Is that a horses' game Pa, do you think they're having fun?"

"I'm sure they are," Pa smiled. It looked like a good game, I thought, I'd have to remember that and play it the next time I had a chance.

We arrive home in the late afternoon and everyone came out to look at the lumber. "I'll sure be glad when it's laid for a floor," Ma told Pa.

"So will I," Pa replied. He told Francis that after supper they will have to dry pile it. "It's gonna take a couple months of good drying before we can lay it."

"Where are we going to pile it?" Francis asked Pa.

"I think over on the west side of the icehouse, it will get plenty of wind and sunshine there. If we keep re-piling it every few days and put a new layer on top, it will dry faster. If it looks like rain, you be sure to cover it with that old tarp," Pa told Francis.

They watered and put the horses away and fed them, by then Ma had supper ready. Ma read the letter from Aunt Midrease out loud to everyone. She asked Pa how Bill was and how good the lumber was. He told her that he and Bill were friends again and that the lumber was very nice. After supper Francis and Pa piled the lumber and all we had to do was wait for it to dry.

"I have to make a long jack plane to smooth those boards down some," Pa told Francis. "That little six inch block plane that I've got is just too small to do the job." They talked about getting a piece of birch and making a plane out of that. Francis said that he knew where there was an old broken truck spring to make a knife for the plane. Pa said that should work really well.

By then it was dark and we all went inside. Ma made another pot of tea and poured Pa and Francis a cup. Pa had a smoke with his tea and Ma read the news from the paper.

Helen had brought home a book of nursery rhymes to read to me and help me learn how to read. As she read them to me I thought that they were really scary. Who would put a baby in a cradle in a treetop? How did they get it up there? I thought about that big old poplar tree in front of the cabin, *boy I'd sure hate to crash down from there!* Old Mother Hubbard must live in our area, what was such a big deal about her cupboard being bare.

Helen got very upset with me and the comments that I made about the stories. Who would be so mean as to cut the tails off three blind mice? And what was all this crap about Jack and Jill, it sure must feel good to put vinegar on a broken head! And that Little Boy Blue, his Pa should have whipped his arse, my Pa sure would have. It seemed to me that all these rhymes and stories were just pure violence. I couldn't imagine why anybody would want to scare a kid half to death just before bedtime.

That big wolf that just gobbled up a grandmother and then waited to eat a little girl. Another wolf wrecked some poor little pigs' houses not to mention some dumb little girl in the Three Bears house. And all the bears did was complain, it's too hot or too cold, too hard or too soft, what a bunch of whiners. That old lady living in a shoe, who ever heard of that? I thought that the whole thing was terrible. Helen was really miffed at my attitude. "I was trying to do something nice for you and all you're doing is finding fault."

"But Sis, they are all bad stories," I tried to soothe her.

"Well you don't have to worry about them anymore," she slammed the book shut and walked away kind of stiff legged.

I must have missed something because she thought that they were good, I just didn't see it. I was tired and said my prayers and went to bed. I tried to explain the whole thing to Tim. He looked at me and sort of made his head go up and down. *At least he understands.* I lay down thinking about that girl and the wolf, her last name is the same as mine. So, deep in thought I went to sleep and waited for a new day to dawn.

Chapter 8
What a Pretty Girl

It was early summer and the evenings were long and warm. After supper Pa lit a smudge pot to keep the mosquitoes away and everyone sat outside. Ma and Pa finished their tea and Pa relaxed with a smoke. They sat and reminisced about the past and talked about the future. Pa wondered what they would do if the damn depression ever ended. I liked these times, I played and listened and wondered what things were like when they lived in Ontario.

One evening as we were all sitting outside I heard a sound. It was somebody whistling. Alf always whistled when he was alone. *It must be him coming home*, I thought. "It's Alf," I hollered, and I ran down the road to meet him. He smiled when he saw me and reached down to scoop me up and put me on his shoulders along with his pack.

"Hi, you little squirt, how is everything?" I started talking a mile a minute, I was so glad to see him. We made our way into the yard and he put his pack and me down, everybody was talking at once. He hugged Ma and Helen and gave Pa and Francis a slap on the shoulder. "Damn, it's good to be home again."

"You must be starving," Ma said. "How about some fried potatoes and eggs?"

"Sounds real good to me Ma," Alf said as he sat down.

We all sat and talked for a while until Ma called that Alf's supper was ready. We all went inside and the talking continued while Alf dug in. "Charlie had money to pay me this spring," Alf said, "and I think I know where we should spend ten bucks of that money."

"What have you got in mind," Pa wanted to know.

"When I was in the store in Tupper today I saw a notice on the wall. Halverson's down by Demmitt have milk cows for sale, most of them in calf. They want ten bucks each for them, if we could get one that's gonna freshen in a month or so we'd be getting a cow and a calf."

"That's a hell of an idea," Pa said.

"Oh but wouldn't it be so nice to have milk and cream and butter once again!" Ma exclaimed.

"We had better go first thing in the morning and hope that they haven't sold them all," Alf said to Pa.

"We could go through the bush and lead her home," Pa suggested. "It would be a lot shorter than going around the road."

The next morning they left right after breakfast. School was nearly over and it was the last year for Francis. It wouldn't be long before he was out looking for some kind of work, but in the meantime there was an awful lot of work to do at home. Time passed quickly and the miles dropped away for Pa and Alf. After two months away, Alf and Pa had a lot to talk about.

"With a cow and three horses we've got to get a corral made and some pasture fenced in." Pa planned. "We should get some kind of a dugout made for water if we can." It was an enjoyable walk through the woods and the fresh morning air smelled good.

At home Ma was in the garden, it was growing nicely and she carried water from the well to sprinkle on the little plants. She had made a sprinkler from a tin can with the bottom punched full of little holes. She hadn't been sure if the seeds would be any good. They were so old. So she had tested them out before spring by putting a few seeds between sheets of newspaper and keeping it damp. In a few days they had started to sprout so she knew that they were good seeds.

Ma had gotten some rhubarb roots from one neighbor and some horseradish roots from another. She also had some flower seeds and winter onions from Mrs. Erickson. On the east side of the garden they took a strip about six feet wide. This was separated from the rest of the garden by a long row of winter onions and rhubarb plants. At the end they planted the horseradish and the rest was planted in flowers. Oh, how they brightened up the place. There were multicolored Sweet Williams, bright red Poppies and pink Bachelor Buttons and a profusion of shorter colorful flowers but I had no idea what they all were.

Ma liked to have bouquets of fresh flowers in the kitchen. She said that it cheered her up. She was quite happy with her garden, the little red French

Breakfast radishes would soon be ready to eat. She said that it wouldn't be long before the leaf lettuce was ready as well. That was going to be a treat for me! I had never eaten lettuce or radishes before. Ma said that the garden would be a big help this winter.

I didn't know much about cows, up until then I'd only seen them at the neighbors, never up close. "Tell me about cows, Ma."

"What do you want to know?"

"You get milk from cows, right Ma?"

"Yes, and cream and butter too."

"The milk comes out of those things that hang down in the back, don't it Ma?"

"Those are teats," she said. *Oh ick, she said that word.*

"Ain't it bad to say that word Ma?"

"What word?"

"Tits, Ma, isn't that a bad word?"

"I said teats, not tits and when you're talking about cows its fine to say that."

"But aren't they the same thing Ma, how come we call them tits on cows and *ninnies* on people?"

"They are really called breasts on people, we just say *ninnies* to little kids."

This is getting confusing for both of us, I thought. "How do you get the milk out, Ma?"

"You pull and squeeze at the same time and the milk comes out."

"Oh that's got to hurt! Don't the cows get mad?"

"No," Ma said, "they don't mind at all." I pinched my nipple, *ouch that really hurts!*

"I'm glad that I'm not a cow Ma."

"Me too," Ma said.

Helen and Francis came home from school, Helen helped Ma prepare supper and Francis brought in the wood. He was making a gun for me that would shoot little wooden bullets. He found an old spring and a piece of pipe somewhere and with that he could make a gun. He could make nearly anything. He said that it should be finished in a couple of days and I could hardly wait.

We had supper and Ma was wondering when Pa and Alf would make it home. "Well cows don't hurry, especially one that's in calf," Francis said.

"I suppose you're right," Ma answered.

I wondered what *in calf* means and decided to check that one out later.

The dishes were done and Helen was working on her homework. Ma and I were putting the chickens to bed when Pa and Alf came around the corner of the barn. They had a white cow with them. "Meet Snow," Pa said to Ma.

"What a pretty girl," Ma said as she pet the cow. She really was pretty, her coat was kind of a curly dappled white color. She had a wide soft muzzle and big brown eyes with long lashes. Ma pet her on the head and she pushed her nose against Ma leaving a wet spot on her apron. "She seems so gentle," Ma smiled.

"She really is," Alf said "and she should freshen in a couple of weeks."

I didn't know too much about cows, so I touched her gingerly, reaching from behind Alf's leg. She felt soft and warm, kind of nice. I snuck a peek at her teats and wonder how butter would come out. "Does she give milk now, Pa?" I wanted to know.

"Not until she calfs, then there will be lots." I was confused about this calfing thing and sometimes they called it freshen. I wondered *where does this calf come from? Maybe a big stork like the one that brings kids brings it.*

They put Snow in the barn and gave her some hay, and then Pa and Alf went in to have some supper. As Ma was warming up their supper, they told her about their trip and the deal that they had made for the cow. After they ate, they sat back and smoked and drank tea. They all seemed to be really pleased about this cow.

"Having milk again will be so good," Ma told them. "We've got eggs now and the garden is growing, it's going to be so much easier to cook now."

Another great day! I thought, *I learned a whole lot of things today.* I still didn't want to say *teat* I was too embarrassed. I said my prayers and thanked Jesus for all the good things that were happening for our family. I checked Tim's sparks and his battery seemed to be okay. I told him about the cow and we fell asleep.

School was out and Francis was helping Pa and Alf make a corral and fence off some pasture. For pasture they cut poles and fastened them to the trees. It really made a crooked fence but Pa said that it was a quick way to do it. The corral was coming along nicely as well. Francis had my gun finished and I was shooting little wooden bullets at tin cans. Sometimes I even hit one. I thought that gun was the greatest thing that I'd ever had. *Someday,* I thought, *I might even get to shoot a moose with it.*

The first of July was coming soon and everyone was excited about it. That year we could all go to the park at Tupper for the holiday. The horses and wagon made that possible. The park was a park in name only. It was a piece of land that the government had set aside for a little park. It was only a few acres. The local people built a dance hall and cleared an area for picnics. They made a baseball diamond and set up some booths for soft drinks and ice cream. Dominion Day was a day when all the neighbors could visit and the kids could play together.

The day before the picnic, Ma told Pa that she thought we had one rooster too many and that one would be great fried up for the picnic. Pa agreed. I hadn't had fried tame chicken before and I could hardly wait. Ma made a big potato salad to go with the fried chicken and a big crock of lemonade made with ice from the icehouse. *What a day this was going to be!*

With everyone dressed in their best clothes, we climbed into the wagon and drove off to the park. We arrived there in about an hour and a half. Pa found a good place to park the wagon in the shade of a big willow tree. The horses were unhitched and tied to the wagon wheel and Pa had brought some hay to feed them later on.

I'd never been to a picnic before so I stayed close to Ma for a while until I got a feel for the place. Some younger people were playing softball and I watched them play for a while. I didn't quite understand what they were trying to do, but they seemed to be having a good time. I met some neighbor kids that I sort of knew. We played and ran in some races. Everybody's legs were longer than mine and I didn't win anything.

Supper was what I'd been waiting for, as usual I was starving and that potato salad and fried chicken was totally delicious. I washed it down with a big glass of lemonade and that really finished off the meal. Ma had bought those lemons especially for this day. It was a great day for Ma as well. She visited with all the ladies that she hadn't seen for quite some time. Pa talked to some of the men and Alf played ball. Helen and Francis went off with some of their friends and everyone really enjoyed the day.

Later Pa took the horses to the river for a drink and gave them some hay for their supper. There were more ball games and visiting and around nine o'clock the dance started. The local boys took turns playing the music. Jim LaForge played the sax and his brother Bob played the fiddle. Gord Fossum and Alf took turns on the banjo. Norval Hayes could really saw off some mean tunes on the fiddle as well. There were several others who could play and they all took turns playing and dancing.

Seeing as it was Dominion Day, they started off the dance with 'God Save the King' and 'Oh Canada'. Everyone stood to sing. It seemed that everyone was proud to be Canadian. Then the hoedown began. They played Fox Trots and Waltzes and some good old Square Dances. I played outside with the other kids in the dark. I couldn't remember when I'd had so much fun!

At midnight the music stopped and it was time for lunch. On the stove they had big copper wash boilers full of hot coffee and there were boxes of sandwiches that all the ladies had brought. They put all the sandwiches together and passed them around to everyone. There were roast moose sandwiches, jam and peanut butter, egg salad and salmon. They were all so good! After the lunch break the music started up again and the dancers were back on the floor. With a bellyful of sandwiches and the time approaching one o'clock in the morning, I couldn't stay awake any longer. Ma put me up on a corner of the stage with a lot of other kids. With the music playing and the foot pounding of the musicians keeping time, we were all asleep in minutes.

The bouncing of the wagon woke me up. It was dark and I could see the stars covering the sky. I was lying on a blanket in the wagon box. Helen and Francis were lying there too. Ma, Pa and Alf were sitting on the wagon seat and the horses trotted towards home. The air was fresh and cool, the blanket felt good. The rumbling of the wagon was so soothing that I just fell back to sleep.

It was late when I woke up the next morning. Ma made me a couple of pancakes for breakfast. I ate one with lard and a little sugar and the other one with a little syrup. I loved Ma's sourdough pancakes and she let me have a little weak coffee to wash them down.

"Did you have a lot of fun yesterday?" She wanted to know.

"Oh I did Ma, I played with a lot of kids and the lady at the booth gave me an ice cream cone for turning the crank on the freezer."

"Did you like it?"

"It's the first one that I've ever had Ma, it was really good but they make your head ache if you get too much on the roof of your mouth."

"Yes they do," Ma laughed.

"When we get milk from Snow, will we be able to make ice cream?"

"Yes, we will."

"Ma, I'd like to have running shoes like the other kids, you know the ones with that round rubber thing on the ankle."

"I know the ones you mean, son."

"I could probably run faster if I had running shoes, my moccasins slip on the grass. I might even be able to win a race!"

"Maybe someday when there's enough money, but for now it's bare feet or moccasins."

I knew that she would get me some if she could afford it and so I told her, "It's okay."

"Go see Pa, he's working on the corral, ask him to show you what's in the barn."

"What's in there, Ma?"

"Go and see."

I ran out to where Pa was working and told him that Ma said he should show me what was in the barn. We walked over to the barn and Pa opened the door. Standing right next to Snow was the most beautiful little black and white spotted calf. She was still kind of wobbly on her legs. Her eyes were big like her mother's and she had knobby knees. Lord, she was cute! I reached out and touched her and she put her nose on my hand. Snow looked on approvingly and let out a *Moo*.

"What do we call her Pa?"

"I think that Spot sounds pretty fitting, don't you?"

"Oh yes, that sounds real good to me, are we gonna have milk now Pa?"

"The calf has to get the first milk," Pa said. I really wanted to know where she came from but it seemed to be some sort of a secret so I didn't ask. I ran back to the cabin to tell Ma how nice the calf was. I was already thinking about ice cream but I didn't know how we could make it without a freezer. Ma told me that a lard pail inside of a larger pail with ice and salt in between would work nicely. She said that you just have to turn the inside pail back and forth with your finger. I sure hoped that she was right because I could hardly wait.

Ma was so pleased about Snow and her new calf. "What a difference this will make, cream for the tea and coffee, milk for the porridge for the kids to drink." She said, "Having milk to cook with is going to be great."

"Is milk good on porridge Ma?"

"You'll find out in a few days," she replied.

They finished building the corral and Alf and Francis started cutting wood for winter. They cut the poplar trees with a Swede saw into blocks and then split and piled them. Pa was planing the boards for the floor, they were dry enough on the outside to plane he told us. The shavings curled out of the plane in long ribbons and the wood was white and smooth behind the plane. "Will the lumber be dry enough to put down by fall?" I asked Pa.

"I sure hope so" Pa said, "It will really be nice to have a floor again." Ma brought out some tea and we sat on the freshly planed boards and had a drink. She ran her hand over a nice smooth board and smiled.

"You do a good job, Joe," she said. He put his hand on hers and smiled. It gave me a good feeling to see the tenderness in their eyes.

"The garden is doing really well," Ma said, "it's sure going to help this winter and with the milk and eggs we are going to eat a lot better than last year."

Pa told her that even if there was still no money things were slowly improving. She agreed. Tea was over and Ma returned to the cabin and Pa to planing the boards.

Ma worked in the garden during the day when she was not busy inside. In the evening she mended our old worn out clothes. As she put patches on patches, she said that if we didn't get some new ones soon that there wouldn't be anything left to patch.

I could hardly wait for that first glass of milk. Then one morning Pa brought a whole pail full into the cabin and put it on the table. "Here's our first pail full," Pa smiled. Ma poured some into a pitcher and some into a glass.

She handed the glass to me and said, "Try this." And I drank my very first glass of milk.

"It's good Ma, really good." Ma put the rest of the milk in a crock and put it in the icehouse. She covered it with a tea towel and smiled. I thought that she was really happy. Tim was meowing all over the place so she put a little milk in a saucer and gave it to him, he lapped it up like it was his last meal.

The next morning was wonderful, we had milk on our cracked wheat mush. It was so much better with milk instead of water. Ma and Pa had cream for their coffee and Tim and I each had a little to drink. After breakfast, Pa brought in another pail of milk and suddenly we had lots of the stuff.

They skimmed the cream off the milk in the icehouse. "Look at this cream, this milk is really rich," Ma told Pa.

Pa poured the skim milk into a pail and took it out for the calf. She had to learn to drink from a pail. Pa put his fingers in the milk and then in Spot's mouth. She sucked on his fingers and he moved her head into the pail. In a few minutes she was drinking by herself straight from the pail. Pa had done that before, I thought.

Ma washed out the crock and started all over with the morning milk. "It won't be too long until we have enough cream to make butter," she told Pa.

"We'll have to make a churn," Pa said "but in the meantime we can just shake the cream in a sealer." Ma looked at me and told me that then I would be able to drink some buttermilk.

"Is buttermilk good, Ma?"

"You just wait and see!"

I headed outside and lay down in a bunch of foxtails out by the barn. The sun felt good and the foxtails were soft as could be. I watched the clouds drift over the pine trees. Some of the big fluffy ones looked like they might catch on the tops of the tallest trees. I could hear the flies buzzing around the barn and I could smell the new cut hay piled close to the barn. I thought that I was the happiest, most contented kid in the whole, wide world. *What more could I want, I love this place, it is my home.* Tim came and lay beside me and then it was truly perfect.

Chapter 9
Never Play Horse

Just when everything seemed to be going so well I somehow fell victim to a series of small misfortunes. Ma told me that my guardian angel would always guard me and guide me through my life. Well I think that he must have been sick, on holidays or something. One thing was for sure, he wasn't helping me at all.

Pa and I were home alone. While he was busy planing the floorboards I was just playing around. Noon came and Pa told me that we had better get something to eat. Pa wasn't much of a cook but he could boil water and fry eggs. He lit the fire in the cook stove and put some water on for tea. Pa didn't know where Ma kept things but he finally managed to find the bread and butter. He handed me a little pail and sent me to the hen house to get a few eggs for dinner.

I was really pleased to be able to help and I ran off to get the eggs. I found four eggs, put them in my pail and headed back to the cabin as fast as I could run. I was nearly there when I stubbed my big toe on a root. I went tumbling head over heels on the ground and with one mighty swing I threw the pail of eggs right up against the cabin wall. Pa heard the crash and me hollering my head off as I hopped around on one leg holding my throbbing toe with both hands.

"Now what the hell happened?" Pa asked me. Between yells I showed him my toe, it was split right down the middle and the blood was squirting out. "Shit kid, why in hell don't you look where you're going, get your arse in here and let me fix that toe." Pa didn't have any patience with things going wrong and he looked pretty disgusted. He put some clean water in the washbasin and added a handful of salt. "Stick your foot in there," he said.

"Holy smokes Pa, that really smarts," and I jerked my foot out.

"Get it in there and leave it in there," he told me in no uncertain terms. "Where in the hell does Ma keep the rags?" he barked as he looked around. Then he looked in the dirty clothes box and he took out a ten-pound salt sack that Ma had just emptied. With scissors he cut about an inch off the top of the bag. He dried my foot and wrapped up my split toe with the salt encrusted strip of cloth. Well, if I thought that the salt water hurt, it was nothing compared to the bandage.

I was really trying hard not to cry because that seemed to make him really mad. "Quit your sucking and take it like a man," Pa said. I didn't feel like much of a man. The eggs were broken so he made some toast on top of the stove. I was not feeling very good so I just went to lie on my bed. Pa had his tea and toast and a smoke and I fell asleep with Tim lying beside me. That was some comfort to me anyway.

When Ma came home she came in and woke me up. "Let me see that sore toe," she said. She was gentle and I knew that she wouldn't hurt me. The bandage was soaked with dry blood and it was stuck to my toe. She got some warm water and carefully soaked the bandage off. "My Lord," Ma said "that toe should have some stitches in it, it's split wide open."

"You gonna sew my toe Ma?" Just thinking about that gave me the willies.

"No, but I'll try to tape it so that it will be together." She put some tape on it and some salve, then she wrapped it up with a clean bandage. It felt a little better after Ma fixed it up but I went around limping all that I could for the next few days. In a couple of weeks it was as good as new.

One day a neighbor lady and her granddaughter came over for a visit. I'll call her Mrs. Brown and she brought her granddaughter, Jane. Mrs. Brown and Ma looked at the garden and the flowers and then they went in for tea. Jane and I were playing. We didn't have any toys so we played house and tag and any other games that we could think of.

I told her about this new game that I saw the horses playing. "Let's play that," she said. So we played horse, down on our hands and knees, taking turns on top. It was my turn to be on top, and I tried to figure out why the horses thought that this was so much fun. Oh well, it was my turn so I decided to do my best and then we'd play something else.

Just as I was at my best with my arms on her rump and my head going up and down, "Whee, he, he," I did my best to sound like a horse, Mrs. Brown came outside. She grabbed me by the arm and flung me to the ground.

"You dirty little devil," she screamed "just what do you think that you're doing?"

Ma heard the ruckus and came outside. "What's going on?" she asked.

"That dirty little devil was riding her like a bull on a cow."

"No I wasn't Ma, we were just playing horse."

"Don't make a big deal out of nothing," Ma told Mrs. Brown, "they were only playing." She complained some more and I could see that Ma was starting to get mad. "Just let it go," Ma told her.

"Hmmp, I've never been so humiliated in all of my life," Mrs. Brown said.

"Oh I'll bet you have," Ma replied.

"Come Jane, we're going home."

"Goodbye," Ma said in a kind of sarcastic tone.

"Where did you learn that game?" Ma asked me.

"When I went with Pa to get the lumber." I told her about the horses in the field and that Pa said that they were playing.

"Well, maybe you shouldn't play that game any more."

"Oh, I won't Ma, I'll never play horse again with anybody, Jeez Ma, she nearly tore my arm off."

At bedtime I knelt down to say my prayers. I asked Jesus to help me be a good boy and I told him that I didn't know why horse was such a bad game but I promised never to play it again. I told Tim about my day and this horse business. He couldn't have cared less. I checked him for sparks and he still had lots, he purred like a tiger and we both fell asleep.

Helen was growing up, she was fourteen and starting to look like a girl. She acted differently and I thought that maybe she had started to like boys. I was outside playing and I saw her walking down the road towards the neighbors. I knew that she was going somewhere special because she was kind of gussied up. I ran to catch up with her, "Where are you going, Gug?"

"None of your business."

"I want to go with you, Gug, can I, huh?"

"No you can't, you just stay at home and behave yourself."

"Oh let me come Gug, Ma won't care."

"I said 'no' and I meant it, go home!"

Boy is she ever cranky today, I thought. *Well, I've got a plan that will sure fool her!* I waited until she went around the corner and then I followed her. I didn't see her looking back so I was sure that she had no idea what I was up to. I kept behind the bushes until she was out of sight and then I ran until I could just see her again.

Am I ever fooling her, she thinks that she's so smart. We were just about to Fossum's place and she was out of sight. *Around the next corner and we'll be there, and then let's see how smart she is.*

I stepped around the bush at the last corner and she leapt out and was on me like a cougar. "You little arsehole, I'm gonna kick your arse till your nose bleeds!"

"Oh, please Gug, don't kill me," I screamed "you scared me so bad I nearly pooped my pants!" Oh man, was this girl ever mad.

"You'll wish that was all that happened before I'm done with you."

"Let me go Gug," I pleaded with her, "let me go and I'll go straight home."

"Don't call me Gug, you little shit, I can't let you go home by yourself, now I've got to take you with me."

"Look at you. You're dirty as a bloody urchin."

"What's a urchin, Sis?"

"Get over here and hold still." She grabbed me by both ears and spit all over my face.

"Yuck, phooey," I cried, "what are you doing to me?"

"I'm washing the dirt off, you dirty little bugger." She took out her hankie and wiped my face. Man I hated that! "That's a little better," she said, "come on and stay outside and don't you be askin' Mrs. Fossum for cookies".

I was wondering where she had learned all that swearing. I thought, *maybe I should tell Ma about this swearing* but one look at her face and I changed my mind. She'd kill me for bloody sure if she knew what I was thinking. We arrived at Fossum's and I sat outside on the step and pet their old dog. She must have told Ma Fossum not to give me any cookies because she sure never gave me any! She made such good ones too.

When we returned home I was really in deep doodoo. Ma was frantic because she couldn't find me anywhere. She was afraid that a bear or something ate me up. What I didn't understand was that if she was so glad to see me, how come I ended up outside cutting a switch! Sure enough, begging didn't help and I got my arse whipped one more time. I was sure that my left arm was getting a lot longer than the right. That was the one that they always held me up on my tiptoes by while they gave me an adjustment.

Well, Helen was mad at me, Ma was upset with me and after supper she told Pa and he was not happy with me either. "You should be strapped," Pa said. "Don't you ever leave the yard again without telling your mother."

"Oh, I've already been whipped Pa and I promise never to do that again."

"You know what they do with kids that are bad and don't listen to anybody?" Pa asked me.

"No Pa, I don't."

"They send them to reform school."

"What's that Pa?"

"It's like a jail for bad kids, you get whipped ever day and you don't get much to eat and you have to sleep on the floor." This bit of news scared me really badly and I started to cry.

"Whip me Pa, but please don't send me to that place."

"Say your prayers and go to bed," Ma said. "Don't forget to tell Jesus that you're sorry and ask him to help make you a good boy."

Ma said that Jesus died on the cross for our sins and that every time I was bad it's like pushing the thorns deeper into his head. I sure didn't want to do that so I prayed and told Jesus how sorry I was for being so bad. It didn't seem like I was doing anything this bad. "Please Jesus," I cried, "please help me to be better." I crawled into bed and I felt awful, I was only four and a half years old and already they were thinking about sending me to this jail place. I still didn't think that I did anything quite that bad, it was a good thing I didn't poop myself!

Tim seemed to understand so I told him all my problems. He seemed to purr extra loud that night. I lay there and thought about all the things that happened in that one day. I did learn one thing, when you make people that you love mad at you it's not a good feeling. It makes a heavy feeling in your chest and a lump in your throat. I hugged Tim and felt sad and I finally went to sleep. It was not the blissful sleep that I usually have. Somehow I didn't feel quite as loved and safe as I did other nights and I hoped that Jesus wasn't mad at me too.

I got up in the morning and felt pretty ashamed of myself. I figured that I'd better keep a really low profile for a while and give everyone a chance to cool off. I sat quietly and ate my breakfast. Everybody seemed normal and it looked like they may have forgotten the whole thing. I sure hoped so. I didn't want to go through that again.

It was the time of the year to put new hay in the mattresses again. Ma and Helen cut the stitches down the side of the tic and took out the old dry crumpled hay, and then they stuffed it to over full with new hay and then they stitched it up again. I loved it when they would do that. It was so soft and had the fresh smell of new sweet hay. Then the beds were ready for another year. Ma said that some people had mattresses with springs and padding and no hay at all. I sure felt sorry for them, they missed out on the soft hay and that great smell.

One day Pa was coming home from town and he met Bill Cundiff along the road. Bill was an old bachelor who lived alone with his dog and some horses. "Hello Joe," Bill greeted Pa, "how's things?"

"Fine," Pa answered, "how's things with you?"

"I'm kind of gibbled up Joe, I hurt my back last spring and it's still not good."

"That's too bad."

"I need some help for a few days, cutting oats for my horses. You reckon you could spare the time?"

"I can help you next week," Pa said.

"Ain't got no money to pay you, Joe."

"No matter, ain't anybody got any money these days."

"Tell you what Joe, I heard about your escapade with the deer last winter and how you broke your knife in the process."

"I damn near got killed that time," Pa told him.

"Did you get a new knife yet?" Bill asked.

"There's not been any money for one yet."

"I got a real good brand new one that I bought years ago and ain't ever used it. If you want it you can have it for pay."

"Sounds good to me, I'll see you first thing Monday morning."

Monday morning found Pa over at Bill's place, it was going to take three or four days to do the work as Pa had to stook the oats as well as cut it. Bill did the cooking and Pa did the work. It was too far for Pa to come home every night and Bill had an extra bunk in the corner that he just needed to move some junk off.

Now, Pa could feel a bedbug a mile away and as soon as the light was out he stared to itch. He sat up and lit his lighter. The wall was crawling with bed bugs scurrying away from the light. "What's wrong Joe?" Bill asked.

"Holy shit Bill! You got enough damn bed bugs to carry a guy away."

"I know but I'm used to them, they don't bother me none."

"Well they bother me, they just eat me alive, and I'm going to sleep in the barn." Bill told Pa to suit himself.

So Pa spent his nights sleeping in the barn but those damn bugs get in your clothes and they are hard to get rid of. Pa finished the work and Bill gave him the knife and sheath. It was like new. Pa was happy with the knife and Bill was happy with the work so it was a good deal all around.

Pa came home and stood outside the door, "Delma!" Pa hollered, "Come out here a minute."

"Come on in. What are you standing out there for?"

"Bring me some clothes. Bill's place is crawling with bed bugs. The damn things like to have eat me alive. I'm not bringing these clothes in the house. I'll get a tub of water and wash me off and then I'll soak these clothes in it." Pa took the tub to the barn and carried some water for it. Ma got him a pail of hot water to put in it and some lye soap.

After a while Pa came in and got ready for supper. Pa showed the hunting knife to all of us. Ma told Pa that it was a real beauty. We ate our supper and Pa told us about the bed bugs. "I don't know how in hell he lives there!" Pa said.

"Maybe he's so dirty they won't bite him," Ma replied.

Pa said that that was altogether possible.

Bed bugs are not something that you want to have and if you live in a log cabin it's even worse. They get into every nook and cranny and lay eggs and pretty soon you're over run with the bloody things. We tried hard not to have any but once in a while some neighbors would visit and put their coats on the bed. Pa would be in bed only a few minutes and he'd be swearing. In winter there's only so much that you can do. Ma would wash all the bedding and sprinkle sulfur powder on all the joints in the bed. If you're lucky you might get rid of them, if not then you would have to fumigate the whole house when spring comes.

I like it when we have to fumigate. Pa has an old tarp that he made kind of a tent out of. We take all the food out of the cabin and close everything up tight. Then Pa takes a pound of sulfur and puts it in an old pail. He sets the sulfur on fire and puts the pail up on the stove. Sulfur burns very slowly with a blue flame and an acid smoke that would kill anything. It burns for hours and the blue smoke pours out of every crack in the cabin.

It's just like camping out for us kids. Ma cooks over a campfire and we all sleep in that makeshift tent. I always think that it's just great and Tim is happy to sleep anywhere that I sleep. The next morning they open the door and all the windows and let the cabin air out for a few hours. Then all the bedding and clothes that we had outside have to be washed and we'd be free of bed bugs until somebody else brought us a new batch.

Chapter 10
Murder and Massacre

Pa rode ole Bird to town to get the mail one day and came home with some pretty startling news. "Old man Schwartz just shot and killed a guy named Hoover down at Watson's ranch."

"Why did he do that?" Ma asked.

Pa told us that Schwartz was looking after Watson's horses and that he was supposed to leave today and Hoover was going to take over. Hoover showed up the afternoon before and Schwartz shot him as he walked up the drive.

"What did Schwartz do after he shot Hoover?" Ma wanted to know.

"Well, after he shot him, he burned down the barn with the horses in it and just disappeared into the bush."

Schwartz only lived a mile and a half from our place. He had a little log cabin in the bush. He has always been a strange acting little guy. Whenever there was a community function going on and there was a camera around, he would just disappear. Ma was easily worried and asked Pa, "What if he should show up at our place."

"Its not likely that he will but everybody had better keep close to the cabin, if old Ranger barks, pay attention. The police are looking for him but there are no tracks to follow and he's a sly old bugger, we'll keep the rifle right here by the door."

Fortunately, Schwartz didn't show up at our place or any place else for that matter. The police never found him and from what people said, they never looked very hard for him either. It was kind of ironic because at the same time as the shooting there was a serial in the *Free Press* about Albert Johnson, the mad trapper of the Yukon. It took several Mounties to capture him and then only after he had killed several of them.

So with one eye out for Schwartz, Pa finished planing the boards for the floor. They needed something to nail the boards down to so they cut some straight little poles and hewed the top flat. Pa leveled them out about sixteen inches apart and started nailing down the boards. Oh they looked so good, all white and clean. When they got to the center of the room, Pa said that they had to stop and dig a cellar.

Pa and Alf took turns digging and everybody else carried the dirt outside. Ma gave me a little pail so that I could help. Pa told us to use the dirt to bank up the cabin. He said that would make it warmer for winter. It looked funny, digging a hole in the kitchen. It took all day working to dig the cellar but by suppertime there was a nice six-foot square hole. Pa put some boards over the hole until the floor could be finished.

The next day Pa and Alf finished the floor and made a trap door for the cellar and Helen and Francis walked to town to get the mail. Weeks before, Helen had sent twenty-five cents for an introductory offer of cosmetics and she was sure that it would be in the mail by now.

Pa and Alf put the last board down on the floor. "Well Ma, your new floor is down, what do you think?" Ma beamed and said that it was beautiful.

"Can I run around in my sock feet now Ma?" I asked. Of course it was summer and I was barefoot but in the winter with a dirt floor you have to wear moccasins all the time. It made the cabin so much brighter inside but it made noise when you walked on it with shoes.

Helen and Francis came home with the mail and Helen was all excited. Her cosmetics arrived and she couldn't wait to have a good look at them. They also had a surprise for Ma. They had pooled their little bit of money and bought Ma a brand new broom for her new floor. Ma twirled around the room with it making imaginary swirls on the floor. Ma hugged and kissed them both and I wished that I could give her something.

Helen finally unwrapped her little parcel, inside was a small orange box with a small lipstick, a little box of powder and some rouge. It had 'Tangee' in big letters on everything. Her face glowed as she admired her prize and she and Ma smelled the powder. "It's lovely," Ma told her. I didn't think that it was fair that Helen and Ma didn't have to wash their faces like I did. I was sure that girls just covered the dirt with powder.

Helen had quite a few friends that were her age. They visited back and forth pretty often and this day Bernice Sullivan was over for a visit. I tried to hang around to see what they were talking about but they chased me away. When I did manage to get close they whispered, I thought that they were talking about boys but I was not sure.

They looked at Helen's new makeup and they 'oohed' and 'aahed' about it. They put on a little lipstick and made their lips go funny. Then they admired themselves in Ma's little hand mirror. They had a picture of some movie guy named Robert Taylor, I thought that he was just a guy but they seemed kind of silly over him. I told Tim that girls are silly and he seemed to agree.

Mid afternoon arrived and it was time for Bernice to go home. Helen told Ma that she was going to walk part way home with her. I asked if I could go and Helen gave me *the look* and after the last episode I decided to forget it. After they left, I went in the bedroom and lo and behold she left her makeup on the bed. I really never had a good look at it before and this seemed like a good time. I put a little lipstick on my lips and tried to wiggle my lips like they did. *Oh but this stuff is smooth.* I made a little mark down my cheek. *Oh this stuff is great! I'll use a little for war paint and play Indian, what a great warrior I'll be!*

I took the lipstick out behind the icehouse, stripped off my few clothes and painted stripes all over myself. *Oh but this stuff goes on smooth!* As I was whooping it up behind the icehouse, Helen came home and found the box open and the lipstick gone. She only had to listen outside to know where I was. When she saw me with that war paint on it was Custer's last stand all over again, only this time it was going to be the Indians that got killed. She took one look and the chase was on. "You little arsehole, wait till I get my hands on you."

I was thinking that I should be someplace else, any place but there. I was streaking through the brush in my nudity with her in hot pursuit. "I'll knock those stripes right off of you," she hollered. *Jeez, that's got to hurt,* I'm thinking. *God but that girl can really run fast!* Anyone who's ever been in Alberta knows about the wild roses that grow there. They are beautiful to look at but they really scratch the hell out of your lower extremities when you run through them nude.

After a long painful chase, I stubbed my toe on a stick and sprawled head first into the brush. *That didn't feel good either.* She pounced on me like a hawk on a chicken, and then she laid some marks on me that wouldn't wash off. "Don't kill me Gug, please don't beat me all up." Once more I was begging for my life, I wondered how I get myself into these fixes.

"I should kick your little arse till it barks like a fox."

Will it really do that? I thought. *Where in the world did she learn all this violence anyhow?*

To add to my indignities, she dragged me by the arm to the cabin to burden Ma and Pa with this little problem. *They are probably gonna whip my arse again, no wonder that it's so small.* She wouldn't let me get my clothes but made me suffer the embarrassment of being dragged nude to the cabin. I was probably the only Indian brave who yelped and bawled so much because of his sister. Ma looked up again and her eyes sort of rolled back in her head. "Whatever is going to become of you son?"

"I don't know Ma but one thing for sure, I won't ever play Indian again." I promised never to touch lipstick again and not even kiss a girl if she has lipstick on. *As if I'd ever kiss a dumb girl!*

Another day was over, pretty much the same routine as every day. I was sore all over and had rose stickers in places that I wished they weren't. After supper, in spite of my begging, they told Pa. Lord, I wish that they wouldn't tell him everything, this time it looked like he was having convulsions, some day I'm afraid that I'm going to kill him. It was bedtime again. I said my prayers again and asked Jesus one more time. I didn't think that he was listening because I didn't seem to be getting any better like I kept asking. Maybe he was just tired of listening to me. I got into my bed and once more I reviewed the day in my mind. Tim was already snoring so it was no use talking to him. All told, it was a pretty good day, except for getting beaten up. I couldn't help but wonder what my guardian angel does all day. He wasn't helping me too much. So, deep in thought, I faded out in that wonderful thing they call sleep.

Needless to say, I was not my sister's favorite person for a while. Every time she looked at that little stub of lipstick she got riled all over again. I was really pussyfooting around trying not to tick her off any more than she already was. I already found out that she can run faster mad than I can scared and that can hurt but in spite of my good intentions, harmony was destined not to last long.

A few days after the lipstick incident, Ma decided that she could leave Helen and me alone without her killing me. I was not too sure but I had no choice. Helen was reading a romance magazine that all the girls passed around and I was trying to draw a horse like Alf had shown me, and trying hard not to irritate her. I looked out the window and there, not twenty feet from the cabin was a nice pair of white tail deer. I quietly went over and touched Helen and pointed out the window. She slipped off her chair and softly crawled towards the bedroom. I didn't know what she had in mind but I thought that this was a good time to vindicate myself.

Without a sound I slipped over and got my gun that was kept by the door. I loaded a wooden plug in it and carefully pulled back the spring. I crept over to the open window and took a good aim at that buck's rump. I just knew that would knock him down and I'd be a hero. *Wrong!* Just as I pulled the trigger and hit him square in the butt, I saw Helen creeping out of the bedroom with the rifle. *Oh my Lord, so that's what she was doing!* She looked up just in time to see me shoot. "I hit him right in the bum Sis," I hollered. To my dismay and total surprise, he and his mate just bounded off. Oh Lordy, I'd done it again!

"I'll hit you right in the bum, you dumb little turd," and the chase was on again.

I headed for the door. If she caught me again I'd be a goner for sure. She jumped at me and I took a detour around the heater and made it to the door. *Oh feet, don't fail me now!* I was running so fast that my feet and legs looked like wheels. I thought, *if I can just make it to the barn and climb up the logs on the end of the wall maybe I can get on the roof and have a chance.*

I was nearly up the wall when a hand grabbed me by the seat of the pants and threw me on the ground. *I guess that's it for me.* I was too scared to holler and I looked up and saw the sky. I was sure that it was the last time that I'd ever see it. Then something strange happened, she gave me that *look*, the one that makes little holes in you and she said, "You make me so damn mad." She turned around and walked away. I was really sorry, but I didn't think that it was a good time to try to explain that to her. I decided I'd just stay outside until Ma came home.

Of course, the first thing Helen did when Ma got home was to tell her the whole story. I figured that I was safe so I tried to tell her that I thought my gun would kill that deer. Besides, I didn't know that she wanted to shoot a deer. She never did that before. "That's just a toy pop gun, you little idiot."

"Oh, let it be, you two will drive me crazy," Ma exclaimed.

I tried to tell them but nobody understood that I really thought that my gun would kill that deer. After my prayers and my talk with Jesus, I crawled into bed. Things hadn't been going too well for me lately. I wondered if Henry would have had so much trouble. *When everybody's mad at you it feels like maybe it would be better if you could die.* Maybe then they would like me better. I talked to Tim. I was really lucky to have one good friend that wasn't always mad at me.

The men were getting ready to go harvesting and this was the year that Francis was big enough to go with them. With them gone, Ma, Helen and I were alone. Ma milked the cow and Helen helped her with the other chores. They watered the cow and calf and the horses. They cleaned the barn and looked after the chickens. It was my job to gather the eggs and carry in the wood. It was also time to pick raspberries and blueberries.

I liked picking berries. I always ate more than I put in the pail because they just tasted so good. One day after lunch we headed down an old trail to pick blueberries. About a half-mile down the trail we slipped a little ways into the bush and there was a nice little blueberry patch. The berries were really ripe and I ate them like a bear. After a while I started to get a bellyache and I told Ma that I had to do a big job. She sent me over behind some bushes to do my thing.

For some reason the wasps were building their nests in the ground and that turned out to be a bad thing. I went behind the bushes and took down my pants and just got started on my big job when all hell broke loose. Apparently wasps don't like it when you poop on their nest. They came out of their hole in full force and bit my bum and stuff all over. I started hollering and dancing around trying to get out of there and slapping my butt with both hands. It's hard to get far away jumping around with your pants down.

Ma and Helen heard me screaming and they came running, it looked a lot like they might laugh. *Boy, they better not!* Ma scooped me up and ran away from there with a few mad wasps still following us. My butt and stuff was really smarting so she took me out to the trail, where there were wagon ruts with water in them. She scooped out a handful of mud from a rut and smeared it all over my behind. Lord, that was nearly worse than the bites but it did take some of the sting away.

That about took care of the berry picking for the day. Ma carried my pants and I had to walk home with my little bare arse all smeared up with mud. I was sure hoping that we didn't meet any of our neighbors. Helen wasn't helping either, every little ways she jumped up and down and slapped at her butt and yelled Ow, Ow! That really aggravated me. We got home and Ma washed the mud off. She made a paste with baking soda and put it on all of my bites. I had over twenty bites and I was pretty sore, so I lie on my belly on my bed and fell asleep. Ma woke me for supper and I felt a little better until I tried to sit down. I thought, *I'll eat standing up for a few days. I have a lot to tell Tim tonight.* I told him that I made a solemn vow never to poop in the woods again

I recovered in a day or two and the berry picking continued. We were down on the side hill picking raspberries. They were plentiful, big and juicy. I lie on my back under the bushes and picked the big ones that were hanging underneath. *What a life, I think, what could be better than this? The day is warm and the berries are delicious.*

"Helen," Ma said, "quit shaking those bushes. You're knocking all the berries off."

"I'm not shaking them Ma, it must be Lewie."

I wasn't shaking a thing! I held the bush with one hand and took the berries off with the other. The bush never moved a bit. Besides that, I was fifteen or twenty feet away from Ma so how could it have been me. I kept on eating and soon I heard Ma again and she was getting mad sounding. "Lewie, stop shaking those bushes right now!" Then I heard her scream again and some big black thing ran right over top of me, rolling me around in the raspberry bushes. *Those things are really scratchy.*

"What was that," I hollered at Ma.

"Are you all right?" she screamed.

"Yes, but what was that Ma?"

"Oh, it was a big bear. We were picking on the same bush. Let's get out of here," Ma said as she held me closer to her.

"But the bear's gone now Ma," I told her. She was really scared and shaking so we hurried home.

By the time we got home, Ma had a migraine headache. She lay down for a while and Helen lit a fire and I got a cold cloth for her forehead. Helen made some tea and gave her a couple of aspirins. After a while she felt a little better. We didn't pick any more berries that fall.

It must have been the time of year that the animals move around an awful lot. When we went to bed that night, Ma left the bedroom window partly open, as it was an unusually warm night. We were only in bed a short time when there was some noise outside. Suddenly there was a really loud snort right in the window and a lot of crashing against the cabin and then all was quiet. Ma was up in a flash and closed the window. She lit the lamp and checked the door. Helen got up too, "What was that noise, Ma?"

"I don't know, but it really scared me," Ma said. We sat up for a while and listened but there were no more noises so we went back to bed.

I don't know if Ma or Helen fell back to sleep but I soon powered out and fell fast asleep. Besides the noise didn't seem to bother Tim, so I felt pretty safe. When morning arrived we only had to look out the window to see who the noisemaker was. Right by the window were the tracks of a big Bull Moose. It was mating season and I guess that he was curious and not afraid, however when he stuck his nose in the window and got a smell of people, he snorted and hit his horns against the cabin as he took off. Ma said that she would sure be glad when the men came home.

LIVING ON A HILL

Christmas 1938
Back Row: Helen, Joe, Alfred, Francis
Front Row: Lewis, Delma

Chapter 11
Winter Preparations

The days were getting shorter and Ma said that it was time to dig the spuds and get them in the cellar. Helen was back in school so Ma and I dug the garden and Helen helped when she got home. Ma dug the potatoes and I put them in a pail and carried them to a little depression that Ma had made at the end of the garden. She said that spuds keep better if they cure for a few days in a pit covered with dirt.

First we did the potatoes and then the carrots. There were turnips as well and to be honest about it, I don't like turnips very much. Ma always says that I have to eat them because they are good for me. I sure hope so because they taste yucky. Finally we had all the vegetables dug and in the pit all covered with dirt. Ma said that we'd put them in the cellar the next week. There were a few beets but they didn't do too good. They were kind of woody but Ma said that we'd keep them anyway. We may need them before spring.

We had run out of coal oil for the lamp and Ma said that we had to wait for the men to get home before we could get some more. In the meantime we had to use a *bitch*. (That's when you put tallow in a can with a rag and light it. It makes light but it smokes like a bitch, hence the name.)

We had to check the chinking and plaster between the logs on the cabin, those cold winter winds would find every crack that wasn't filled. The logs were chinked tight with moss and the crack on the outside plastered with mud. Ma and Helen chipped the loose mud off and redid it with fresh stuff. Ma mixed up some clay from the cellar with water and a few ashes and spread it on the cracks with a thin stick. I tried to help but most of the mud ended up on me.

Ma said that it would soon be time for the men to come home from harvesting and she was right. A couple nights later we just finished milking the cow when the dog started to bark. There were Pa and Alf and Francis walking down the lane. We all ran to meet them and everyone was talking at once. They looked thinner and tired, their clothes were pretty well worn out and it was their best ones that they were wearing.

Ma made tea and put some supper together for them. "It's sure good to be home again," Pa said. Alf reached in his pocket and gave me a big shiny nickel. I admired it, with a picture of a king on one side and a big five on the other.

"You better put it away before you lose it," Ma told me. No sooner did she say that than I dropped it on the floor and it rolled right down a crack between the boards. *Damn that floor anyway!*

"Take the board off," I told Alf.

"We can't do that, it will ruin the board and we don't have another." *So much for my happy time and my nickel!*

We all turned in early, what with everyone being tired and that bitch for a light. In the morning after a good night's sleep and a big breakfast, everybody was in a good mood. Alf said that Francis and he would go to town and get some groceries and some coal oil. Ma and Pa relaxed and talked for part of the day and Ma washed some of their dirty clothes. It was good to have everyone home again. It didn't take long to put the vegetables in the cellar with everybody helping. Pa said that it was really good to see a winter's supply of grub down in the cellar. It seemed to take some of the worry off of their faces. They counted the money left after buying groceries and there was about sixty dollars left. "That has to do until we have some fur to sell," Pa said. They needed a few clothes and they studied the catalog for the best prices and tried to figure out what they could afford and what they needed the most. Ma wrote out an order and it came to nearly forty dollars. Pa said that would have to do.

They checked their traps and snowshoes to make sure they were ready for winter. They wouldn't have long to wait as the wind was blowing cold from the north. Alf and Francis made a trip over the trap line to make sure that everything was okay. They went to the little lake where there was a small cabin and got it ready. By the time they got home the snow was already starting to fall. Winter had arrived.

Then it was my birthday and I had made it to five! Ma made me a cake and Helen made me a card. I was glad to be five but I wished that I were bigger. I still could hardly see on the table and I couldn't seem to get over thirty pounds. I weighed myself every time we went to Erickson's and I never seemed to change. "How come I'm so little," I asked Ma.

"Oh you'll grow one of these days, don't worry about it," she told me. *Easy for her to say, try walking in three feet of snow when you're only two and a half feet tall. When I say my prayers tonight I'll ask Jesus to try and make me bigger.*

It was a cold winter and that made trapping difficult. When the traps were set they had to go and check them every day or two, cold or not. Ma was teaching me to read and write my numbers. She said that she talked to the teacher and she would let me start Grade One in May if Ma taught me at home. I did my work on old paper bags from the store. Ma cut them open and ironed them flat. We used the wrappings from Eaton's parcels as well. Sometimes Ma had to write letters on bags and make envelopes out of them too. It was hard to see the pencil marks on those brown bags.

When the men weren't trapping or doing chores they were building a big sleigh for the horses. The previous fall they dug some birch trees out by the roots and sawed them two and a half inches thick with Pa's old ripsaw. By cutting them the right way the roots had a natural curve for the runners. Pa said that makes them really strong and they won't crack if they hit something. They wanted to build a logging sleigh. There wasn't enough room in the cabin but it was too cold outside so they planed and sawed and shaped all the parts in Ma's kitchen. She had a lot of patience as she worked around them.

They sold some fur and bought some flat iron to shoe the runners and made the other metal parts. They also bought a can of red paint and a little can of yellow. They painted all the wood pieces red and then they painted a little yellow stripe on them. Oh, it did look beautiful! They made a good fire outside and got the iron red hot in the coals and bent it to shape. Then they were ready to put the whole thing together. They made it so that the wagon box would fit right on. Finally it was finished and we could all go places in the sleigh.

Like the previous year they took the fur to Hythe to sell it and buy groceries. They ordered another box of fruit from Woodward's as well. We had more food but money seemed to be harder to come by than the previous year. The men who smoked had trouble finding enough money for tobacco. Francis was glad that he didn't smoke, that was one thing that he didn't have to worry about. I smoked moss rolled up in old newspaper out behind the icehouse. It makes me cough and my eyes run but I do it anyway.

Alf took an address from an ad in the paper where you could send for natural leaf tobacco somewhere in southern Ontario. They got together with a couple of neighbors and for only few dollars they ordered twenty pounds of tobacco. It surely was cull tobacco. They sorted it out and some wasn't too bad and some was black and moldy. They wiped the mold off with vinegar and put it aside to dry. They used to call it dog bedding and with good reason. Ma said that it smelled like horseshit. Pa said that it tasted like that too. I wondered why they just didn't go to the barn and find a nice horse turd and save some money.

At night they rolled a leaf of tobacco up and cut it into little strips with a razor blade, then they put it into an old tobacco can with a piece of potato to keep it moist. Ma said that she wouldn't smoke if she had to go through all that trouble. I thought that she was probably right.

I begged Francis all the time to pull me on the sleigh. He tried to ignore me but I didn't give up easily. Ma told me to go and play and leave him alone. Finally he said that he'd give me a ride if I lay on my belly on the sleigh. I agreed and he ran as fast as he could toward the barn. When we got to the barn he stepped aside and the sleigh and I crashed head first into the barn. Boy, did that make the top of my head hurt and my eyes go crooked and water! He asked me if I wanted another ride and I was so stupid that I said yes. Well, two head firsts into the barn was about all that I could take for one day. He went back to what he was doing and I went to lie on the bed for a while and wait for the pain to go away. Ma asked me what was the matter and I told her that my head hurt and why. "What's the matter with you anyhow?" she asked Francis. "Are you trying to kill your little brother?"

"But he's a bloody nuisance, Ma." He told her. She told him not to do that anymore. *I guess that's the end of my sleigh rides.*

I liked to go out and play after supper. It was really cold and the moon shone so brightly that it made the snow sparkle. I liked to watch the Northern Lights flash and dance across the sky. They changed colors from yellow to green and blue and white and orange. Sometimes they were so bright I couldn't see the stars.

The coyotes were howling over on the rim of the hill, the whole thing was awesome and I loved the wild feel of the wilderness. If I watched long enough, sometimes I'd see a shooting star streak across the sky. I stayed out until I couldn't stand the cold any longer. It feels so good to go in and stand by that old wood stove when you are really cold.

I asked Pa what makes Northern Lights, he said that it was the sun shining on the ice burgs at the North Pole and we can see the reflections in the sky. That made sense to me but I also believed that it was the trees moving that made the wind blow. That must be right because the more the trees move the harder the wind blows.

Alf said that it was time for me to learn to shoot and make campfires. He spent thirty cents on an extra box of twenty-two shorts for me to practice with. "Come on Souris, let's go kill some cans," he told me. (Alf calls me "Souris" most of the time. It means mouse in French. I'm not very flattered by it but I'm used to it.)

He showed me how to aim, "Just nestle the front bead in the groove in the rear sight," he instructed. "Now get the bead on the target and squeeze the trigger." I aimed real good and shut both eyes and jerked the trigger. "No, No, squeeze I said and keep your eyes open, shit, if you jerk like that you'll shoot yourself in the back of the head!" I tried again and I did better.

"Now take your time," he told me "try to hit the can, not every tree in the bush." After a couple careful shots I finally hit a can. "That's good," he said "take your time and make every shot count." He showed me how to load the gun and how to carry it. He also showed me how to put it down when I crawl through a fence so I don't shoot myself in the ass.

"Enough shooting for today, let's make a campfire and warm up a little." We gathered some dry twigs from under a big spruce tree and he took a little bark off of a birch tree. We got some bigger sticks from a dead willow. "Now pay attention, this could save your life some day." He kicked the snow away, right down to the ground with the side of his foot. "Get your back to the wind, so it won't blow your match out." He peeled the birch bark into thin layers and sort of stacked it up and with his hand cupped he lit the match and set the bark on fire. It caught quickly and he broke up the dry twigs and put them on top. Soon he put on the bigger sticks and we had a nice fire going.

"Don't make your fire too big, it just wastes wood and it's so hot you can't get close enough to cook on it."

"What if I can't find birch bark?" I asked him.

"You make shavings or prayer sticks. I'll show you next time." After we warmed up for a while, he kicked snow on the fire and we headed for home. *Oh, I've got a lot to tell Tim tonight!*

"When can we go again, Alf?"

"In a while, when I have time we'll do it again, in the meantime you can practice making little fires." I told him that I would. *Man, it feels good to be growing up.*

I practiced making fires in the bush behind the barn. Sometimes I held the match too long trying to get the birch bark to light and burnt my fingers. I was getting pretty good at it and I wanted to learn how to make shavings. I watched Pa at night when he made shavings to start the fire in the morning. It looked so easy. He took a kindling stick and with his razor sharp knife, he peeled about a dozen long shavings like a rooster tail on a stick. I tried but I could never cut the stick. "Why can't I do it Pa?" I asked him.

"Let's see your knife," he said. "Well it's no wonder, your knife is so dull you could ride it all the way to Winnipeg and not cut your arse." So Pa took out the whetstone and showed me how to sharpen my knife. He told me to be careful now because it was really sharp and I could cut myself really badly. He showed me how to cut away from myself, and then if the knife slipped I wouldn't cut myself. It took a lot of practice to make shavings and I kept on trying.

It was Christmas time again and Helen and Francis let me go with them to get a tree. They were so fussy about finding the right tree. I saw lots of good ones but they always found something wrong with it. Finally they found one and both agreed that it was the one. Francis cut it down and they carried it home. I felt sorry for people who lived in the city because they don't have trees to cut for Christmas, I didn't think that they could have Christmas in cities because of that. Helen said that they did and I wondered how she knew.

They got the tree put up and once more Ma opened the trunk and all the wondrous contents appeared. Oh but that tree looked so beautiful all decorated in the corner of the cabin! Ma baked some cookies and pies and we had a big rooster for Christmas dinner. Ma had saved him just for that occasion. She told me that we'd have a lot more chickens next year because the hens would be old enough to hatch out chicks on their own. I'd never seen that before but it sounded good to me.

A few nights before Christmas we all got dressed up and went to the Christmas concert at the schoolhouse. Ma stood me on the kitchen table to finish dressing me. I really hated that. *How can I be big and grown up when she stands me on the table? She doesn't do that with Alf.*

Helen was in the concert and I'd been memorizing a little poem that I was going to recite. It was only four lines long but I was still pretty scared. My turn came and I went out on the stage to say my poem. *Holy smokes! There must be a hundred people out there.* Helen had told me to look past everybody and look at the door and say my piece. I did, "Santa is a fine old man, Santa is a dandy, he always fills my stocking up, with toys and nuts and candy." Everybody clapped and I make it off the stage. I felt weak and wobbly and I thought that I might pass out.

After the concert was over came the big part. Santa showed up and had a little paper bag with a few candies and an orange for all the kids. I thought that Santa must be Norwegian because he sounded a lot like Olaf Fossum. After he left they moved the seats and put them up against the wall and they had a dance. I played with some kids that I knew and ate my candies. I finally fell asleep and when I woke up we were on our way home. Ma said that I did a good job of my recitation and that made me feel good. *I'll tell Tim about it if I can stay awake long enough.*

Christmas day finally arrived and just like the last year I could hardly wait. I got a little coloring book and some crayons. I also got a big scribbler with an orange cover with a big five on it. I was really going to be able to do my schoolwork now. Christmas dinner was wonderful, that big rooster was a real hit and with all the vegetables that Ma had this year, she surely outdid herself.

Some of the neighbors visited over the holidays and there was a New Years dance at the school. I liked dances. I liked the music. You could hear the musicians keeping time with their feet a mile away. There was a cute little girl named Irene and I mustered up enough guts to ask her to dance. She said yes and we tried to dance around the floor without getting stepped on by the grown ups. Of course neither of us could dance but we thought that we could. I kind of liked her, and after that night we danced together at every dance that we both went to. I told Tim about her and he gave me a look like maybe I was crazy. *I don't think that I'll talk to him about girls anymore.*

It was a whole new year and all the festivities of the holidays were over. My hunting lessons resumed and Alf took me out to shoot my first rabbit. There were a million snowshoe rabbits, at least it seemed that way. Everywhere you looked there were some. Alf said that they were starving to death because there were so many of them and not enough food. They sat very still, snow white in the snow and they thought that you couldn't see them. Alf told me that they didn't seem to know that they have a big black eye. "Make the first shot count and you won't have to shoot again," Alf said. I rested the rifle barrel on a branch and tried to remember all the things that he'd told me. I got a good bead right on that black eye. Took my time and slowly squeezed the trigger. The rabbit just fell over and didn't even kick.

"I got him!" I shouted, "Alf, I got him!"

"Yes, you did, and that was a really good shot," he told me. That made me feel so good because he is a crack shot and for him to say that was really high praise. He could put a match up on a fence post and light it with his twenty-two rifle. I hoped that maybe someday I'd be that good. He gave me a lot of lessons as to the danger of a rifle and the great need to use tremendous care and caution. After that I was allowed to go hunting squirrels and rabbits and partridges all by myself. The best thing that he ever taught me was to never point a firearm at anything that you don't intend to shoot.

The Cabin in the Pines

School Kids at Independent Valley 1939
Back Row: Helen Houde, Eva Gammon, Bessie Hamilton, Joyce Rule
Centre Row: Merv Staggs, Nona Staggs, Bob Hamilton, Dave Hamilton
Front Row: Opal Staggs, Charlie Hamilton, Lewis Houde, Daphne Rule

Chapter 12
Chickens and Eggs

It was a nice day in February, and I convinced Pa to take me with him to one of our neighbors. We took old Bird and the stone boat, and off we went. Along the way we met another neighbor and of course they stopped for a talk and a smoke. Just as we were parting he said to Pa, "Say Joe, are your hens laying?"

"No," Pa told him, "I guess it's the time of year that they take a rest."

"You'll have to pound salt up their arses," he said to Pa. *I didn't know that*, I thought. That night as I lay in bed I got to thinking about those hens. If that was all that it took, I'd take care of that tomorrow. It seemed to be a job just my size and boy would they be surprised when I started bringing in eggs again.

After breakfast I snuck out with Ma's saltshaker, I didn't want her to know, as I wanted these eggs to be a surprise. Now all that I needed was something to pound salt with. After looking around for a while I came up with an old round headed clothes peg. So with the saltshaker and the clothes peg I set off to the hen house to get those lazy hens back in production.

For the first hen I picked out a big fat red hen that looked like she should be a good layer. She simply didn't agree with me and she put up a heck of a fight. After a lot of scratching and flapping I finally got her subdued and I sat on the floor holding her by the feet. I gave her a good shot of salt and I proceeded to pound it in with the clothes peg. Apparently this really upsets old hens as the scratching and squawking got real violent. It seemed to make the other hens uneasy as well. When I thought that I'd pounded in enough salt, I let her go and she ran around the coop taking funny high steps. *Maybe the eggs are coming already*, I thought.

For the second one I got a nice barred rock hen, I guess she was watching the first hen because she didn't seem to want any part of the procedure and she was extremely adamant about that. By then I was beginning to understand why no one else was doing this job. I was not sure if the eggs would be worth it. My original plan was to have one egg a day for everyone in the family and that meant six eggs a day and seven if Uncle Fred was home. At that point I was thinking that maybe one egg every other day would be okay.

I was getting pretty beat up by this time so I looked for a nice quiet gentle hen. I spied a nice tawny colored hen that seemed unruffled by the goings on. She sat quietly on the second roost at about eye level. I realized that maybe I'd misjudged her because as I reached for her legs she pecked me really hard right on the lower lip. I let out a hell of a yell and the fight was on. I grabbed her by the neck so that she couldn't peck me but that left her feet free. With her feet kicking and her wings flapping she just about turned me into a girl. By then all the hens had gotten into the act, flapping and squawking and making an awful mess.

Ma heard the noise all the way to the cabin and came running to see what was wrong with the chickens. She took one look and crossed herself, "Sweet Jesus, what in the world are you doing?"

"I'm fixing to get these hens to lay Ma."

"Oh Blessed Mother, give me strength," she said and she looked up at the ceiling. I looked up but I didn't see anything. I also made a mental note of what she said. I thought she must be tired lately because she had been saying that a lot lately. I'd have to try to help her more.

"Look at you, you're covered with straw and feathers and chicken crap and your lip is bleeding down your chin, get to the house right now! You wait till I tell your Pa about this."

"Do you have to tell him Ma?"

"I'm afraid so," she said. Sometimes the talks she has with him resulted in me getting an attitude adjustment with Pa's razor strap. That's not something that I was looking forward to. "What were you doing to those hens anyway?" she asked.

"Harold Rule told Pa yesterday that if the hens weren't laying to pound salt up their arses and I was trying to help."

"That's just a stupid saying, it's not true," she said.

"Why would he say that if it's not true Ma?"

"Who knows son, just don't believe everything that you hear."

"But Ma, how do I know what's true and what's not?"

"If you don't know you should ask somebody," she told me. I thought, *she might be right. It might save me a lot of trouble.*

After supper she told Pa about my escapade with the hens. He was really upset this time, his eyes squinted and he clapped his hand over his mouth and he made some queer snorting noises. Ma also seemed to have a pained look on her face and had a bad twinge in her cheek. *Oh lord, I guess that I've really done it this time, maybe Pa's having a seizure or something.* After a while they both seemed to recover except that Pa's forehead kept wrinkling up and down.

"Are you gonna lick me Pa?"

"Not this time son, but don't you ever do anything like that again."

"Oh I won't Pa, not ever again," I promised.

With that Ma told me to say my prayers and go to bed. "Be sure to ask little Jesus to help you to be a good boy," she added. She put some salve on my split lip and as I went to the bedroom I heard her say to Pa, "I really don't know what will become of that boy." I knelt down and said my prayers and I wondered if little Jesus ever did anything that got him into trouble and if he did, who did he pray to for help?

"Is Tim in bed with you?" Ma asked.

"No Ma," I lied, but I was sure that she knew that he was because he was every night. Tim and I lay there in the dark and I rubbed his fur backwards and he still sparked. I wondered how that happened. I thought of my day and felt my swollen lip and all of my scratches. *The only thing that I learned today was things not to do. Maybe tomorrow I would learn something useful.* So with peace made with Ma and Pa and little Jesus and my guardian angel watching over us, Tim and I drifted into that wonderful sleep that comes only to kids and cats.

After breakfast the next morning I was playing with Tim while Ma mixed bread dough. I was wondering about Jesus. Ma finally sat down with a cup of coffee and I told her that I needed to know some things about Jesus. "Okay," she said "what would you like to know?"

"How old is Jesus, Ma?"

"Oh, nearly two thousand years old I guess."

"Is he really small, Ma?" I asked.

"I don't think so, what makes you ask that?"

"Well, we always call him little Jesus, maybe if he's big and that old he might want to be called Mr. Jesus."

Again she looked at the ceiling and rolled her eyes. I still didn't see anything, maybe her neck was sore. "Why don't we call him Dear Jesus, I think that would be nice," Ma said. I think about it a little and I agreed, Dear Jesus sounded real good and that's what I'd call him from then on. Another problem solved. I asked her if her neck is sore. "No son, why do you ask?"

"Just wondering Ma." Did Joseph, Mary and Jesus have chickens, Ma?"

"I don't know," she said.

"Couldn't God just make chickens if he wanted to?"

"Yes, he could," she answered.

"Wouldn't God make chickens and give them to his son if he needed some Ma? Pa would give me chickens if I didn't have any, wouldn't he Ma? I'd give my son chickens."

"I'm sure you would," she said, "but for now go and feed the dog and that old tomcat in the barn." Our old barn cat's name was Pug. Pa named him that because he had six toes on each front foot. Ranger, our dog was part German shepherd and part wolf. We had to keep him tied up because he chased the cow and tried to hamstring her. His wolf heritage was showing through.

Ma took the pancakes that were left over from breakfast and a little pail of warm water and gave them to me to go feed them. As I put on my coat and toque, I asked Ma about Pug. "If Pug is a tomcat, how come Tim isn't?"

"He's been fixed," she told me.

"Was he broke?" I wanted to know.

"No, it's something that they do to males sometimes."

"Have I been fixed?" I asked.

"Not yet," and there was that twitch in her cheek again.

"Will I be?"

"No," she said.

"Has Pa been fixed?"

Again she said no, but I thought that I heard her say, "He should have been," under her breath. "Go feed those animals and stay outside for a while, I've got work to do."

Ranger was glad to see me. He wolfed down the pancakes and had a big drink of warm water. I pet him for a while and then I went to look for Pug. There was a real plague of rabbits, thousands of them eating anything that they could find and our haystack was covered with them. Even the dog couldn't keep them away, there were so many that he got used to them and just slept.

Pug liked to play tiger and he hid in the hay until a rabbit got close enough and then he pounced on it. Then there was an awful fight with fur flying all over the place. I could hear Pug meowing as he fought with a big buck rabbit. The wagon box was leaning upside down against a tree and underneath was Pug and this rabbit locked in mortal combat. Pug had his teeth in the rabbit's neck and their front feet were locked around each other as they tried to disembowel each other with their hind feet. "Hold him Pug," I hollered, "I'll help you." I ran to the barn to get a pitchfork and threw it like a spear at the rabbit.

Poor old Pug, I missed the rabbit and pinned Pug to the wagon box by a hind leg. "I'm sorry Pug," I yelled as I pulled the fork out. He gave me a look that said, "Next time don't help me," and he took off for the barn. I must have only got him through the skin because it didn't seem to bother him very much. I decided to keep this incident to myself, I didn't want to ruin Pa's razor strap. Finally another day was over and it was off to bed again. I said my prayers, talked to Jesus, same thing every night. I was thinking, *he must be getting awful tired of hearing this.*

For a while Pa had been complaining about sharp pains in his lower stomach. Right after breakfast as he was getting ready to go out to do the chores, he doubled over in pain. "What's wrong, Joe?" Ma said as she hurried to his side.

"Oh, that one hurt like hell," Pa said. Ma pressed his stomach and he hollered.

"You've got bad appendicitis," she told him "you've got to get to a doctor right away."

Alf and Ma took Pa to the train and Francis stayed home with me. Ma went to Pouce Coupe with Pa and Alf brought the team home. He'd go back and pick her up the next day. Alf said that it was a good thing that they still had a few dollars left so Ma could stay at the Hotel over night. It seemed awfully strange with both Ma and Pa gone. Helen made supper and Alf and Francis did the chores. Supper was quiet. Nobody seemed to have anything to say. "Do you think Pa will be okay?" Helen asked.

"I'm sure that he will," Alf assured her. Alf and Francis discussed how they would do the chores and run the trap line as well. "We'll have to hustle our butts." Alf said. "Money is real short and we have to come up with some for this." We said our prayers and went to bed.

The next day after breakfast, Alf went back to town to meet the train and pick up Ma. Helen had supper already made when they got home. Ma looked really tired and everyone wanted to know about Pa. "They operated this morning but I had to leave before he came to. Doctor Hollis said that they really had to come out and that he would be fine, he said that he would phone the store if anything goes wrong and they would get the message to us."

It was nice to have Ma home but she seemed to be worried. They always said the rosary at night but I was usually asleep by then this night was different. They said it earlier, Ma leading and all the rest of us answering. I'd never done this before and it seemed awfully long. I had a hard time staying awake and as soon as it was over I went right to bed. I hugged Tim and went to sleep.

Ma told us that the doctor said to come and get Pa in a couple of weeks. That seemed like a long time when you didn't know how he was doing. Ma and Alf talked after supper and she seemed to depend on him a lot. She seemed to be really down and said that every time things seemed to be going better, something knocked them down again. Alf told her not to worry, that everything would work out. She seemed somewhat comforted by that.

The two weeks finally passed and they went to get Pa. Ma walked into his hospital room and he was so glad to see her that tears filled his eyes. "Take me home, Hon," he said. It was quite a ways from the hospital to the train station and they had to spend another quarter to get there. Pa was really tired by the time they got home but he was so very glad to be home. Ma put him to bed and made some tea. All of us kids were glad to see him and we sat by his bed. He told us about his stay in the hospital and Helen and he compared her stay with his.

Everybody was at ease with Pa at home and on the mend. The doctor said that he should take it easy for a couple of months. Every day I went with him for a little walk like I had with Helen. Each day we walked a little farther and he got a little stronger.

That winter we just seemed to be plagued with one problem after another. Just as Pa was recovering nicely, Helen got a severe case of tonsillitis. They had to come out. This time a friend of hers, Bessie Hamilton, had the same problem so they went to the hospital together to get their tonsils out. They removed Helen's but Bessie had a cold so they left hers until her cold was better.

All of these problems had Ma beside herself. "Where is the money going to come from to pay for all this?" Pa assured her that it would all work out and not to worry herself sick about it. After a few days they brought Helen home and her throat was really sore.

She didn't look good to me, real pale looking. In the middle of the night she called for Ma, "It's bleeding real bad Ma." Ma went to her bed and looked at her throat.

"My God, she's hemorrhaging, get some ice quick!" By then everybody was awake. Alf got some ice and packed her throat. "I hope that works," Ma said. I didn't know what to do so I prayed to Jesus to help my sister and I told him that this time I really meant it. The bleeding finally stopped and everybody went back to bed. Ma left the light on and she probably didn't sleep very much. By morning Helen seemed to be on the mend and said that her throat felt better. Ma made her some warm cocoa and some soft porridge. That seemed to make her feel better still. In a few days she was back to normal and Pa was also doing well. Soon all of the problems were a thing of the past, something to talk about next year.

Spring arrived and the trapping season was over until next year. Pa and Alf made the trip to Hythe to sell the fur and buy some groceries. Pa said that it was time to send some money to the hospital and the doctor. Things seemed to be going much better again.

It was a nice spring morning and Ma and I were in the kitchen. She looked out the window and said, "Oh look at that nice big red breasted robin." I ran to the window and looked.

"I don't see one."

"April fools," Ma told me.

"April what, Ma?"

"April fools, it's a trick you play on people on the first day of April," she explained.

"What for?" I wanted to know. After an hour of trying to explain it she said that she wished she had never brought it up. After a while I sort of grasped the idea and I spent the next week doing April fool tricks on Ma.

"It's only the first day of April," she told me. I didn't care. I was going to make the best of this.

"Here comes Pa, the cow is out of the corral, there's a bear looking in the window." She ignored me and it was no fun anymore.

Ma had been teaching me Grade One at home and she had made arrangements with the teacher for me to start school on the first of May. I could hardly wait. The day arrived and I had my little yellow lard pail for my lunch and off I went with Helen. I could do everything that the teacher gave me to do. I had never played with modeling clay before and I thought that was wonderful stuff. I could make people and animals and all sorts of things. Mrs. Sullivan was my teacher and it made me feel good when she said that the things that I made were good.

I really liked art class and they had good crayons at school. I did a wonderful drawing of a baby deer hiding in the grass. I proudly showed it to the teacher. She looked at it and turned the paper around like she couldn't make it out.

"What is all the green?" she wanted to know.

"It's a baby deer hiding in the grass."

"I don't see a deer," she said. *God, sometimes she's stupid for a teacher*, but of course I didn't say that out loud.

"Of course you can't see it," I tell her. "If you could see him he wouldn't be hiding."

"Don't act smart," she told me. I made a face. "You will stay in your seat all through recess."

"What did I do?" I asked. She gave me a look and I thought that she was getting mad so I shut up. When I got home I told Ma what happened and she told me to be a good boy and listen to the teacher.

It was the time of year for Alf to go work on a farm again, this time he went to work for a farmer named Frank Smolick up north of Dawson Creek. It was closer to home than when he went to work down by Grande Prairie. The cow had gone dry and Pa said that she would be until she calved. Spot, last years calf was getting pretty big. Pa said that in another year he could get her bred. I thought, *what she's going to do with bread, I'll never know*. The hens were laying again and some of them were sitting on eggs. Ma said that they'd hatch in about three weeks.

Francis made some little peaked houses for the hens to set in, they had slats across the front so the hens couldn't get out and the coyotes couldn't get in. One day we heard an awful lot of squawking going on and so we ran out to see what was wrong. There was a big black snake going around and around the little house. When he put his head through the slats the hens pecked hell out of him, he didn't like it but he was determined to get those eggs. Ma changed his mind when she cut him in half with the axe. Lord, but he was an ugly big thing. *I really hate snakes, they give me the willies*. His tail kept twitching and Ma said that it would until the sun went down. I asked her how come and she said that she didn't know but that it just would. I thought, *I'll keep checking to see if she is right*.

Alf came home around the middle of June and of course we were all glad to see him. He had promised me before he left that he would take me fishing when he got home and I didn't let him forget it. Early Saturday morning he said that today was the day. Ma made us a little lunch and Alf got out the green line and a shiny spoon hook. "Let's hit the road, Souris," he said and we headed off to Erickson's place at Swan Lake.

It was three miles to Erickson's and my legs were short so it took us a couple hours to get there. It was great walking down the trail with my big brother. I liked those mornings, the air was cool and fresh and it made my chest feel good just to breathe it in. The pea vine along the trail was as tall as me and it was wet with dew. We went down the trail past all the familiar places. We walked down the detour hill and out the west gate. We walked down past the bear pen and along the creek. We could see Charlie Gordon's little cabin way up on the hill. I wondered how he got water up there. We came down to a little flat that went right to Erickson's house. We visited with Ma and Pa Erickson for a little while and she gave us some iced tea and shortbread cookies. She made really good cookies and I tried to be a gentleman and not eat too many.

They live right on the shore of Swan Lake where Callison Creek runs into the lake. They dock their boats in the creek where it is quiet. Carl Erickson is a Swedish boat builder extraordinaire. He has five beautiful lap strake boats tied to the dock.

Alf told Carl that he wanted to take me fishing and Carl said to take any boat we wanted. He is a very nice man and speaks quietly with a soft Swedish accent. Alf picked a small white boat with blue trim and we rowed down the creek. On the way he stopped by an overhanging willow and cut a nice little fishing pole. He tied the green line to the pole and tied the hook onto the line and we rowed out on the lake.

Swan Lake is a beautiful lake surrounded by hills on the east and gently sloping woods on the other sides. I noticed that the surface of the lake was a mirror image of the sky. It was the same color but one shade darker. It was warm and blue and completely still and the boat hardly disturbed the surface of the water. The oars made little round swirls as Alf rowed quietly along. All along the shoreline the ducks paraded their new babies and the redwing black birds gave us a serenade as they flashed their red patches among the reeds. The serenity and beauty of it all had me mesmerized until Alf broke the spell.

"Are you going to stare off into space or are you going to fish?"

"Oh, I want to fish," I told him. He showed me how to hold the pole and how to feed out the line. I'd never seen a hook in the water before and this one was a marvel to see. As soon as it was in the water the spoon started to spin, shining and flashing in the sun. Soon the line was all out and I could feel the hook pulse like a living thing as I held the pole.

"Now if you feel a bite, give the pole a little jerk to set the hook."

"Okay, Alf," I wanted to do this just right so that he'd be proud of me and tell everyone what a good fisherman I am.

I felt a tug on the pole and my enthusiasm took over. I gave the pole a jerk and the hook flew out of the water just missing Alf's head. "Shit, Souris, I said a little jerk, not try to throw the damn fish all the way to shore!"

"I'll do better next time," as I fed the line out again. Well not much better but I was lucky and I missed Alf's head again.

"Forget about setting the hook, just let the fish catch themselves." I felt really sheepish so I didn't jerk on the pole any more, I sure seem to have a hard time to learn how to do things right.

I was just about ready to feel sorry for myself when the pole was nearly torn from my hands, I tried hard but I could hardly hold it. "I've got a big one," I screamed, "now what do I do?" Alf took the pole and reached out and grabbed the line. He put the pole in the boat and pulled the line in, hand over hand, until a big pike was thrashing up a storm right beside the boat. With one deft move he flipped the fish right up into the boat.

"He's a dandy, maybe four or five pounds," Alf smiled.

"Look at those teeth," I told him, "they look really sharp."

"They are really sharp so keep your fingers away from his mouth." He held the fish up by the gills and poked the hook loose with the end of the pole and then he put it in the front of the boat.

Alf was about to start rowing again when he stopped, "Wait a minute, I forgot about these." He reached in his pocket and took out a little blue roll with silver ends. He opened one end of the roll and took out a little round white thing and handed it to me.

"What is it?" I asked him.

"It's candy, peppermint. I bought them in Dawson just for our fishing trip."

"They are so good, what do you call them?"

"Marvels," he said, "we better not tell anybody else about this because they didn't get any, it'll be our secret."

"Okay," I told him and I thought, *boy this day just keeps on getting better and better, fishing, candy and now a secret with my big brother. Man but this is great.*

Fishing was really good and in another half hour we had five more nice fat pike. Alf said that was about all the fish that he wanted to carry home so we headed back to shore. After we tied up the boat, Alf cut a little forked willow and slid it through the fishes' gills so that we could carry them. We thanked Erickson's for the boat and they admired our catch.

"Fishing has been good this spring," Carl told us. We set off for home and I was on top off the world. I'd caught my first fish and I was sauntering along the trail with my big brother. We talked and we had a secret and we were just plain enjoying the day. I hoped in my heart that we'd have more days like this, but if we didn't, I'd remember this one forever.

By the time we got to the top of detour hill, I was all pooped out. Alf put me up on his shoulders and I rode the rest of the way home. We showed our catch to Ma and she said that fresh fish would be nice for supper so we had better get them cleaned. We took them out behind the icehouse and cleaned them on a log. Alf got some water and washed them off and took them in for Ma to cook for supper.

After a big feed of fish for supper I was ready for bed. I said my prayers and thanked Jesus for such a great day. I hope he doesn't mind me using up his time because I talk to him a lot since I found out that I can talk to him anywhere. He's like my invisible friend that I could ask for help anytime. I crawled into bed and told Tim about my day, even the secret. I checked Tim for sparks like I did every night and once more I went to la la land.

Chapter 13
Holy Men and Summer Camp

School was out and I'd passed into Grade Two, I was feeling pretty good about that. The hens that had been setting were parading their new chicks all around the yard, showing them off. They clucked and scratched and acted like fussy old mothers as they tried to show the chicks where to find the food. The chicks ran around pecking at flies that they couldn't catch.

We'd been to the first of July picnic again and as last year it was great fun. The only thing that wasn't fun was my foot. On the morning of the picnic, Pa and Uncle Fred took the hayrack off the wagon so that they could put the wagon box on. That way we could all ride in comfort to the picnic. They got it off and it was sort of lying on its side and I was playing around on it. I was in my bare feet and as I stepped on one of the wheel covers I stepped on a spike that came right through the top of my foot. That really hurt! I thought that I would probably cry, whether Pa liked it or not. I tried hard but I couldn't get my foot off of the spike. I hollered for Pa who was putting the box on the wagon but he didn't hear me. I tried some more and I finally got my foot free and I ran to the cabin yelling bloody murder all the way.

Ma looked at my foot, "Oh my God, what have you done now?" I told her between yells as she got a pan of water and a handful of salt. Oh boy, this was reminiscent of the split toe thing only on a larger scale. Looking at the blood stringing around in the water nearly made me sick, I felt like I was going to pass out and fall off the chair. After a good soak in the salt water, Ma put some salve on it and wrapped it up. I still had a good time at the picnic but there were no races for me that time.

My foot healed up in a few days without any complications and I was able to run and play as usual. I loved this time of the year, it was warm and the days were long and lazy. All I needed to wear were overalls, no shoes, no shirt, just a life of freedom. Tim and I sat and dozed in the sun. It was quiet, just a breeze in the trees and the buzz of those blue bottle flies enjoying summer as well.

Right after lunch, the priest drove up in his Model A Ford. Ma made him a cup of tea and a sandwich and they visited for a little while. He said that he wanted to talk to Pa. "Joe's down in the hay meadow putting up hay, Lewie can show you the way if you want to walk down there."

"How far?" he wanted to know.

"Only two or three miles."

So we set off walking, "You sure that you know the way?"

"Sure," I told him. "I go down here all the time." This was the first time that I'd been alone with a priest. Ma says that they are God's representatives and holy and that I should treat them with respect and be on my best behavior around them. We had only gone a little ways when Father Owens asked me to wait a minute. He stepped behind a bush with his back to me. "What are you doing?" I asked.

"I'm urinating."

"You're doing what?"

"I'm urinating."

"It sounds to me like your peeing," I told him.

"I am. That's what urinating means."

"Why are you doing that?" I asked.

"Because I have to."

"Priests don't do that," I said.

"Of course we do. What makes you think that? We have to go just like everybody else."

Well, this revelation brought him down off his pedestal quite a bit. He just didn't seem as holy as he did a few minutes before. "Did Jesus pee?" I wanted to know.

"Of course, he was a man."

"I thought that he was God, does God pee too?"

"I don't know, no one has ever seen God."

"Well, how do you know so much about him if nobody's ever seen him?"

"It's written in the Bible."

"That's a book, isn't it?"

"Yes, the Bible is called the good book."

"I don't trust books very much," I told him "I did something that I saw in a book last year and I damned near drowned."

"Don't say damn, that's not a nice word."

"What should I say then?"

"You could say darn."

"I should call a beaver dam a beaver darn?"

"No, that's a different kind of dam."

"How do I know a good dam from a bad dam?"

"It depends on how it is used in a sentence," he said. Two dams, one good, one bad, it just didn't make much sense to me.

"Are there bears around here?" Father Owens wanted to know. He seemed awfully uneasy and kept looking all around and behind us.

"Oh yes, there's lots of bears, Pa said that he saw some fresh bear shit on the trail just the other day."

"Bear dung," he said.

"What?

"Bear dung, your father saw some bear dung."

"No, Pa said that it was bear shit and Pa knows bear shit when he sees it."

Father looked frustrated, "It's the same thing, but a proper word for it."

"Dung and shit's the same thing?" I asked.

"Yes."

"Then what's the difference?"

"There isn't any difference. It's just a nicer word that you can use in public." He seemed to be getting cranky, maybe his feet hurt.

"You mean that if I have to go I should say I have to take a dung?"

"No, people waste is called excrement, you should say, I have to go to the bathroom."

"We don't have a bathroom. We bathe in a washtub in the kitchen. We go to the outhouse for the other stuff that I can't talk about."

I didn't know anything about bathrooms but I knew that Ma always says don't ever pee in the bath water. Boy, if she ever found a turd in there she would sure whip somebody's ass. If he does that in the bath water it's a good thing that he doesn't bathe at our house.

"Did you ever see bear dung?" I asked him.

He said "No."

"I'll watch for some to show you." I thought, *if I watch real close I should be able to find some to show to him.*

"That's fine. I really don't want to see any."

"You got to watch for it in the berry patch, they eat berries and then they poop all over. You got to watch." I told him. "If you step in it, it's worse than chicken shit." His forehead was getting up and down wrinkles. I thought that maybe he was getting a headache. Maybe the sun was too hot and he should have worn a hat.

"Did you ever see a bear," I asked him.

"In the zoo."

"What's a zoo?" I asked.

"It's a place in the city where they keep animals in cages."

"Why do they do that?"

"So that people can come and see them." "But you can see them here. Why put them in cages?"

"They just do." He seemed to be getting impatient. I was beginning to think that this Priest was a pain in the butt, begging your pardon, Lord.

"What if we see a bear?" he asked.

"Do you think that a bear would eat a priest?" I asked him. He said he was afraid that they probably would. I thought that a bear would spit him out. He was so sour. "Couldn't you just ask God to make the bear go away?"

"It doesn't work that way," he said.

"Maybe you could throw some Holy Water on him and bless him and then he'd be nice and wouldn't want to eat you." I imagined a bear on his hind feet holding his front paws together, praying. I started laughing, boy that would look funny.

"What are you laughing about?" he asked. I told him that I thought blessing a bear would be funny. "That's not funny. You don't laugh about Blessings and Holy Water." We saw Pa cutting hay a little ways away, I was sure glad. That guy was one big barrel of laughs. He never smiled, nothing was ever funny and he was hard to talk to because I never said anything right. I was beginning to understand about some of those monks that Ma told me about that take a vow of silence, it would be less trouble.

Father Owens and Pa talked for a while and had a smoke. Father smoked Players and he took quick little puffs and blew the smoke out right away. I wondered why he bothered to smoke at all. Pa said it was getting on in the afternoon and we might just as well go home. Pa hitched the team to the wagon and put some hay in the box to feed the cow and calf. Father Owens and Pa sat on the seat and talked, I lay on my back in the hay and looked at the clouds. As we rode along, I thought about this dung business. If he wanted a nice word we could call it bear candy. I laughed to myself as I thought about that. If we called it bear candy I could ask him if he'd like some. I'll bet then he would agree that it was bear shit.

We got home and Ma had supper on cooking, with new potatoes and deer steak even a priest could put away a good meal. After we ate Father Owens asked me if I want to go to summer camp. I said that I was not too crazy about the idea. Ma and Pa said that I had to go to learn my religion and get ready to make my first communion the next year. For a day that had started out so good it sure went haywire after that priest showed up. Helen had to go to camp too so that would make it a little better. I really didn't want to go and I told that to Tim as we settled down for the night. Just when things were going so nicely, how come somebody had to interfere and mess up your whole life? I had trouble sleeping worrying about it.

A few days later we got ready to go. Pa took some potatoes and carrots and meat to help feed everybody at camp. Helen and I took a blanket and a few clothes in a box. We were supposed to be gone for two weeks. On the ride there I was really feeling down, nobody listened or seemed to understand that I really, really, didn't want to go.

The parish had five acres on the west side of Swan Lake and that was where the summer camp was located. There was a small church with an upstairs and that was where the girls stay. There was a big old house with several rooms downstairs and a big attic, that was where the boys slept. The nuns cooked and slept downstairs. There was a big veranda facing the lake and the windows from the attic overlooked the veranda roof. We arrived just before lunch and the sisters showed Pa where to put the food. Pa unloaded the wagon and our stuff and then he headed for home. I watched him go until he was out of sight. Sister Lucy brought me back to reality in a hurry. "Get your stuff up in the attic right now and make a bed." I went upstairs to the attic. It was one big room with kids' blankets all over the floor. There were no beds.

"Find a spot and make your bed" Sister Lucy said "then put your towel and things at the head and roll it up from the foot."

I'd never made a bed before but I did the best that I could, I thought that it looked pretty good.

Sister Lucy came up for inspection and took one look at my bed and kicked it across the room.

"Now do it right, what's the matter with you," she said. I didn't like this treatment at all but there was not much that I could do about it so I picked up my stuff and did it again. This time seemed to satisfy her.

"Get down stairs for lunch," she said, and I did.

I didn't know where to go and I couldn't see Helen anywhere. A friendlier Nun saw that I was lost and she showed me where to go.

We sat around a lot of tables on the veranda. I'd never seen so many kids before. Someone said that there were seventy kids, some were little like me and some were fifteen years old, this was their first chance to make their first communion. Lunch was a piece of dry bread and some kind of soup that looked like dishwater. My first impressions were not too favorable and I wondered where all the fun was that Father Owens said there would be.

After lunch we had lessons until suppertime. Supper consisted of boiled fish, bones and all and potatoes all mashed together. There were kids gagging all around the tables on the bones. I wondered where all the good food that Pa brought went. After supper we had prayers and Benediction, I was praying to Jesus to help me to survive this ordeal for the next two weeks.

It took about two days and all seventy kids had summer complaint. That was what the Nuns called it but I knew that it was just the shits. All night long it was a steady stream of kids running down the stairs and trying to make it to the outhouse. There was a big stone that stuck up about four inches on the trail. Lots of kids stubbed their toe in the dark and dropped their load right there. By morning there was a streak of shit from the attic to the outhouse. Some bigger boys just opened the window to the veranda roof and blew a brown stream all over the shingles.

The days dragged on, we were up at six for mass, washed in cold water and shivered though a breakfast of sloppy oatmeal and a piece of bread. We did our lessons and some kids had to help the Sisters. We carried water from the lake, got wood for the stove and helped with the vegetables. A farmer brought a washtub full of green peas and they put me, and a girl named Doris to work shelling them. We were sitting opposite each other working away when Sister Lucy walked by. She hit me up side the head and knocked me off my stool and spilled my peas. "You dirty little devil, sitting there looking at Doris with no underpants on!"

"I wasn't looking at anything," I tried to tell her but she'd got a mad on and whacked me again.

She sent Doris to put some underpants on but Doris said that she didn't have any.

"Well, you put something on or I'll pin your skirt together between your legs."

Doris left and I went on shelling peas and wondering what I should have been looking at. I wondered where the nice friendly Sisters were that used to come up to our homestead. I was thinking about the Jesus that I know and the one that they kept talking about. Theirs seemed to be different than mine.

We learned the Ten Commandments, about Jesus in the temple and the story about the loaves and the fishes. They taught us about the mystery of the Holy Trinity, the Father, the Son and the Holy Ghost all in one. We didn't understand and they said that no one did that was why it was called a mystery. I thought about it and I told the Sister that I thought I understood it. She asked me to explain and I did.

"See, Pa has this little can of oil that he oils his rifle with, he also oils hinges and anything else that needs oil, it's called three in one oil, three different oils in one can."

Sister said that was just plain stupid, that it was not like that at all. How did she know I'm wrong, when she didn't know the answer herself?

Finally the two weeks ended and Pa came to get us, I could hardly wait to get home. The bigger boys stole my soap and my toothbrush and somebody took my towel and left me with an old ripped dirty one. I was tired and hungry and I'd had the shits for two weeks, I just wanted to get home. I was so homesick that when we got home and Ma came out to meet us that I ran to her and hugged her and I burst into tears. She had tears in her eyes too. She hugged Helen and me and took us into the cabin. Helen told her that we had summer complaint real bad. She boiled some pepper in milk and gave it to us to drink. That soon slowed things down. At supper I wanted to eat everything on the table, I hadn't remembered that Ma's cooking was so good.

I was really happy to see Tim and he seemed happy to see me, he rubbed on my legs and purred. I sure had a lot to tell him. I went out and fed old Ranger his supper. He was glad to see me too and I pet him and played with him for a while. He seemed lonely so I spent some extra time with him. I felt sorry for him, he was always tied up and nobody bothered much with him. I told him that if he didn't chase the cows that he could be loose but I don't suppose that he understood. I told myself that I'd have to play with him more.

I said my prayers to the Jesus that I know and got into bed. It felt so good after sleeping on boards for two weeks. Tim was glad to sleep in bed again. He had to sleep in the sock box under the bed while I was gone. I checked Tim's sparks and I told him all the stuff that went on at camp, he purred and in a few minutes we were both sound asleep.

It was the lazy hazy dog days of summer. The days were hot and the sun was a big red orb with the smoke from forest fires turning the green hills into blue. The men were making a dugout so that there would be water for the stock. Pa borrowed a slip and a plow from the county and they plowed the ground first and then scooped the dirt out with the slip. It was slow going but the hole was getting deeper every day. Pa said that when it was six feet deep they would quit.

Some of the berries were getting ripe and Ma and Helen and I picked them, we picked some chokecherries down by the canyon and Ma made syrup with them. It really tasted good. Pa said that when they got the dugout finished they had to get a supply of wood put up for winter. The garden was doing well and Ma said that it'd be a good feeling to have the cellar full again.

I lay on my back in the patch of soft foxtails and enjoyed the hot August sun. High overhead a pair of red tail hawks circled lazily as they had a free ride on a warm updraft of air. Pa said these foxtails were a damn nuisance and they weren't good for anything but they sure were nice to lie in when they were green.

Chapter 14
Aristocracy and Weasel Bait

Ma was a member of the Women's Institute, as were most of the ladies in the area. I guess it was their only chance to associate with each other and have a little break from the homestead chores that they spent their life doing. Once a month they had a meeting at one of the homes, each taking a turn

There were about a dozen ladies altogether. There was Mrs. Fossum, quite a big woman, much like my Ma and probably Ma's best friend. She was a lovely lady. There was Mrs. Erickson, older but still a beautiful Swedish lady with just a little accent to her voice. Mrs. Sullivan was a small, tough little Irish woman who seemed to carry the weight of the world on her shoulders. There was Mrs. Rule, Mrs. Hamilton, Mrs. LaForge, Mrs. Gammon and a few more. Then there was Mrs. Watson, she was the elite of the group and I always wondered why she associated with the rest. She was the wife of Alf Watson who owned the store, the ranch and was the Post Master and also the local fur buyer. They were about the only ones in the whole area that had any money. Mrs. Watson was a prim, trim English lady and she held her head up high and looked down her sharp hooked nose at everyone. She never wore a print dress like the other woman but instead always wore a suit with a white blouse. She wore a little fur thing around her neck that had a little head and beady eyes.

She had a small brimmed hat with the front brim turned down and the back brim turned up. A sharp little feather protruded from the hatband and she had a pair of half glasses hanging from a gold chain around her neck. She may have been a nice lady but she seemed as out of place with these other women as a turd on a dinner plate.

I was a little older and a little bigger and I planned to catch a lot of weasels in the coming winter and really help out with the money end of things. At least that was my plan. I was big enough to set a trap by myself if I was careful and I could hardly wait for winter to get here so that I could start trapping.

Now anyone knows that to catch anything you need good bait and weasels are no exceptions. I started in the spring to make my bait for the coming winter. Great bait required great ingredients: some chicken innards, some fish, a drop or two of oil of anise and a couple drops of beaver castor oil and you are all set. The last couple of ingredients I borrowed from my brother's trapping supplies. The real secret of good bait is to put all of these fine ingredients into a jar, put the lid on tight and half bury it in a safe place for a couple months. As it ferments it all blends together and looks like thick grease. A little of this taken out of the jar with a stick and smeared on your trap is all that it takes. The smell makes your eyes run and your nose turn inside out. Weasels can smell it for a mile and people can smell it for quite a distance also.

Now I knew that Mrs. Watson was a very prim and sophisticated lady, but I also reasoned that if her husband was a fur buyer she must have quite an interest in the fur business. She should have also appreciated the smell of really good weasel bait.

The ladies were having their meeting at our place this warm summer afternoon. The meeting was over and they were having tea and cookies when I decided to treat Mrs. Watson to the aroma of my weasel bait. I brought in the jar and walked over to Mrs. Watson. I carefully took off the lid and popped the jar under her nose.

"Have a whiff of my weasel bait," I told her.

Well, if weasels would react to my bait the way that she did I would be rich! Her head snapped back and her hat flew off, her eyes crossed and her arms fell limp at her side as her legs shot straight out in front of her. I saw Ma head my way with both arms outstretched and a look of sheer horror on her face. I didn't think that she wanted to hug me with those outstretched arms so I side stepped her and made it out the screen door to safety, safety for the moment only. The other ladies were making strange sounds, some gasps, some shrieks and I thought maybe even a giggle or two.

I really didn't know what was happening but the ladies left shortly afterwards with some of them helping Mrs. Watson to the car. I steered clear of the cabin for quite a while as it seemed another one of my wonderful ideas had gone awry. I finally had to go in and I got a really severe chewing out and was threatened that if I pulled one more stunt like that at her meetings that I'd probably end up in reform school.

Of course when Pa got home she had to relate the whole episode to him. *Lord, she's got to stop telling him this stuff or the pain of me being so bad is going to kill him.* It was the same routine as always, his eyes went funny, his forehead wrinkled and he clapped his hand over his mouth as those awful snorting noises came out of his nose. I didn't know what a stroke was like but I thought this might have been one.

Ma didn't seem happy with his condition either. She seemed to get madder.

"What will ever become of you?" she said to me with a look that I'd never seen before on her face. I was starting to wonder that myself. *Everything that I think is a good idea turns out to be a disaster.* So one more time she sent me off to bed with the same instructions. I said my prayers and I was ashamed to ask Jesus to help me be a good boy again. I told him that I didn't try to be bad I just used bad judgment. I asked him to help me with that, as it seemed to be one of my biggest problems.

I lay in bed and pet Tim, his purring was really comforting. I remembered back to last year's ladies meeting. There were a lot of skunks around. I looked out the screen door and saw Alf coming home from fixing the fence. Trying to act grown up and impress the ladies I hollered out the door,

"Hey Alf, did you see any piss cats today?" I didn't know if I impressed the ladies but I sure didn't impress Ma. I started to think about next year's meeting and decided that I'd spend the day picking berries, catching frogs or anything except being around those fussy old ladies.

It was late fall and once again it was time to do all the things that must be done. The wood was all stacked up and the vegetables would soon be in the cellar. There was a new calf that we called Roany so the cow was milking again. The men were harvesting down by Grande Prairie and Helen and I were going to school again. It was the last year for Helen. I was glad to go to school again. I liked to learn and have other kids to play with. My very favorite game was 'Auntie-I-over the schoolhouse' we played it with an old basketball, when it wasn't flat.

This year I learned something totally new, I learned about racism. I didn't understand it and I didn't like it. For some reason the kids treated us differently this fall, they called Helen and I frogs and damn Catholics. They called us catlickers, I didn't understand and so I asked Helen why they did this. She said that they called us frogs because we were French. I thought that our parents were Americans because they were born in the States as were their parents. I thought that we were Canadians because we were born here so what was with this frog stuff? Helen said to try to ignore them.

One day we were playing in the bush out behind the school at noon recess. Just before the bell rang, some kids grabbed me, pushed my back against a tree and tied my hands and feet behind me. The bell rang and they all ran to the school laughing, saying that maybe a bear would eat me. That thought crossed my mind as well and I felt pretty scared and helpless. I tried to wiggle my hands free but they had done a good job and I couldn't get loose.

When I didn't show up Helen and the teacher asked where I was. The kids said that they never saw me and maybe I went home. Helen knew better than that and came looking for me. When she got close enough I heard her calling my name and I hollered back. She came and untied me and asked which kids did it. I liked these kids even if they were mean to me and I wouldn't tell. The teacher said if I didn't tell everybody, including me would have to stay after school. I still wouldn't tell and we all had to stay after school. Helen was mad at me for not telling, she said that she should have left me tied to that tree.

Helen said that when she and Francis were going to school a few years before that it had been quite bad but in the meantime the family that instigated most of it had moved away and that now it wasn't so bad. Francis was proud to be French and one day a kid was calling him names and Francis punched him in the eye. The kid ran to the teacher crying,

"Francis knocked my eye out!"

The teacher told him, "You had better put it in your pocket before you lose it." They didn't bother them so much after that.

I had a couple of friends at school that didn't call me names. David Hamilton was one, he was a nice guy and I liked him. He was tall for his age and he was smart, he was a good artist and he got good marks in school. He was about a year older than I was and a grade ahead of me. I asked him how come he didn't call me names. He said that it was stupid and he had better things to do with his time. Another good guy is Merv Staggs. He was about three years older than me and he was a very sensible acting fellow. He went to the Calgary Stampede when he was quite young and I was in awe as he told us about it.

After a while the name calling stopped and everything was back to normal. I liked school and I liked this time of the year. The hills looked so beautiful with the leaves all red and yellow and the ducks and geese were flying south in big Vs. The air was fresh and crisp as we walked to school in the mornings, when we went home in the afternoon the sun was warm and the sky was blue these kinds of days just plain made me feel good.

Winter got closer and the days grew shorter and colder. In the mornings there was a thick white frost covering things like icing on a cake. The men came home from harvesting and finished getting things ready for winter. Uncle Fred came home in the fall as well and he and Alf went down to the moose lick and shot a nice fat moose. We'd have meat for quite a while. They hung it in the icehouse and it was cold enough to keep.

Francis and Alf came home from town with some good news. Frank Donald from Grande Prairie had a tie contract with the railroad and was hiring workers for his logging operation. Joe Goodwin was the foreman and Alf and Francis both got jobs there for the winter. Uncle Fred got a job in a sawmill at Buffalo Lakes. Pa stayed home and looked after the stock and the trap line. He told Ma that things were finally looking better.

The road to the logging camp went right by the school and Frank Donald had a big shiny new truck to haul the railroad ties. A young fellow named Art Mohr was the driver and he was a kind of hero to all the young guys who wished that they could drive a truck. He dressed in western clothes and all the girls at school had a crush on him. When he drove by the school they all waved and giggled and he blew the horn. I liked the truck, it was about the only one around and it was a nice blue Chevrolet Maple Leaf. I hoped that some day maybe I could drive a truck.

I had my little trap line set up and my weasel bait was working pretty well. I caught a few weasels but Helen made me give her the first two to pay for the lipstick that I wasted. I was glad to give them to her, now maybe she'd quit bugging me about it. I couldn't skin them very good yet so I got Pa to help me. I couldn't pull the bone out of the tail and sometimes I pulled the tail right off. Pa just put his thumbnail against the skin and pulled the bone out. Maybe the next year I'd be able to do that.

It was a long cold winter but everybody seemed to be having a good time. Some Saturday nights they had dances at the schoolhouse and sometimes they had box socials. All the ladies and girls each made a nice lunch and put it in a fancy decorated box. They'd decorate them with crepe paper and paper flowers. I'd be glad when I get big enough to bid on them.

At suppertime the Auctioneer would get up on the stage and start to auction off the boxes. Of course the girls who had boyfriends told them what their box was decorated like so that they'd bid on it. There was very little money and sometimes they bid with squirrel skins. Everyone knew who was dating who and when a young fellow suddenly started to bid on a box, all the other guys would bid him up. He would start turning red and getting mad and they all quit bidding just in time. He and his girl would be all smiles as they went off to eat their lunch.

A couple of guys always came from Tupper to the dances. They both worked on the railroad so they had more money than anyone else. One little guy named Chuck would buy five or six boxes and then try to sell them to the other guys after he found out which girl went with which lunch. The girls hated that because he was a little short, fat guy about fifty and he spoke very poor English.

These dances were a lot of fun and went on until the wee hours of the morning. It was a cold ride home with the sleigh and the horses but no one seemed to mind. Most times I couldn't stay awake that long and I was sleeping long before the dance was over.

The Christmas concerts were always a big hit and the young people tried to go to all of them. Alf and Francis were no exception they went to the one at our school, to North Swan School, South Swan School, Gundy and any others that they could get to. Most of the time they had to walk but they didn't seem to mind as they went anyways.

There was a kid named Bucky who went to another school but came with his parents to our concert. Bucky was a real little glutton. He got a bag of candy like the rest of us that he would eat and then he would come and beg us for ours. This year we devised a plan for him. We pooled our pennies and bought a five cent chocolate bar. We got a bunch of nice round rabbit turds and we melted the chocolate bar and carefully rolled them in the chocolate. They looked really good, we kept them in a cold place until the concert so that they wouldn't melt or stick together.

On the night of the concert Bucky was in his usual form. We waited until we saw him coming and we all pretended to be eating from the bag. "Can I have some?"

"Sure Bucky, help yourself." He ate a couple handfuls and we pretended to eat some more.

After a few minutes we said, "We've had all we can eat, do you want the rest?"

"Oh yes," Bucky said, "these are delicious." We were a little disappointed that he found them so good but pleased that we fooled the little pig.

Chapter 15
A Winter to Remember

The old timers all said that this was the coldest, meanest winter that they could remember. The snow was deep and we'd had lots of blizzards. Right after Christmas the temperature dropped down in the fifty to sixty below zero range. The windows in our cabin were thick with white frost and we couldn't see out. Sometimes I held my hand on the window and tried to melt the frost off. My hand always froze before the frost melted from the glass.

Pa said that we'd be lucky if we didn't run out of wood. Our old heater was made from a thirty gallon drum and in this kind of weather it would take both the heater and the cook stove going full blast to keep it warm in the cabin. We heated water for the cows, horses and chickens to drink and we gave Ranger hot water and hot porridge to eat as he huddled in his doghouse.

One morning Pa came in from the barn and when he opened the door you could see the cold air sweep across the floor. "It must be some kind of record," he said, "the thermometer is sitting at seventy-two below!" It was so cold there was frost on the logs on the inside of the cabin. A big old porcupine had climbed high up in a pine tree right by the cabin. He stayed up there for weeks eating the bark from the tree. I wondered why he didn't freeze to death.

Most days Helen and I still went to school. It was freezing in the school and it took until noon to get warm enough for us to sit in our desks. We all stood around the big old heater in the back of the school doing oral lessons. We kept turning around to warm one side and then the other. By the time we got home we were nearly frozen, we came around the last corner on the trail and saw the little cabin in the trees with the smoke going straight up and the light making a warm glow on the frosty windows. It looked so warm and inviting and we knew that in a few minutes that we'd be inside warming up.

Ma gave us a cup of something hot to drink and a piece of bread. We sat on a chair in front of the stove with our feet on the open oven door to thaw out. Heat feels so good when you're really cold, and is one of the little pleasures of life. After we warmed up we brought in the wood and helped with the other chores. I wondered if we'd ever see spring again.

We had something new to amuse us on the long winter nights. Francis was always inventing something and he'd made a sort of a radio. At first he had only one earphone and we took turns trying to hear something on it. Then he made a loudspeaker out of a tobacco can lid and an old magnet that he scrounged somewhere. It sounded pretty tinny but it really worked. I thought that it was amazing what this brother of mine can make out of junk. Like Pa said, "He can make chicken salad out of chicken shit."

When March arrived the days began to grow longer. Winter was really reluctant to release its icy grip and hung on as long as it could. The longer days and the warmer sun pushed back on the cold air and spring slowly emerged. Every living being was so glad to get out and soak up some sun. The snow melted and the frozen ground gave way to spring. Little green shoots sprouted from the soil and the miracle of the season once more made itself shown.

Uncle Fred came home from working in the bush and brought an old white horse with him. He said that he got him in a trade. Pa said that he probably got drunk and somebody suckered him into buying it. Pa was not too happy about this horse. He said that we didn't need another nag and mouth to feed. Uncle said that his name was Roy and warned to watch out behind him because he kicked like crazy. Pa said that Uncle would have to get rid of him but in the meantime they'd put him in the barn. The barn was small and with the cows and three other horses in there they'd have to tie Roy in the aisle between the stalls, with his rear end up against the back door of the barn. Pa told me to stay away from there because he kicked real bad.

I really wanted to see a horse kick so I tried to figure out a way to see him kick without getting hurt. I cut a long slim willow and poked him in the rump through a crack by the door hinges. Well, a couple of pokes and Roy came unglued. I stood in awe as he kicked both hind feet at a time. He was a little too close to the door and every time he kicked he hit the door. Bam, Bam, he was really going to town and I jumped back just as he kicked the door right off the hinges.

Pa heard the noise and came running to see what was going on.

"What the hell, I might have known it was you." He grabbed me by the favorite arm and commenced to change the color of my butt with my own stick. Between jumps, I thought how stupid I had been not to get rid of the stick.

That night after my prayers and my talk with Jesus I consoled myself talking to Tim. I tried to explain to him what it's like when a horse kicks and told him don't ever get involved with it. I didn't care if I ever saw a horse kick again. I was glad that I seen it once but I was not so sure that it was worth the lickin'.

Spring turned into summer and everyone was busy with summer things. With Alf and Francis both working in the tie camp there was a little more money around. Pa bought a big old sow pig named Frankie. I thought it was a pretty funny name for a pig. Pa said that by fall we'd have lots of pigs when Frankie farrowed. They kept on using words that I didn't understand.

One beautiful summer day only Ma and Pa and I were at home. It was right after lunch and Ma was cleaning away the dishes and Pa was having a snooze in his rocking chair. Ma gave me some pancakes that had been left over from breakfast to take and feed to the dog. I took my time and enjoyed the day as I strolled out to feed Ranger. As I went by the barn I heard a strange sound and I went to look in the open door. Oh my Lord! My eyes nearly popped out of my head and I ran to the cabin as fast as my legs will go. *Oh boy, Pa sure ain't gonna believe this!*

"Pa, Pa, come quick and see the cow, there's something trying to crawl up her arse, just the feet are sticking out!"

Pa laughed, "I think it's trying to get out, not in." Pa headed for the barn and I was right behind him.

"What is it Pa? How did it get in there?" When we got to the barn the head was out and a minute or two later a slippery, slimy calf slipped to the floor. "It's a calf Pa, how did it get in there?"

Pa wiped the calf off a bit with a gunnysack and then carried it up to the front of the cow. She made mooing sounds and started to lick the calf. Yuk, she licked all that yucky stuff off! Pa told me to go tell Ma that we got a new calf and to ask her how it got in there.

Ma sat me down to explain about sex and the miracle of birth. "Is that how people get babies," I asked her.

"Yes, that's how everything gets babies." Well, the whole thing sounded pretty gross to me and I was quite sure I was never going to be involved in making babies.

This must have been my summer for learning because new things seemed to happen every day. Pa told Uncle Fred that Eagle, our old white horse was constipated and they needed to give him an enema. *Oh, I've got to see this!* Ma gave me one once with a hot water bottle and a little rubber hose. *What are they going to use on a horse?*

They took him in the barn and tied him up in a stall. I wanted to see real good so I sat on a stall across the aisle right behind him. They got a five-gallon pail of warm soapy water, a big hose and a funnel. Uncle soaped up the hose and pushed it up the horse's rump. The horse danced around a little like maybe he was not too crazy about the whole thing. Pa got up on a box and Uncle handed him the pail of water. Uncle held the funnel and Pa poured in the water.

Eagle danced around some more and I could hear his belly growling. They waited a couple of minutes and Uncle pulled the hose out. Then all hell broke loose. I was right behind the horse and in the direct line of fire. I got hit in the chest with a full stream of soapy, poopy water. Every couple of feet there was a hard horse turd. I was slapping at the water and getting pulverized with water and horse turds. Pa and Uncle sat in the aisle busting a gut. The tears ran down their cheeks as old Eagle grunted and squirted me a couple more times.

Of course they had to tell everyone else about it and they all had a good laugh at my expense. Anyway, now I know how to give a horse an enema and I learned where not to stand. I told Tim about it and he even seemed to have a grin on his face.

Father Owens showed up again and said that it was time for me to go to summer camp and make my first communion. This year Helen wasn't going and I had to go alone. That summer camp thing sure took the fun out of my summer. Ma got my blanket and things ready and put them in a box. I couldn't take very many clean clothes because they would be stolen. Pa loaded some potatoes and vegetables in the wagon along with some eggs and meat. I hoped the food would be better than the last year. I gave Ma a tearful hug goodbye and we set off for camp. The wagon wheels rumbled doom all the way. We stopped at the store on the way and Pa bought me a couple of big black jawbreakers.

When we got to camp there were kids all over the place. I helped Pa put the food that we brought in the kitchen where the Sister said to put it. I got my blanket and box of clothes and said goodbye to Pa. I couldn't cry in front of everybody and Pa didn't hug me goodbye. He climbed up in the wagon, told me to behave myself and drove off. I was left standing there among a hundred people but I felt alone.

As soon as Pa was out of sight a Sister told me to get upstairs and make my bed. She also added that I should make it right the first time and then report to her. I took my stuff upstairs and found a place in the middle of the room to make my bed. All the space next to the walls was already taken. I didn't like it in the middle but it was the only choice I had. I rolled out my blanket and put my box of clothes at the head. That board floor sure looked hard with only a blanket for a mattress.

I reported to the Sister and she sent me over to a group being taught by another Sister. I asked what they were studying and she told me to shut up and listen. After a while I learned that they were talking about mortal sins. My mind wondered off and I was thinking if I had any mortal sins that would condemn me to hell forever. I thought of the food and the bed and I wondered if maybe I was already there. I was brought back to earth with a whack on the head and told to pay attention. I thought, *things haven't changed much from last year!*

Suppertime came and I was really hungry. I was hoping for a nice meal but the slop dish was the same as last year. Fish and potatoes boiled together, bones and all. I thought it was no wonder these ladies became Nuns no man would ever marry one of them if they cooked like that. I came to the conclusion that if you're cranky and can't cook, you become a nun.

After supper we went to Benediction and then we were allowed to play until nine o'clock then it was bedtime. I found my friend Frankie. He had just arrived today as well. We talked until bedtime and then went upstairs. Somebody had already been through my stuff and taken most of it. This was going to be another wonderful two weeks, I was sure.

A few days passed and soon everyone had summer complaint again. I was not a happy camper and I wanted to go home. Frankie got appendicitis and had to leave. I wished I could get something so I could get out of there. One evening, I was sitting watching the big kids play ball when all of a sudden this big kid jumped on me. He grabbed me from behind and knocked me on my back and scratched hell out of my face. I hollered for help but nobody paid any attention, he punched me in the face a few times and then left. I was covered with blood from my nose and I had a really nice black eye. I didn't even know who this kid was so I asked some other kids and one kid knew him. He said that his name was Ralph Wilbert. I filed that name and face in my memory bank, one day I'd grow up and I'd be bigger and if I ever meet him again then he would take one hell of a beating.

They had arranged some sporting events along with our studies. The girls played badminton and the boys had wrestling and boxing. They paired me up for a sparing match with a kid from Dawson Creek. I'd never seen boxing gloves before and when they tied them on they felt really clumsy. Pa used to spar with me and he said that in sparring, you never really hit the other person very hard. This kid didn't know about that, he was a flurry of gloves and then he gave me a haymaker in the eye. I fell on my back and they declared him the winner. I was left with two black eyes and tears running down my cheeks.

The other kids slapped him on the back and pointed at me laughing. Sister saw the tears and called me a big suck. This place was really starting to get to me. Everybody laughed at my black eyes. "You look like a raccoon," they laughed. Once again I wished that I were home. All night I thought about that kid and by morning I'd made up my mind to do something about it. That afternoon I asked if I could box with him again.

"Haven't had you had enough?" the priest asked as he tied the gloves on. I didn't say anything but I knew that in a minute that little smart ass was going to get his.

The bell rang and I was on him before he knew what was happening. I gave him two good ones to the face and he fell on his back. I jumped on him and pounded his face and eyes some more. His eyes started turning black and he started to cry. The Priest grabbed me by my belt and lifted me off.

"You're not supposed to get on him when he's down," he hollered at me, "what's wrong with you, you're a real spoil sport."

I didn't care what he said, that little bastard got his and nobody was laughing at me any more. They had omitted to tell me the day before that this kid had been boxing in the gym in Dawson Creek for three years. I was really ticked off at the Priest and Sister. They helped him up and wiped his face. I was thinking, *yesterday they called me a suck and today when I win they call me a spoil sport. What do they want from me anyhow?*

That night I made my plans to get away from the camp and go home. By my calculations if I went around the south side of the lake and through the bush trail from Erickson's it would be five or six miles home. I crawled in my blanket with all my clothes on. Around midnight everyone seemed to be sleeping. I crept over to the window and crawled out on the veranda roof. I couldn't go down the stairs because the Sisters would see me. I had to get over the veranda roof and shinny down the post without falling and breaking my neck. After a few scares and the loss of some skin I made it safely to the ground.

I snuck by the kitchen and then by the church and finally I made it to the road. I walked as fast as I could around the lake, past Cornock's and over to

Erickson's. The moon was bright and I could see pretty well until I got on the bush trail. The shadows from the trees made it pretty dark and there were a lot of noises in the bush. I heard snorts and brush cracking as I hurried along. Being that scared and having summer complaint was not a good combination. By the time I got to the bear pen the moon was fading and the sky in the east was getting lighter. I heard noises and hoped it wasn't a big bear like the one they caught in the pen.

Maybe if I sing and make some noise it will scare things away. I couldn't remember any songs except Jingle Bells, I didn't think that I should sing it in the summer time but it was an emergency so I tried it. "Jingle Bells," my voice sounded small and funny. *Maybe I would be better talking, that's it, I'll talk like I'm with someone and the animals will think that there's two and get scared and run away.* My voice still sounded small but I started to talk as if Alf was with me. "Pretty dark tonight," I said. "Yes it is," I replied in as big a voice as I could muster. I kept talking on past the west gate and up the detour hill. By then the sun was just peeping over the horizon, I'd never seen the sun come up before and so I stopped and watched as the rays of light came up over the hill and spilled out into the valley. It was beautiful!

I was really tired but I was almost home so I hurried along the trail and I came into the yard just as Pa was coming out to milk the cows. "Pa, Pa," I yelled and ran to see him.

"What in hell are you doing here and how did you get here?" I told him how I ran away and came home through the bush. "Go see your mother," he said, not very happy sounding.

He went to the barn and I headed to the cabin. Tim was on the step and came running to meet me. He rubbed on my legs and purred like a truck. I hugged him and went into the cabin, Ma hugged me and I was so tired I just wanted to melt in her arms and stay there.

She asked me the same questions that Pa did and then she saw my black eyes. "My Lord, what happened to you?"

I sat down and she gave me some breakfast and I told her the whole story. The food was so good and I was so hungry it was awfully hard to talk between mouthfuls. Pa came in with the milk and as they ate their breakfast Ma related to him what had happened. Pa said that I have to go back and Ma tearfully agreed. I was worn right out and I fell asleep with my head on the table.

It was noon when Ma woke me up from the bed where she had moved me after I fell asleep. "Pa is taking you back this afternoon."

"I really don't want to go, Ma."

"I know son, but you have to make your first communion."

"But it's a different Jesus that they talk about. The one we pray to here is kind and gentle but theirs seems totally different."

"It's the same one. It just seems different because you're away from home."

We had some lunch and Pa hitched the horses to the wagon to take me back. I climbed up the wagon wheel and got on the seat next to Pa. I could hardly say goodbye for the big lump in my throat. Ma had tears running down her cheeks as she told me not to run away again and to be a good boy. Pa made a little whistle sound and the horses headed on down the road. I wanted to look back but I knew if I did I'd cry and Pa don't like crybabies.

When we arrived at camp the Nuns were relieved to see that I was fine but I could tell that they were mad too. Pa told them that he wanted to talk to them and they went inside to the kitchen. I stayed by the horses until he came out. He climbed up in the wagon and without a word he set off for home. I don't know what they talked about but the nuns didn't bother me too much for the rest of my time at camp.

After what seemed like an eternity the day for our first communion arrived. Some of the boys' parents brought them white shirts and clean pants to wear. My clothes had been stolen so I had to wear what I had on. We had rehearsed this for a couple of days and we tried hard to get it right. We had to line up and march into the church and kneel down in an orderly fashion.

The night before we had to go to confession, I tried to think of some bad things to tell the Priest. I said that I used some bad words sometimes and stole a spoonful of honey from the cupboard when Ma was outside. I said that I was sorry for running away and that it was a bad thing to do. I couldn't think of anything else so I told him that I had kicked the calf in the arse when it wouldn't move. He gave me penance of one Our Father and five Hail Mary's and told me not to do those things again.

Some kids' parents arrived in time for the communion Mass but Ma and Pa didn't get there in time. I was pretty excited when the Priest put the Host on my tongue. The Nuns had told us not to bite it because we wouldn't want to bite Jesus. As I went back to my seat the Host stuck to the roof of my mouth. I tried to get it off with my tongue without making to strange a face. It was stuck so when I knelt down I bowed my head and pried it off with my finger. *I sure hope that I don't go to hell for that.*

After Mass was over the Nuns put out sandwiches for the parents and acted nice and congratulated us. Ma and Pa arrived in the middle of lunch. They had a sandwich and some tea and we went home. I'd never wanted to go home so bad in all of my life and I swore to myself that I'd never leave again.

We got home and Tim was glad to see me. I pet him and he purred like we should never be apart again. I went and saw Ranger and he was glad to see me too and I played with him for a while. Ma made supper and I ate till I was ready to bust. She gave me some more boiled milk with pepper for my summer complaint. *I sure hope it works.* We sat around after supper and I told them my experiences and they filled me in on what had been going on at home. Pa went out to milk the cow and I dried the dishes for Ma. I just wanted to be close to her. I didn't know that I loved her so much. I wished that I knew how to tell her.

I was tired and I went to bed early. I said my prayers and had my little talk with Jesus. He seemed so much closer to me here. Tim was glad to get to sleep in the bed again and crawled in beside me. He purred so loud I could hardly go to sleep. I thought over the last couple weeks and I decided that I'd changed. In only two weeks I'd learned that people steal and most can't be trusted. I'd also learned that it feels good to punch somebody out that is mean to you. I wasn't sure if that's a good thing or if Jesus would like that, I decided to ask Ma in the morning.

I thought, *I've learned a little about God and a lot about people. Most of what I've learned about people I don't like, I don't like people very much. I hope God doesn't punish me for that, somehow I feel a little harder and I don't understand why nor do I like to feel this way.* I went to sleep wondering what life would be like when I grow up and leave home for good. It gave me a deep sad feeling.

Chapter 16
Smoking, Eating and Having Fun

After a few days at home I recovered from my ordeal at camp and forgot the whole thing. Helen had a job working in the hospital in Pouce Coupe and came home for the weekend. I was so glad to see her. I hadn't seen her for a couple of months. She knew that I like to read so she brought me a book. Tom Sawyer, oh how I liked that story, I really related to it, except that I didn't have a friend like Huck Finn to play with. I sure wished that I did. I sat and daydreamed about them sitting around smoking and talking. I thought maybe I should smoke but I didn't have a pipe.

I tried to smoke moss rolled up in some old catalogue pages. It worked but it sure tasted bad. I had to come up with a pipe. Tobacco might taste better than moss but it was hard to get any. Pa would probably notice if any of his went missing.

Sometimes it seemed that I was just plain lucky. Francis brought home a Popular Mechanics magazine and it had an article on how to make a pipe. It said that I needed a piece of briarroot. I didn't know what that was so I asked Francis where I could get some. He said that it grows in Greece or some far away place like that and that I had no chance at all of getting any.

Well, if I couldn't get briarroot, I'd just have to use something else. I got a piece of root from an alder bush. I got Francis to help me drill a hole for the bowl and then I tried to whittle it to look like a pipe. After a lot of work I thought that it looked pretty good. I had to make a little hole in the stem to the bowl. I did this with an old steel knitting needle that I got red hot in the stove and then I burned the hole. It was hard to do and I had to hold the needle with a pair of pliers and try not to burn myself.

Ma said that I was making an awful smell trying to burn that thing and she asked me what it was that I was trying to make anyhow. I told her that I was trying to make a bubble pipe. I finally got it finished and I made it brown with shoe polish. Oh, it was a work of art. I could hardly wait to try it.

I had a little shelter that I'd made in the bush behind the barn and I ran out there to try it out. I stuffed the bowl full of moss and lit it. It worked pretty darn good! After a couple of smokes, the bowl charred on the inside and it worked even better. Life was really great, *now I can sit and smoke my pipe and daydream, just like Tom and Huck.*

After another pipeful, I was as green as the moss that I was smoking and as I barfed in the grass I wondered if this ever happened to Tom and Huck. I wobbled to the cabin to lie down and Ma wanted to know what was wrong with me. I told her that I ate a white turnip and it made me sick. She told me not to eat white turnips anymore. She smiled and I think that maybe she knew that I'd been smoking.

I had a sleep and by suppertime I felt better. I decided I'd only smoke one pipe full in the future. At bedtime I was sure she knew that I'd been smoking when she told me to say my prayers and ask Jesus to help me not to eat white turnips anymore.

There's a nice creek that flows right beside the hay meadow and we go there quite often. There were lots of minnows in the creek and I caught as many as I could and put them in a pail of water. I'd made a little dip net from a piece of old screen from the screen door and I caught them with that. Ma wanted to know what I was going to do with them. "I'm gonna cook 'em and eat 'em," I told her.

"You're going to kill yourself eating things like that," she said.

"No I won't Ma. I'll cook 'em real good." I had a little frying pan made from a tobacco can lid and Francis made a handle for it out of an old coat hanger. I cleaned my minnows when we got home and made a little campfire. I got a little lard and salt from the cabin and those minnows fried up real nice.

Tim helped me eat them and he seemed to think that they were pretty good. Ma came out and had a little fit. "My Lord," she said, "whatever is going to become of you? Why do you eat that crap? You'll kill yourself for sure."

"It's real good Ma, you want to try some?"

"Oh no," she said, "I wouldn't eat that."

"It's better than the squirrel that I fried last week."

She turned her hands palm side up and looked at the sky. "I really don't know what will ever become of you." She seemed to say that a lot and I wondered if she knew something that I didn't.

'The summer went by and I kept on frying minnows and squirrel legs and partridges and Tim and I ate them. I ate all the berries I could find and smoked my pipe. Ma worried needlessly because nothing bad seemed to be happening to me.

Summer faded into fall and Uncle Fred came home for a while before harvest started. It was good to see him again even though he teased me like crazy. He smoked his pipe after supper and I thought I would like to try some of his pipe tobacco. He smoked something called "Old Glory." It came in a hard plug and he cut some off with his knife for his pipe. I thought it smelled good.

One night after supper Uncle and I went down the hill to get the cows for milking. It was nice walking and talking to Uncle. He told me about the tugboat that he worked on. He said it was named the 'Gator.' I thought that was a pretty good name for a boat.

We found the cows and got them headed for home. They knew the way and walked down the trail single file ahead of us. We started walking up the big hill behind the cows when I got a brain wave. I decided that I could hold a cow's tail and let her pull me up the hill. I got hold of Snow's tail and it was going real good until I turned my head to tell Uncle what a good plan this was. When I turned my head around again the cow had stopped and I stuck my nose right in her butt. *Oh, Lordy, what a smell!* I jumped back just in time for her to relieve her bladder all over me, from my chest on down to my bare feet. Shit, this was a disaster but it got worse. I looked back at Uncle and thought he must be having a heart attack or something because he was rolling on the ground grabbing his chest and making strange sounds.

I ran down to where he was only to discover that he was just having a laughing fit. Somehow I failed to see the humor in this. I had this smell in my nose that might never go away and I was soaked with cow piss from the neck down. How funny could that be? Anyway it confirmed my idea that all bulls are stupid. They must be because they always seem to be smelling cows' arses and I don't know why, they smell really, really bad.

Uncle finally recovered enough that he could walk and we hurried to catch up to the cows. Of course when we got home Uncle had to tell about my misfortune. He had a hard time telling it between fits of laughter. Everybody laughed and it didn't make me feel too brilliant. Ma made me take my clothes off outside and put them in a tub of water. Then she scrubbed me down until my tan was almost gone. *Damn that smelly cow anyhow.* I told Tim about it as we lay in bed and he purred and I thought he was smiling. *Damn silly cat.*

September arrived and with it came the new school year. The first day of school all the kids went to get enrolled and meet the teacher. They call it Labor Day and they must be right because we had to spend the day cleaning the school and the yard. We raked the leaves and the big boys cut the grass and the weeds with a scythe. Our new teacher's name was Miss Hill and she was not very nice.

The second day school really started and boy was I proud of myself. Ma had bought me a new pair of overalls and a new red shirt. It was the first new clothes that I'd ever had. I got a new yellow lard pail for my lunch and a new cap too. I was ready to go and Ma said that she wanted to take my picture. I stood there waiting for her to get the camera and I saw Pug, the old barn cat, sauntering over to me. Ma had the camera and she told me to smile, just as I smiled I felt something hot running down my leg. I looked down and good old Pug was marking his territory on my new pants. I was really mad! I kicked his ass and hollered, "You stupid son of a bitch, I'll wring your bloody neck!" Ma stood there with her mouth open for a second and then she came to life.

"Don't you ever use that kind of language!"

"But Ma, he pissed all over my new pants and even on my lunch pail!"

"No mind," she said, "you don't swear like that."

"Pa did when the cow kicked him," I complained.

"Well he shouldn't and you better not again."

So I had to put on my old pants from last year and wash my leg. I figured when I got home from school I'd slap hell out of that stupid cat. I told Ma that it must be my summer for all the animals to relieve themselves on me. First the horse, then the cow, and now that stupid cat. Miss Hill was not the best teacher in the world. They said that it was her first year and I believed it. She had no idea how to get along with kids and she really got off on the wrong foot. She said that us boys were worse than a bunch of wild coyotes. She got so mad one day she said that she'd shake our shoes off. Charlie Hamilton sounded like a little Texan and he told her, "I'll tie mine on with bag strings and sack strings." Everybody laughed except Miss Hill.

Chapter 17
A Trip to Grande Prairie

Miss Hill wrote a lot of our lessons on the blackboard and it was giving me a lot of trouble. When I tried to read what was on the board I saw double. One image seemed to be about two inches higher than the other one and two inches to the right. I'd never had this problem before or when I played outside. The marks on my first report card were bad and Ma asked me why.

I told her that I couldn't see the board and about seeing double. She checked my eyes by covering one and then the other. I could see perfectly with my right eye but to my surprise I could hardly see anything with my left one. I wondered how come I never noticed this before. Also when I closed one eye and then the other the image moved back and forth.

Ma went to the school and had a talk with the teacher about it and in a few days a school Doctor came around and checked my eyes. He said that I had a lazy eye and that I had to wear a patch over the good eye. He said that would make the lazy one work. I wore the patch for quite awhile and I couldn't see to do anything. I could hardly find my way to school and I couldn't do my schoolwork at all. Ma and Pa talked to the teacher again and somebody arranged for me to see an eye specialist in Grande Prairie.

A couple of weeks later, Pa got a letter from the school board with two train tickets and a letter for Pa and I to stay in a hotel. They gave us a date to be there and the letter said that I was supposed to see a Dr. Levie at the Grande Prairie Hospital.

I was scared and excited all at the same time. I'd never been on a train before or in a hotel. When the day came for us to go we were up early. Ma put a few things for Pa and me in an old suitcase and Alf took us to the station. The train left mid morning so we had to stay in Grande Prairie for two nights.

We stood on the platform and the locomotive came rolling by us. Steam was coming out in a lot of places and made little clouds in the cold air. The train rolled to a stop and a conductor stepped down with a little stool and put it on the platform. Pa and I got on and I held his hand tight until we got to a seat. I looked around and there were quite a few people on the train, some were reading newspapers and some were looking out the window. A couple of men played cards on a suitcase. Pa said that they looked like traveling salesmen. The conductor called, "All Aboard," and came in with his stool. There was a little jerk and we started to move. In a couple of minutes the platform and Tupper Creek were out of sight.

I looked out the window at the trees and farms as we passed by. The seats had some sort of fuzzy material on them. Pa said that he thought that it was plush. We stopped at a lot of little places on the way. The conductor came through the coaches calling names. "Next stop, Demmitt… Lynburn… Hythe…" There seemed to be a lot of places between Tupper and Grande Prairie.

After a while, Pa said that he needed to go for a smoke and that I'd have to stay here while he went to the smoking car. I was not too thrilled with that idea but I had to do as he said. Ma had packed us some lunch and Pa said that I could eat a sandwich while he went to the smoking car. It seemed like he was gone for a long time.

A black man in a white jacket with a box of sandwiches wrapped in wax paper came down the aisle. He was the first black man that I'd ever seen and I guess that I was staring at him. He stopped at my seat, "Good day young master," he said. "Perhaps you would like a chocolate bar or a soft drink?"

"Oh no Sir," I replied, "I have no money for anything."

"Do you mind if I sit down?" he asked.

"No Sir," I said and I wondered why he asked me, it wasn't my train. He sat across from me and put his tray on the seat.

"Traveling alone?" he asked. I told him that Pa was in the smoking car. "What's your name, young master?"

"My name is Lewis and why do you call me young master?"

"That's what we call young people," he told me. He said that his name was Benjamin and he had some boys. We talked for a while and he said that he better try to sell some sandwiches and he left. He seemed like a very nice man.

Pa finally returned and I told him about Benjamin. Pa said that black people are nice folks. As we got closer to Grande Prairie the fields got bigger and there was less bush. Sometimes the smoke from the engine came back by the window and I couldn't see anything.

We arrived in Grande Prairie late in the afternoon and walked to the hotel. Pa gave the man at the desk the paper that came in the mail, the man nodded and handed Pa a pen and a big book. Pa spent a long time putting his name in it. The man gave us a key and we went upstairs to our room. On the way Pa showed me where the washroom was in the hallway. Our room had a bed and a washstand with a basin and a big pitcher of water. There were towels hanging on a bar by the stand. I thought that it was a nice room. There was paper on the walls with flowers on it and a picture above the bed. Pa told me to stay here while he went downstairs for a little while. I was scared here alone. I looked out the frosty window at the cars and the people below and thought, *I'd rather be home.*

After a while Pa came back and we went down to the dining room for supper. We had some hot stew and bread and it was quite good. After we ate Pa told me that he had a surprise for me. He said that we were going to see a moving picture. I couldn't imagine how a picture could move but I sure wanted to see it.

We walked a little ways to a building that Pa said was a theater. There was a girl at a little window with a hole in it and Pa gave her some money. She gave him a couple of little pieces of cardboard and we went to another door. *Boy, this moving picture thing sure is complicated.* At the second door a man took Pa's cards and tore them in half and he gave half of them back to Pa. I wondered what that was all about. We went through the door and it was really dark inside. I held Pa's hand so I didn't get lost. Another girl had a flashlight and she took us to some seats. *This must be an old place because the floor seems to go down hill towards the front.* We sat a few minutes and suddenly there was music and the biggest picture I'd ever seen appeared on the wall.

There was something called a newsreel first and then some funny pictures. The movie started and it was about some guys going down a river on a raft and some bad guys on shore shooting at them. It was scary and I didn't understand what was going on. Anyways, at least I could say that I'd been to a picture show.

We walked back to the hotel and Pa told me to go to bed and that he'd be back in a little while. There were even electric lights in this room. I was sure learning a lot on this trip. I went to bed and it was cold, I didn't like being here alone, I wished that Tim were here. I remembered to say my prayers and I fell asleep while I was saying them.

Pa woke me and we washed and went downstairs for breakfast. Pa said that we had to be at the hospital early to wait my turn to see the doctor. It was bitterly cold out and it was a long walk to the hospital. We got there and Pa showed a lady at a desk a paper, she pointed and told us to go downstairs. There was a long hallway with people sitting on benches. At the end of the hall was a small room with another lady sitting at a desk. Pa showed her the paper and she handed him a paper and a pencil. Pa looked at it and leaned over and quietly told the lady that he could neither read nor write. He looked embarrassed, she smiled and asked him some questions and she filled in the paper. She said that there were no appointments and that I would have to sit in the hall and wait my turn.

Pa told me to wait and he left again. I sat and waited. A nurse in a crisp white uniform and a little white hat kept coming out of a room and taking people back with her. I wondered when my turn would come. I was getting hungry and my bum was sore from sitting on the hard bench. I could see a big clock on the wall in the little office and it said three o'clock. I'd been waiting since nine.

I was daydreaming when the nurse touched my shoulder, "It's your turn," she smiled. Dr. Levie was a little white haired man. He looked tired and cranky. I had heard people talking in the hall that he was a specialist from Edmonton who came once a year. He looked in my eyes with a really bright light and had me read the eye chart. He put some drops in my eyes and the nurse took me back out in the hall and told me to wait until she came back.

While I was waiting in the hall, Pa came back. He asked the nurse how much longer it would be and she told him about an hour. He sat down with me to wait. The drops made my eyes run and they felt like they had sand in them. I couldn't see how this was going to do me much good. After a while the nurse came back and took me into the room again. Dr. Levie looked in my eyes again and then had me look through a machine. I looked at letters and numbers and lines going every which way, he kept changing lenses until he was satisfied that it was right. He told me that I was lucky that my right eye was nearly perfect the left one was healthy but had very little sight.

The nurse took me back to where Pa was waiting and she told him that my glasses should be in the mail in about two weeks. We walked back to the hotel and Pa had me wait for him in the lobby. He said that he was going to have a beer and then we'd go for supper. When he came back we went to the dining room and had supper. I was starved and supper tasted good. After we ate we went upstairs to our room and Pa lay back on the bed and had a smoke. I looked at a bible that I found on the table by the bed. It belonged to some guy named Gideon. Pa said that he was going downstairs again. I lie on the bed and fell asleep, Pa came back and woke me and I undressed and went to bed.

We got up and had breakfast and Pa said that we had some time to kill before the train left. We walked around town on the board sidewalks and looked in the stores. It was late November and they had some Christmas things out already. I'd never seen so much Christmas stuff before. We went in a grocery store and Pa bought some bananas. I'd seen them before but I hadn't tasted one. When we left the store Pa gave me one. *Are they ever good!*

We waited at the station until our train came along. Quite a few people got on and I saw Benjamin walking down the aisle. We rode for a while and Pa had to go to the smoking car again. I watched the farms as we passed by, sometimes people waved at the train. I saw the farmhouses, and I wondered who lived there and what they were like. It was getting dark and the conductor came in and lit a lamp at each end of the car. They were up on the wall and they didn't give much light.

There was a kid that was acting really stupid, running up and down the aisle and his parents didn't try to stop him. He started to aggravate me real bad. I was still eating bananas and I asked Pa if it was true that you could slip on a banana peel. He told me that it was. It was dark on the floor and the next time the kid came by I slid a banana skin in the aisle. He stepped right on it and his feet shot out and he fell on the back of his head. The skin flew under the seat out of sight. He started bawling his head off and his Pa came and carried him back to their seat. I smiled at Pa and he smiled back, the kid didn't run any more.

It was dark when we got to Tupper and Alf was waiting for us with the team and sleigh. We rode home in the dark. I was so glad to be home, I missed Ma terribly when I was away. Tim was glad to see me again and after a late supper we lay on the floor by the stove and fell asleep.

Chapter 18
A Very Lonely Christmas

I'd just started home from school when Pa caught up with me. He was riding old Bird and he had been to town to get the mail. He had two gunnysacks tied together over the horse's neck in front of him. He had supplies and mail in those sacks. "Grab my arm," he said and he swung me up on the horse behind him.

"Did my glasses come?" I asked him.

"I think so, there's a little package in the mail."

"Is it from Edmonton?" I asked.

"I don't know," he said and I didn't ask anymore as I remembered that he couldn't read.

"Did you learn anything in school today?"

"Yes I did, Pa."

"That's good, you learn to read and write real good."

"Oh, I will Pa, I will." I knew why he wanted me to learn, he didn't want me to be illiterate like he was. I knew that he was embarrassed, not being able to read or write.

We got home and Pa stopped in front of the cabin. He let me down and then he handed the bags down to me. "Take those in to your Mother, while I put the horse in the barn." Ma took the things out of the bags and put them on the table. There in the mail was the little package wrapped up in brown paper. Ma handed it to me to open. I was so excited that I could hardly open it. I finally got it open and there were my new glasses. The lenses looked so clear and the frames were a nice gold color.

Ma told me to put them on, I did and I was amazed at how good I could see. I could see things that I never noticed before. Ma said that I looked very dignified with them on, whatever that meant. The next day was the last day of school for the week and I could hardly wait to see how good they worked at school.

I was really pleased at how well I could see the blackboard at school. My new glasses were going to make a big difference in my schoolwork. Some of the kids made fun of my glasses and called me a four-eyed freak. I didn't know why they would do that. David Hamilton wore glasses too and he told them to leave me alone. It was nice to have a friend like Dave.

Ma wasn't feeling well. She had a headache and a fever and she seemed to be getting red blotches on her skin. Alf came home from work on Saturday night and he saw how sick that Ma really was. "We've got to get her to a doctor," he told Pa. Early the next morning Alf went to Tupper and called Max Miller in Pouce Coupe. Max had a taxi and Alf made arrangements with him to pick up Ma. He couldn't get to our place on account of the snow and the big hill, but he could get as far as the schoolhouse with his car.

Alf hurried home and they got Ma ready to go. Pa got the team and sleigh ready and they bundled Ma up in quilts for the trip. I had to go along as well and we got to the meeting place just as Max arrived with his taxi. Alf and I told Ma goodbye and her and Pa went off to see the doctor. Alf and I went home. When we got home, Alf did the chores and I got in the wood and water. Alf came in and we made us some supper.

"Will Ma be all right?" I asked my big brother.

"Oh, I'm sure that she'll be fine once the doctor gets a chance to look her over."

"I sure hope so," I told him, "what would we do if she should die?"

"Don't worry. She'll be better and back home in no time."

"I really hope you're right, but in the meantime I'm going to say some prayers for her, that should help, right?"

"Well it sure couldn't hurt," he told me. When supper was over and Alf went out to milk the cow I stayed in to do the dishes. After the work was finished we sat and talked and Alf made us a pot of tea. He lets me have tea when we were alone. It seemed awfully quiet with just the two of us.

"Do you think that Ma will be home for Christmas?" I asked.

"I doubt it, it's only a few days away and I don't see how she can be home that soon."

"It's not going to be a very good Christmas if Ma isn't here," I told him.

On Monday I got ready and headed out to school. Pa was expected home and he would let us know how Ma was. I didn't have a very good day in school because I was worrying about Ma. Alf was doing the chores when I got home from school. I helped with the work and just as we were going in to make supper, Pa came walking home. He looked really tired.

We all went into the cabin and Alf made a pot of tea. "Well, what's the matter with Ma?" Alf asked.

"She's pretty sick," Pa said, "the doctor says that she has something called Erysipelas, he says that it's going to take her quite a while to get over it but she is going to be fine."

"That's good to hear," Alf said, "I wonder how long she's going to be in the hospital."

"The doctor says probably a month," Pa told us.

At least with Helen working in the hospital Ma wouldn't be lonely.

Alf had to go back to work and Pa and I would be home alone until Alf and Francis came home for Christmas. Alf was working at Donald's tie camp and Francis was working for Pete LaForge at his sawmill. I finished up the last few days of school before the Christmas holidays. I was supposed to have a part in the concert at school but I wouldn't be in it because Pa wasn't going and I couldn't go by myself in the dark.

Once I was home from school it was really lonely at home. When Pa was busy working, I was home by myself. Of course, Tim was there with me and I talked to him a lot. I missed Ma something awful and I said a lot of prayers to Jesus for her. I hoped that he heard them. I wondered what Christmas would be like without her here. Sometimes I wondered what it would be like if something should happen to her. When I thought about things like that the tears ran down my face and I felt like I must be a big suck but I couldn't help it. I wondered if big men cry. It made me really mad when I cried and I wished that I was tough and didn't do that.

My brothers came home for the holidays and it was a lot nicer with them home. It was not as lonely with them around. Pa went to town and phoned the hospital to see how Ma was doing. The doctor said that she was doing fine but it would take a couple more weeks before she could come home. I was glad that she was getting better but two weeks seemed like a long time to wait till she came home.

It didn't seem much like Christmas, there was no tree and no decorations around the cabin. I asked Pa and he said to forget about it. I wondered how we could forget about Christmas. I was wondering if there would be any presents this year. I didn't believe in Santa anymore but I would have liked to, it was more fun that way. On Christmas Eve I told Pa that I was going to hang up my stocking. He told me to forget it because there wouldn't be any presents this year. I wondered why he was acting so strange, maybe he was just fooling me, so I hung up my stocking anyway.

When I got up Christmas morning, I realized that he wasn't fooling. *Well, maybe he was.* When I reached down in my sock to see what was in there, I found three small potatoes, that didn't make me feel very happy. This was my worst Christmas day ever. Francis tried to find something to cook for Christmas dinner. He found some chicken parts in a crock in the icehouse and tried to cook them. Bad move. They had been in there too long and they were spoiled. Once they started to cook they smelled terrible! Francis didn't give up easily. He decided that he was going to make Christmas dinner no matter what. He peeled some potatoes and carrots and put them on to cook. Then he went to the icehouse and cut some little steaks from a frozen piece of deer meat. Dinner was a pretty tasty meal and it sure was the best that we'd had since Ma had been gone. Pa didn't cook very much, mostly fried eggs and bread. I made myself a solemn promise to learn to cook when Ma came home.

Alf and Francis didn't have to go back to work until after New Years, and that made it a lot better around home. Pa and Alf went over the trap line together and Francis and I stayed home and did the work around the house. We all wanted to know how Ma was doing but it was really hard to find out. Alf and Francis would go to town in a day or two and phone the hospital to find out. In the meantime we just waited and wondered.

It was bedtime and it seemed strange without Ma here. When Ma was here, we always said the rosary before we went to bed. Now that I was bigger she let me stay up later and say it too. With her gone I said my prayers at bedtime and crawled into bed with old Tim. I'd spent a lot of time talking and spending time with Tim this last couple of weeks. I knew that he didn't understand but he seemed to care. I went to sleep asking Jesus to help Ma get well.

Alf and Francis came home from town with good news. The doctor had said that Ma was making an excellent recovery and would be able to come home in two weeks. I could hardly wait. New Years came and went and Alf and Francis headed back to work. Pa and I were home alone again. Pa had all the chores to do and when he was gone I stayed home by myself and kept the fire going.

It was lonely at home by myself. I got the wood in and keep the reservoir on the stove filled with snow. We used melted snow for wash water and I got ice from the icehouse for drinking and cooking. Francis showed me how to peel and cook potatoes and how to cut and fry deer steaks. It was really not much different from when I cooked in my little frying pan over a campfire. Pa said that I was learning to cook pretty good.

When school started again I had a hard time finding clothes to wear that weren't dirty. Pa said that we were going to have to try to wash some. I hoped that Ma was feeling good when she got home as there was so much to do that I didn't know how to do. I thought, *I sure will help her all I can so she doesn't get sick again.* I had to make myself some lunch for school and we were all out of bread. There were a couple of pancakes left over from breakfast and I put a little jam on them and rolled them up like a little jellyroll.

My new glasses really helped me do my schoolwork. Pa went to town and called the hospital again. This time they told him that Ma could come home. Pa made arrangements with Max Miller to bring Ma home the next day and he would meet him at the schoolhouse to pick her up. When he came home and told me, I was so excited I could hardly wait.

I stayed home from school so that I could keep the fire going and have the cabin warm for Ma when she arrived home. I did my very best to clean the cabin and tried to put things in order. I cooked some potatoes and some meat so that she could take it easy and rest for a while. I knew that she would be surprised when she found out that I could cook. I'd missed her so much that I could hardly believe that she was really coming home. It seemed to take them forever to get here. I kept looking out the window and just when I was about to give up on them, they came around the corner by the gate.

I ran out to meet them and I felt ashamed of myself again because I was crying and the tears were running. I wished that I didn't do that. Pa didn't like it when I cried. He said that big boys don't cry. I didn't care if he saw me crying, I just wanted to see my Mother. We hugged each other and Pa didn't say anything about me crying. Pa helped Ma into the cabin and I carried her suitcase. She said that she was tired and wanted to rest a little. I put the kettle on and when Pa came in from putting the team away, he made a pot of tea.

We sat by the bed and asked Ma all kinds of questions. I could tell that Pa was as glad to see Ma as I was. She told us about Helen and about Christmas at the hospital. She was pretty weak after being in bed for over a month and would have to regain her strength a little at a time. Pa and I left her to have a little rest and Pa helped me finish making supper. I woke her for supper and she said that it was the best meal that she'd had since she left home. That made me feel really good.

That night we said the rosary before we went to bed and for the first time since Ma'd been gone, everything seemed right. I went to bed and Tim seemed glad that she was home too. As I said my prayers I thanked Jesus for making my Mother better and I asked him to let me have her for a long, long time. I went to sleep happy for the first time in weeks.

I awoke to the sounds of the kitchen and Ma was up making breakfast. "Why didn't you call me to help you?" I asked her.

"Oh, I'll be fine," she said, "I'll just take it easy for a day or two." It was nice to have a good breakfast again. Pa said that I should stay home for a few days and help her around the cabin. Ma said that I could stay with her the rest of the week, there was only two days of school left anyway.

Ma recuperated quickly and by the time Monday had arrived she said that she was well enough to be alone so it was back to school for me. I had to work extra hard at school to make up for the time that I'd lost, but the teacher was understanding and before long I was all caught up.

Alf and Francis came home on the weekend to see Ma and have a little visit. Everyone was happy that we were all together again. They all seemed to be talking at the same time. Francis helped Ma in the kitchen and Alf helped Pa with the chores. It was great to have everyone home again the only one missing was Helen. I wished that she were here too. I really missed her.

When I was not in school I helped Pa haul hay from the hay meadow. I liked it when I could do that. Pa pitched the hay up in the rack and I spread it around to build the load. Sometimes on the way home he let me drive the horses. It made me feel good to be able to help out. It was a nice feeling.

When we got home and got the hay unloaded, it was time to go in for supper. Oh, what a great feeling to go into the warm cabin and smell all the wonderful smells of Ma's cooking. By the time Pa and I were washed up, Ma had supper on the table. Ma was a great cook and supper tasted so good. After supper we sat and drank our tea and talked about the day and what we'd do tomorrow.

Pa went out to milk the cow and I got in the wood. It took a lot of wood on those cold winter nights. When all the work was finished, Ma made another pot of tea and she and Pa talked while I did my homework. When bedtime came, I was tired and ready for bed. As I drifted off to sleep I could hear the murmur of my parents talking. It was a nice sound to go to sleep to.

Chapter 19
Wonders of Radio

It had been a long cold winter but in spite of all the problems that we'd had, it had not turned out too bad. Alf and Francis worked all winter and trapping had been quite good as well. Everyone came home for Easter and it was nice to be together again. Helen came home from her job at the hospital for the first time since the last summer. I was so glad to see her. She brought me a book about Popeye and Olive Oyl. It was a funny book with good stories and a lot of pictures.

Easter dinner was just too much! There was a nice big chicken, mashed potatoes with gravy, parsnips with butter and a lot of other great things. It always makes me mad that I can't eat all that I would like to. By the time that I got to the pie, I was so full that I didn't have room for any. After dinner they sat around and talked about old times. They reminisced and laughed and laughed. I'd heard these stories so many times that I felt like I knew all the people they were talking about. Even though I'd heard them before, I never tire of hearing them again.

There wasn't anyone that was very hungry when it was time for supper, so Ma and Helen just put on a little lunch. After we ate and had some tea, it was time to do the chores. The cow had to be milked and all the stock had to be fed. It was also time to get in the wood and water for the night.

After the work was finished, they talked some more. They talked about the fact that they had made a little money this winter. They all agreed that they were better off than they had been for a long time. Ma said that it was nice to have a little money around for a change. Alf said they should buy a radio. The radio that Francis had made, worked, but not very well. It had poor reception and was hard to understand. Everyone thought that was a great idea but Ma worried about spending that much money. Pa said that it would be nice to hear what was going on once in a while.

The decision was made and Ma got out the Eaton's catalog. We all gathered around the table and looked as Ma turned the pages until she came to the radios. There were floor models and table models, expensive ones and cheaper ones. To Ma they were all quite expensive. Francis knew the most about radios as he and Eric Erickson had built small ones and some crystal sets. After a lot of discussion they decided on a six-tube Viking table model. The price was $39.95. They had to order a battery pack and an antenna also. The total cost was just a little over fifty dollars, Ma thought that it was too much but she made out the order for Pa to mail the next time he went to town.

Alf and Francis went back to the bush to work. They said that they should be back in a couple of weeks. The radio should be here by then and they would put up the antenna and hook it up. I wanted us to have a radio real bad. The Ericksons had one and the Fossums had one and they listened to all kinds of music and plays. When we got ours we would be able to listen to the Lone Ranger, Superman and all sorts of programs like that. I could hardly wait. Ma told me to have patience, that it would get here in due time. Ma has a lot more patience than I have.

A couple of weeks went by and Pa went to town on Friday afternoon. He wouldn't be home very early because he had to wait for the afternoon train and it didn't get in until quite late. Ma knew that Pa would be late and she said that we had better do the chores so that Pa wouldn't have to do them when he got home. The cow wasn't giving very much milk as she was drying up for a while before she had a new calf. We just finished up when Pa came driving in with the team and sleigh. He stopped by the cabin and unloaded the groceries and a couple of boxes from the sleigh and we helped him carry them inside. The boxes were from Eaton's for sure it must be the radio. I helped Pa put the horses in the barn and we gave them some hay and oats. Pa was hungry and we hadn't eaten either. Ma had supper on the stove and it only took her a few minutes before we could sit down to eat.

I wanted to open those boxes really bad but I knew that I had to wait until Pa was finished eating and had his cigarette. Finally he said that we should open the boxes and see what we got. He took out his jack knife and carefully cut the cord and tape that kept the box closed. There was a lot of paper wadded up and packed around things. Pa said that was to keep things from getting damaged in shipping. He took the packing all out and then with great care he lifted out the radio.

It was the most beautiful thing that I'd ever seen. It had two colors of wood on it, the top was dark wood and the front was light. It was so shiny I could hardly believe it. It had a dial with numbers and a needle and four knobs below the dial. "Let's hook it up and turn it on," I said to Pa excitedly.

"We can't do that yet," Pa said, "we have to wait until we get the antenna put up."

"When can we do that, Pa?"

"We have to wait for the boys to come home to do that."

"What's a antenna, Pa?"

"It must be in this other box with the battery," Pa said. Pa opened up the other box and took out a roll of copper colored wire and a long big battery. "This is the antenna," Pa showed me "it has to be stretched between two tall trees and then it hooks up to the radio. Francis is the guy who knows about hooking it up."

Waiting was really hard but I didn't have a choice. Alf and Francis got home Saturday afternoon around three o'clock. I was after them right away to get that radio hooked up. Alf climbed high up in a tall pine tree and fastened the wire close to the top. Francis climbed up another tall tree by the cabin and stretched the wire between the trees. They ran a lead wire down the tree and through a little hole that Pa had drilled in the corner of the window frame. They also had to drive a little metal stake into the ground to hook the ground wire to. They said that they had everything outside ready and they went in to hook up the radio.

Pa put the radio on a little table and the battery on the floor. Francis hooked up the antenna and the ground wire and Alf hooked up the battery. They gave Pa the honor of turning it on for the first time. Francis pointed to the 'on' switch and told Pa to turn it on. It must have been tuned in to a religious broadcast because the first thing it said when Pa turned it on was, 'Jesus Christ.' Pa jumped back a bit, "What in hell kind of a radio is this?" he wanted to know.

The sermon carried on and everybody laughed like crazy. Pa laughed and said that he thought that it was swearing at him. Francis tuned it in to different stations and they all said what a good tone it had and how good the reception was. I didn't know about any of those things but I was truly amazed by it. That night after all the chores were finished and supper was over, we all sat and listened to the new radio. We listened to Amos and Andy, the Great

Gildersleeve and Abe's Irish Rose. At ten o'clock we listened to the news. It was late and time to say the rosary and go to bed. What a day that had been!

I woke up in the morning to the sounds of some great singing and guitar music. Alf told me that they were listening to something called the Grand Ole Opry. I didn't know what that was but it sure sounded nice. Ma seemed glad that we had this radio she said that it was good company when she was alone. I thought that it was nice for everybody. My brothers had gone back to the bush to work and Helen had gone back to the hospital to work. It was back to school for me and I was glad to go back.

The days were getting longer and the sun felt warmer. It was nice to know that spring was not far away. We were just sitting down for supper when Francis came walking down the road. Ma took one look at him as he came through the door and knew that something was wrong. "A log fell on Alf's leg and it really messed up his knee, he's in the hospital in Pouce Coupe," he told us.

"My God," Ma cried, "will he be all right?"

"They don't know how bad it is yet, it's not broken but the doctor says that all the ligaments are torn from the bone."

The next day, Pa went to town and got a ride to Pouce Coupe to see how Alf was doing. Francis had to go back to work and I had to go to school. Ma stayed home and worried herself sick over Alf's knee. *Ma must be the biggest worrier in the whole wide world.* By the time Pa got home she had herself in a real snit. Pa was tired when he got home and sat down with a cup of tea. "It looks like they are going to have to send him to Edmonton for therapy on his knee." Pa said.

Ma started to cry and Pa went over and put his arm around her. "Don't do that," Pa said, "he's going to be all right. He's going to get compensation until he can work again and that will help a lot."

"But he was so big and strong and now he's going to be a cripple, why does everything have to happen to us?"

"Jesus, don't cry," Pa said, "you know that I can't take it when you cry."

"I can't help it, it seems like we just get over one problem and then we get another, I just can't take it anymore."

Pa sat by the table and put his head in his hands. I'd never seen him do that before. He looked like he might break down and cry. I felt so sorry for the both of them that I found that I was crying too. Finally Pa stood up and said that everything would be all right and that he was going to do the chores. He went over to Ma and put his hand on her shoulder. She stood up and they held each other for a little while. Pa held her face in his hands and gave her a little kiss. Then he turned and went out to do the chores. Ma seemed to have gotten herself together again so I went out to help Pa.

I was worried about Alf as well, but somehow I knew that he was tough enough to handle it. Anyway I was going to do some praying to Jesus about it so that should help, it always seemed to help before. With all of this stuff going on, we hadn't had our supper yet and when we went in from milking, Ma had supper on the table. I was glad because I was hungry.

Morning came and after a night's sleep, things seemed a little better than they had the night before. Pa waited a couple of days and then he went to town again and phoned the hospital to find out what was going on. He got to talk to Alf and he told him that he was going to Edmonton the next day. He told Pa that they thought that it would take two or three months. He said that he'd write as soon as he arrived and knew what was happening.

Ma felt bad that she was not going to see him before he went but she felt somewhat better knowing that he was going to be cared for properly. The weather was warming up more each day and it wouldn't be long before the logging camps would be shutting down. Then Francis and Uncle Fred would be home again. I'd be glad to see them home again. It had been a long winter.

Trapping season was over for another year and it was time to pick up the traps that we had set last fall. I went with Pa on the weekend and we picked them up and carried them home for another season. Pa had a hard time getting the ice cut with Alf and Francis both working in the bush. Frank Sullivan had the same problem as his boys were out working as well so he and Pa helped each other and together they got the job done.

Pa liked to listen to the news on the radio and one night as he listened, he suddenly sat upright and shook his head. "Those bastards are at it again," he said, "it sounds like they just took over Poland."

"Who did that?" Ma asked.

"Those goddamn Germans, they just can't leave any damn thing alone, they are gonna frig around until they start another bloody world war."

"What's a world war?" I asked Pa.

"It's not a very nice thing, lots of innocent people get killed all over nothing," Pa said.

"Why do they do something stupid like that?" I asked Pa.

"Just damn greedy is the only reason that I can see, they just want to own the whole world."

"Can somebody own the world, Pa?"

"I don't know son, but I sure hope not."

That night as I went to bed, I had some new things to think about. Things that I didn't even know existed until then. I checked Tim for sparks like I always did, but with everything that was happening it was hard to feel as worry free as I usually did. As I said my prayers I asked Jesus to stop this war thing before it was too late. I fell asleep before Ma and Pa said the rosary.

Francis' First Old 1928 Chev Truck

Chapter 20
Francis Buys A Truck

The warm spring breezes pushed back the cold snows of winter and the patches of black earth seemed to reach for the sun as they expanded bigger each day. The blue and yellow crocuses pushed their little fuzzy faces through the snow as if somehow they must be the first to witness the birth of spring. It seemed like a miracle to me that the warm tenderness of spring could overpower the frigid harshness of winter and push it seemingly right out of existence.

I guess the thing that impressed me the most was the fact that nature goes through this transformation without any help from man. Just as a butterfly emerges from a cocoon, so does spring emerge from winter. These are the things that make me have the feelings for nature that run so deep in my soul. Things that I find that I have no way of explaining to anyone.

I guess that it must have been time for a change for Francis as well. He had just finished working for Pete LaForge. They had been peeling and piling the railroad ties that they had cut through the winter. Now they had to wait for the railroad inspector to come to inspect them before they would be paid for them. For the past few days, Francis had noticed an old Chev truck parked by Vern Stark's general store in Tupper. It had a 'For Sale' sign in the window and the more Francis looked at it, the more he wanted it.

He and Pete were in the store after their last day of work, and he mustered up the courage to ask Vern how much he wanted for the old truck. Vern wanted seventy-five dollars for it. Francis had about a hundred dollars coming in wages, but Pete wouldn't be able to pay him until he got paid for the ties.

Vern told him that if he wanted the truck, he could take it and Pete could give him the money when he got paid. Pete said that was fine with him so they wrote up a deal and Francis was the proud owner of a 1928 Chevrolet truck. He didn't know how to drive so he had to leave it there and walk home. As he hurried home his feet barely touched the ground. This old truck had transformed itself in his mind into a whole new way of life, no more walking everywhere, plus Ma would be able to get out a lot more.

By the time he got home, he was not in very good shape. The excitement of buying his very first truck had his nerves pretty well shot. A couple of aspirin and a cup of tea got him partially recovered and he told us about his new truck. Pa was all smiles over this deal. It was not often that Francis did something that really pleased him but this truck seemed to have gone over big with him. Ma was excited too and I was just about speechless. Pa could drive because he had a car when they lived in Ontario, so in the morning they planned walk to town and bring that truck home.

Morning came and Pa and Francis seemed to get the chores finished in record time. They set off walking the six miles to Tupper. They seemed to have a spring in their step that I had never noticed before. I didn't think that it would take them very long to get there at the speed they were walking. Ma used to drive a car as well, when they lived in Ontario. I asked Ma what it was like to drive a car. "If you want to go straight, do you just hold the wheel tight? How about if you want to stop?"

Ma told me as best she could and I wondered if I'd ever be able to drive a car. It didn't seem too likely.

A couple of hours passed and they still weren't back. Ma said that it took longer than that and not to be so impatient. I wanted to see that truck so bad I could hardly wait. I'd nearly resigned myself to the fact that they would never come home when I heard the rumbling of a motor along with quite a bit of rattling coming down our road. I ran and told Ma that I could hear them coming. She wiped her hands on her apron and came out to the yard with me. The dog was barking as if he was excited too. While we watched, the old truck came around the corner and through the gate. Pa drove up in the yard, he was sitting up straight and had kind of a proud look on his face. Francis was beaming like a Cheshire cat that just ate a mouse.

I asked Francis if I could sit in it behind the wheel. He said that I could but not to touch a thing and not to be cranking on the steering wheel. I promised that I wouldn't touch anything and I opened the door and got in. I'd never sat in a truck before and only once or twice in a car. It was not very big inside and the seat was worn pretty badly. Ma saw that too and she said that she would make a new cover for it.

There were some gauges on the dashboard and I had no idea what they were for. The steering wheel had steel spokes and a big wooden rim. I got out and looked around the outside. It once had green paint that was faded quite badly. It had a box that Francis said was factory built. It too, was once painted green. Pa said that the tires were pretty good and all in all he said that it was not a bad old truck. I thought that it was wonderful.

"When can we go for a ride?" is what I wanted to know. Pa told Ma to get ready and we could go to town right away. It only took her a few minutes to get ready and she and Pa got in the cab and Francis and I got in the box. Pa stepped on the starter and the ancient old engine sprung to life and with a little shudder it seemed to grumble as it carried us down the road.

In all the excitement Pa had forgot to give Ma the mail that was in the truck. She saw it in a box on the floor and that made her happy. There was a letter from Alf. She had been waiting a long time to hear from him. She tried to read it as we drove down the road but it was too rough. It only took about twenty minutes for us to get to town. It usually takes two hours to walk and nearly that long with the horses this had to be some kind of a record.

Ma read the letter as soon as we got to town and Pa stopped the truck. She seemed a lot happier once she had read Alf's letter and found out that he was doing fine. He said that he was staying with Frank Gardener and his wife. Frank used to live near Tupper and he and Alf were friends. Frank had moved to Edmonton a few years ago and had a job there as a milkman. Ma was happy that Alf was staying with friends so he wouldn't be lonely.

Ma bought a few groceries and we headed home again. We rumbled on home and I was amazed by the fact that we'd been gone less than two hours. That old truck was sure going to make going places a lot easier. Ma asked Pa if maybe we could go to church on Sunday. Pa smiled and told her that he couldn't think of any reason why we couldn't go. He said that maybe we could go once a month if the weather was good. That seemed to make Ma real happy.

Pa told Francis that he had better get in that truck and learn how to drive it. I got in with him because I sure didn't want to miss a ride. He started the engine and put it in gear. He let out the clutch and the old truck lurched ahead and stalled. After a few tries he got better on the clutch and we went jerking down the road. He did not too badly until we came to the first corner. We made it around the corner but he couldn't seem to get it straightened out.

It was a good thing that the ditches were shallow, we went in the right ditch and he cranked on the wheel like a mad man. We lurched out of that one and right into the left one. He had an awful time finding the center of the road. I was thinking that he had a lot of practising to do and maybe I wouldn't ride with him anymore until he did some.

After his initial bout Francis got his act and his nerves together and with a few more tries he conquered the old Chevy and he learned how to drive. He didn't use the truck very much though. Pa seemed to use it a whole lot more. It seemed as though that he bought it so that Ma could get to town once in a while and for the family to use more than for him.

Pete LaForge bought himself a new Ford one-ton truck and made a box with a tarp over it and the whole family was going to take a trip for a month this summer. Pete asked Francis if he would stay at their place while they were gone and look after the cow and chickens. Francis agreed so he went and spent most of July over at their place.

The LaForges had a bicycle and Francis learned how to ride it while he was staying there. One day he came home for a visit and he was riding the bike. I thought that it was a pretty nice thing because I'd never had a good look at a bike before. Francis wanted me to go stay with him for a few days and I was really excited about that. When it was time to go Francis put me on the handlebars and we set off. This was pretty exciting, riding up front on this bike. When we came to the first corner the excitement got even greater because he couldn't turn corners! The handlebars of a bike while you're crashing through the brush are not the optimum place to be sitting. After a pile up on the second corner I persuaded him to stop and let me off for the next one. That made it a lot easier on the skin and face.

I stayed with him for a week and it was lots of fun. We walked down by the lake and I found a dead fish that washed up on the shore. It smelled real stinky and had a million flies around it. We took the boat and rowed across the lake to the store to get some groceries. Pete had made arrangements with the storekeeper to give Francis any groceries that he needed while he was staying there. Francis seemed to really love puffed wheat because that was all that he ate the whole time. The week seemed to go by fast and it was time to go home again. The trip home on the bike was the same thing, stop for the corners and walk around them and then ride to the next one.

It seemed like a lot of things were happening this summer. Dauphine Rule, a neighbor girl that I went to school with became very ill and they took her to the hospital. They found out that she had Polio, whatever that is. I'd never heard of it before but they said that there was a lot of it going around and that it is a real bad thing. They said that it can cripple you up, make your legs go all funny and sometimes you couldn't walk after you had it. And some People died from it. I sure hoped that I didn't catch it.

Pa came home from town and told Ma that Mr. Finlay had passed away. He said that the funeral was on Thursday and that we should go. Pa said that he died from gangrene that he got in his foot and it spread through his whole body. The Finlays were good friends and Ma agreed that we should go to the funeral.

Thursday dawned and it was pouring rain. Pa said that it was not a good day to have to go to a funeral. The funeral was to be held at two, and with all the rain and mud we set out right after lunch. The road was really muddy and the mud picked up on the old trucks tires until they were twice their size. Pa had quite a time keeping it out of the ditch and on the road. Ma was nervous about the road and hung on tight to the seat. Her knuckles turned white she hung on so hard. I was a little apprehensive about all of this. I'd never been to a funeral before nor had I seen a dead person. I was not too sure that I wanted to either.

We arrived at the little log church on time. It was a little church sitting among the aspen trees along the road to Gundy. There were a couple other old cars there and some horses and wagons tied up among the trees. We went in and sat down on the old plank pews with the other folk. The coffin was made of pine and sat on a couple of sawhorses at the front of the church. Reverend Golding was the minister and the Finlays were like family to him. He was going to miss Mr. Finlay as much as the family would.

The service began and the Reverend had a hard time doing the readings. He kept breaking down all through the funeral and I felt really sorry for him. It was obvious that he loved this man dearly and he was unable to hide his pain. After the service all the people walked by the coffin and had a last look at the poor unfortunate body inside. When I got up to the coffin I had to stand on my tiptoes to look inside. When I did I was face to face with a dead person who has passed away from gangrene. His face was absolutely green. I froze on the spot. Ma took me by the arm and pulled me away. I saw that green face in my mind and I couldn't seem to get rid of it. This was one experience that would be embossed in my memory forever.

As we got to the door, they put the lid on the coffin and nailed it down. There were rope handles on the coffin and six men carried it outside and put it in the back of a wagon. The rain was still falling and it was a really gray and dreary day. The wagon set off for the cemetery and we all followed. Pa had a hard time keeping the old truck on the road when we were going so slowly. We arrived at the cemetery and the same six men carried the coffin over to where the grave has been dug and placed it on two ropes that were lying on the ground.

The minister stood at the end of the coffin and tried to carry on with the funeral. He tossed a handful of mud on the lid and said something about ashes and dust. Now he was really confusing me. He kept saying, "He is not here, he is not here." *He must be there because we didn't see him fall out anywhere. If he isn't here, I wonder where he is.* After some more sermons, the men picked up the ropes with the coffin suspended in between and lifted it over the grave. Some more talk about ashes and dust and more mud thrown on the lid and they lowered it down into the grave.

Everyone started to leave and Pa got ahead of the wagons so we could go a little faster. We went right on to Tupper to get the mail and a few groceries. There was another letter from Alf and it said that he was coming home next week. Ma looked so happy and I could hardly wait. There was also a letter from the school board that said that the school would be closing due to insufficient students. It said that I must be registered with the correspondence board and that I would be taking my schoolwork at home from then on.

I was a little disappointed with this news but decided that it probably would have some benefits. Ma said that we would have to fill out the papers right away and send them back. We got home and the rain was still falling. I got in some wood and put it in one corner of the wood box so that it could dry out. There was enough dry wood in the other side for Ma to make supper. After supper I helped Pa with the chores. I gathered the eggs and closed up the chicken coop for the night. It was too wet to play outside so I went in and played with Tim.

At bedtime after I said my prayers I got into bed and talked to Tim. I told him about the funeral and about seeing a green dead man. He didn't seem to care but I had to talk to somebody about it. This was my first brush with human death and it bothered me. I thought about the fact that everybody dies. I found that hard to comprehend. I wondered what the purpose of life is if all we do is die after we do all this work. Every time that I closed my eyes, I had the vision of that dead green face. I found it hard to go to sleep.

The next days went by slowly when we were waiting for Alf to come home but the day finally arrived. We got in the truck and motored into town to meet the train. Alf got off and Ma hugged him and he hugged her back. He shook hands with Pa and rubbed my head. He was walking pretty well but he still had quite a limp. He said that it felt not too bad and that the doctor told him to take it easy for a while and let it get stronger. He said that he was sure glad to be home. We were all glad that he was home too.

Alf hadn't seen the truck and he thought that it was quite an improvement over the team and wagon. He hadn't driven before either so he had to learn how too. Just like Francis, it didn't take him long to learn and soon everyone could drive but me. I thought, *maybe someday I'll be big enough to learn how. I sure hope so.*

Chapter 21
Schoolwork At Home

September arrived and it was time to do my schoolwork from my correspondence supplies. The supplies came in the mail in a big box and there were lessons for a whole year in it. They were all numbered and were set up for one week at a time. I liked doing my schoolwork here at home. Ma was a good teacher and she made me study just like I was in school. I started at 9:00 a.m. and went until 10:30, then I had a little recess and it was back to studying until noon. After lunch was the same until 3:30. Ma made sure that I didn't goof off. If I did she got really cross and got out the strap. That was a lesson that I could do without.

This work at home had lots of benefits. I didn't have to go out in the rain or cold and I had more time because I didn't have to spend time walking. I missed playing with the other kids but the good things outweighed the bad.

It was the middle of one afternoon when Father Owens drove up in the yard. He had another priest with him and he introduced him as Father Goetz. Father Owens told us that he was leaving and that Father Goetz would be our new priest. I liked him right away. He was different than Father Owens. He wasn't so stuffy and he told me that he liked to hunt. He said that the next time he came that he and I could go hunting rabbits and partridges if I knew where to go. I told him that I sure did know where we should go.

After they left I told Ma that I liked this new priest and she said that she liked him too. I could hardly wait until he came again so that we could go hunting. He also told me that he wanted me to learn to be an altar boy. I was not sure that I could do that but he said that I could learn to do it so I decided that I'd give it a try.

Alf's knee was still stiff but he said that he could hack ties again if he was careful. That war that Pa was worried about was raging on and it seemed to have put an end to the depression. Suddenly there seemed to be lots of things happening and there was more work than there had been in years. Alf and Francis went to Grande Prairie to see Frank Donald and they got a contract to sell him railroad ties. There were quite a few pine trees on our homestead so they would be able to stay home and cut ties here. Uncle Fred came home to help out.

It was the first winter that everyone had been home for a long time. It was nice but it really made a lot of work for Ma, cooking and cleaning for everyone. I tried to help her when I wasn't doing my schoolwork. Of course they had a trap line and I had a little one of my own. There were still lots of rabbits and the price for rabbit skins had gone up a little so we tried to catch as many as we could. The price was not high enough for us to shoot rabbits as it cost nearly as much for the bullets as we got for the skins. We trapped and snared them but Pa had an idea that he thought would really get us a lot of rabbits.

He made a box about ten feet long and three feet square. On one end of this box he made a trap door and tied some hay on it. When the rabbits jumped on the door to get the hay the door would drop down and they would fall into the box. This worked really well except for one little problem. Pa forgot to figure out how to get the rabbits back out of the box. It was nearly full of rabbits when an idea popped into his head. He put me in the box and told me to catch them and hand them out to him.

This was not a good idea! As a matter of fact it was a real bad idea. I got in the box and there was not much room in there and there must have been fifty wild, scared rabbits in there with me. They were leaping around all over the place. They kicked me in the face and all over my body, I thought that they were gonna kill me if I didn't get out of there right away. I tried to get the door open but those damn rabbits kept knocking me all over the place. I hollered for Pa to get me out and he opened the door a little and asked me if I'd caught one yet. I told him that there was no way that I could catch one of those suckers and asked him to get me the hell out of there. Pa grabbed me by the collar and pulled me out and about a dozen rabbits came thumping out with me. I was all beat up and scratched all over my face and hands. I never knew that rabbits could be so violent.

Pa said that it wasn't one of his better ideas after all and he opened the door and let them all out. If they were as glad to get out of there as I was, they must have been pretty happy. When I got home, Ma took one look at me and I had to tell her the whole story. I didn't know whether she was going to laugh or cry. She washed my face and put some salve on the scratches and the cuts on my hands. She said that Pa should have known better than stick a kid in a box with fifty rabbits. When she said it that way it seemed kind of funny and her and I laughed and laughed.

It was a cold winter and it seemed that a lot of wolves had moved into the area. One night we heard the wolves howling a lot and really loud. They were just down in the valley south of our cabin. Pa was worried that Bird, our old gray mare, maybe in trouble. She had been sort of retired and spending a lot of time down in the valley by the creek. She liked to go in the spruce thicket after she ate to lie down in the soft moss where it was warm and out of the wind. Pa said that he should go see if she was all right but in the pitch dark he wouldn't be able to see a thing.

Early the next morning Pa and Alf went down to see what all the noise was about and they quickly found that the wolves had poor old Bird for supper. She had gotten down in the deep moss and couldn't get away. Pa set some traps out around the kill, hoping that he would catch some of the wolves. There seemed to be wolves everywhere and Pa told me not to be going in the bush without a rifle and he said to keep my eyes open.

I still smoked my pipe but it was too cold to be smoking out behind the icehouse. I thought that I should try some cigarettes instead of my pipe. I was in the outhouse and I rolled a cigarette out of moss and a piece of old catalog. I rolled it up and I was sitting on the seat having a good smoke and watching the cabin through the crack in the door. I was only about halfway through my smoke when I saw the door opening and Ma coming outside. I thought that she might be coming to the outhouse and I didn't want her to catch me smoking so I threw my smoke down the hole and slipped out and over to the barn.

It turned out that she went to the icehouse instead of the toilet so I figured that I'd escaped one more time. Wrong! After a while I went into the cabin and as I was having a cup of cocoa, Alf came in and said that the toilet was burning down. We ran out to see and sure enough, it was blazing like a big bonfire. "How did that happen?" Alf asked, and as he said it he looked at me. I shrugged my shoulders and told him that I had no idea what happened.

He didn't believe me for a minute. Ma looked at him and asked him if he thought that I had something to do with it. "Damn right he did, the little bugger was smoking in there and threw a lit smoke down the hole." Now Ma was on my case.

"Is that true, that you were smoking in there?" I had to tell the truth because they knew it was me. There was no one else around.

"Oh, please don't tell Pa, he'll kill me for sure," I told them.

"How do you expect him not to know about it, do you think that he won't notice that it's burned down when he goes out there?"

"Maybe you could tell him that a spark from the stovepipe started it," I suggested.

"I don't think so, you'll just have to face the music." I didn't know about music but I knew one thing for sure and that was that I'd be dancing when Pa was through with me.

I didn't have to wait long. Pa came home for supper and of course right away he noticed that the outhouse was no longer there. He wanted to know in no uncertain terms just what had happened to it. I was thinking that maybe I could tell him that I had to go so bad that it set the thing on fire, but before I could do that, Ma gave him the full story. Well, I was right about the dancing. Pa stretched my left arm a little more and applied the razor strap to my lower extremities with a force that made me think that I wouldn't be smoking in any buildings for quite some time. Ma wanted to know what we were going to use for a toilet. Pa said that we'd have to use the barn for a while until they had time to build a new one. I wished that they would quit talking about it and let Pa cool down. I was going to have to stay out of his sight for some time.

I'd been looking at an advertisement in the paper for quite some time and I begged Ma to let me write to it. It was an ad from a company looking for kids to sell Christmas cards and earn some fabulous prizes. If I sold just fifty boxes of cards for only fifty cents a box and sent them the money, I could have my choice of several prizes. There was this beautiful shiny silver pocket watch, and that was the prize that I wanted. Ma was really reluctant to let me send for my selling kit and wanted to know who I thought would buy all these cards. I told her that I'd work real hard and for sure I would sell them all.

I finally wore her down and she agreed to let me send for these beautiful cards. I thought that it would be easy to sell them as the ad said that people just couldn't resist them. I wrote the letter and I could hardly wait for my selling kit to arrive. I was thinking how I would show these cards to the neighbors and they would be amazed at the beauty of them and they would be sold in no time. Then I could send them the money and they would send me my big shiny silver pocket watch. Ma said to be patient, as it would take at least three weeks for them to get here. They had better hurry because it was not too long until Christmas.

There was another little thing that I want but I hadn't figured out how to get it just yet. Every night as we listened to the radio, there was a program that was sponsored by the International Tractor Company. They had a promotion for kids that if you sent in seventy-five cents in stamps or coin, they would send you a perfect model of an International Farmall tractor complete with real rubber tires and a steering wheel that actually steered the front wheels. I wanted that tractor so bad that I could taste it but the promotion was only good in the U.S. and besides I didn't have seventy-five cents.

After a lot of brainwork I believed that I had a foolproof plan. It was a little underhanded and I had to tell a little lie but I wanted that tractor so bad I decided to try it. That night I listened to the radio and had a paper and pencil ready to write down the address for that deal. Then I composed my letter. I couldn't let Ma see it or she'd put an end to my plan real quick. I told them that I knew that the deal was only good for the United States but that I was a little crippled boy and if they could see their way clear to send me a tractor I would be ever so pleased and I would try to send them the money if they wanted it.

I got Alf to mail it for me so that Ma wouldn't find out. He asked me what the letter was about and I told him that it was for a pamphlet about tractors for my schoolwork. At bedtime when I said my prayers I felt really bad about this tractor thing and I talked to Jesus about it but it didn't make me feel better. So I decided I would have to tell the priest about it the next time that I went to confession. I wondered how telling a little lie like that could make me feel so bad. Maybe they wouldn't send me the tractor and just telling the lie wouldn't be as bad as if they actually sent it. I didn't tell Tim about it because I felt like some kind of a crook. What if they sent a policeman to check it out and found out that I was lying? I didn't sleep real well that night.

The men were busy hacking ties and piling them up in the bush. After work every night Alf and Francis hauled some to the railway siding in town. The bark had to be peeled from the two sides of the tie that weren't hewed and they told me that they would pay me five cents for each tie that I peeled. I worked hard at my schoolwork and when I finished that and my chores I went to peel ties. I peeled them with a thing they call a spud. It's like a wide chisel with a four-foot handle and it works pretty well. The ties were heavy and I had trouble rolling them around and piling them up after I got them peeled. If I worked hard, I could peel four or five ties a day, after my schoolwork was finished.

I was keeping real busy, what with school and trapping and peeling ties, my time was pretty well all used up. Of course I still had my chores to do as well. When you're busy the time seems to go by quickly and it was the first of December before long. Alf came home from town and he had the mail. In the mail was a box for me. It was the Christmas cards that I was going to make my fortune on. I opened the box and there seemed to be an awful lot of boxes of cards in it. I was sure going to have to hurry to get these all sold by Christmas.

After supper I tried for my first sale. I took a couple of boxes and showed them to Ma. She said that she'd buy one box. It wasn't much but it was a start. I got a little box to put the money in so that I'd have it to send to the card people. On the weekend I walked down to Fossum's place and she bought one box too. I walked to all the neighbors and the best that they could do was buy one box each. After I'd been to all of their places I still had forty boxes to sell. I was thinking that maybe this selling business wasn't as easy as they said in the ad. They made it sound like the people would be just waiting for me to get there so they could buy these cards.

I thought that if I went to town maybe I could sell some cards there. I went in with Alf and Francis on Saturday and stayed in town while they made a couple trips hauling ties. I went to see everybody that I could think of and only sold a couple more boxes. I even sold one box to the storekeeper and he had cards to sell himself. There was no one else to try and sell to so when Alf and Francis came in with another load, I went home with them.

It was just a few days until Christmas and I still had thirty-five boxes of cards left. I asked Ma if she would like a few more but she said that she had all that she needed. I wrote a letter to the card people and told them that I still had all these cards and asked what they wanted me to do with them. I also gave Ma the money for the ones that I'd sold so she could get a money order made out to send with the letter. At the rate that I was going, I'd never get that watch.

Christmas arrived and I got real excited because Helen came home for a couple days. I missed her but Ma said that she probably would never come home for good again. I wished that she would, we always had such good times together even when I got in trouble with her. She got me a couple of books for Christmas and Ma got me a real nice little hunting knife. I'd wanted one for a long time and I finally had one. Christmas dinner was awesome as always and my only regret was that I couldn't eat more.

Father Goetz came out during the holidays and stayed overnight. In the morning he said mass at the kitchen table and I did my altar boy bit. I didn't really know what to do but he was patient and told me that I was doing fine. Of course I had to go to confession and tell him about the tractor deal. He told me that was a very bad thing to do and not to let my greed control my actions. He said never to do something like that again and gave me a bunch of Hail Mary's and some Our Father's to say for my penance.

After mass we had breakfast and then he and I went hunting. I hoped that he didn't mention the tractor thing and he didn't. I took him and showed him my trap line. It was soon obvious that he didn't know a lot about the bush either. He liked the bush and I showed him how to skin squirrels and weasels. He could shoot pretty well and we had a good time shooting rabbits and we even shot a couple squirrels. There sure was a big difference between him and Father Owens. I could even say rabbit turds and he didn't seem to care.

The holidays were soon over and it was back to the normal everyday routine. They came home with the mail and there was a little parcel for me. I was hoping that it wouldn't come but here was a package from International Harvester Co. Ma asked me what it was and I told her that I didn't know. She said to open it and find out. I opened it and unwrapped a beautiful little red tractor. It was even more beautiful than I imagined it would be.

"Why did they send you that?" Ma wanted to know. I told her that I didn't know and then she saw a letter taped to the wrapper. She took it out and read it and as she did I saw her forehead start to get little creases in it. "So now you're crippled. Is it very bad or do you think that you might recover?" I knew that I couldn't lie to her so I told her the whole story. She was really disappointed in me, and that made me feel terrible. I tried to tell her how sorry I was but somehow it just didn't seem to be enough. So I had this lovely little tractor and I couldn't even enjoy it.

I asked her if she was going to make me send it back. She said that she wouldn't because it would probably mess things up with the people who sent it and make them feel bad that they did such a nice thing for such a little crook. I sure hoped that the F.B.I. or the Mounties didn't come after me for this. I had this nice little tractor and I would never enjoy playing with it. Ma said that she wouldn't tell Pa about it because if there is anything that Pa hates it's a thief and she didn't want him to hate me. I swore that I would never cheat or steal anything else for the rest of my life. I told her that I'd already confessed to the priest about it and that I'd talked to Jesus about it and she told me that we'd forget about it but just don't ever do anything like that again. I promised.

Chapter 22
The World Is At War

Everyone's worst fears became reality and war raged throughout Europe. England was being bombed constantly and Germany was running rough shod over many of its neighbors. Canada of course was involved and the government had started conscription and all the young men were being called up to go and do their duty for King and country.

Much to Ma's dismay, Alf and Francis got their conscription notices and they had to go to Grande Prairie to the induction center for their physical. Alf was still having lots of problems with his knee and Francis was turned down because of heart and lung problems. They came home with mixed feelings about the results of their tests. On one hand they wanted to go and do their part in defending their country and on the other hand they also wanted to stay home. I guess that all the young men who went to war had the same feeling.

A lot of the neighbor boys were going and some had already finished basic training and had come home on leave before going overseas. I saw some of them at the store and at some of the dances we went to and they looked very sharp in their new uniforms. I wished that I were big enough so that I could go. Ma said that she was glad that I was not. It seemed to me that I was always too small for everything that I wanted to do. I wondered if I'd ever get big enough to do anything.

Germany had taken over Czechoslovakia and many of the people escaped with only their lives. Several families of them had come to our area and were placed on homesteads by the Government. The area that they settled was on the way to Pouce Coupe and was known as Tate Creek. Most of them were professional people: accountants, lawyers, shop owners and even a doctor. They had a hard time adapting to this way of life, but they liked the freedom and they all worked very hard.

The set up for them was that they had to all work together and help each other. They lived two or three families to a house until they could build more houses for the rest of them. We got to know some of them and they seemed like very nice people but they couldn't speak English and we couldn't speak German so there were a lot of hand signals going on. Pa said that they were going to make good neighbors.

It was getting close to spring and the winter work would soon be over for another year. Pa was feeling happy. He came home from the trap line and he had a big black wolf. Pa said that maybe it was the son of a bitch that helped kill old Bird. He was frozen stiff but I went and kicked him anyway just to get even. I felt a little better about poor old Bird since they had caught one of those suckers.

They had hauled all the ties to town and when they got paid for them, I'd get my money for the ones that I peeled. The way I'd figured it, I'd made just a little over ten dollars. With the money that I'd made from trapping this winter I was feeling pretty well to do. I always had grand plans of saving my money until I had enough to buy a bike but somehow I always seemed to piddle it away on candy and twenty-two shells. Sometimes I bought myself a book or magazine if I could find one that had something that interested me. I had to go to Dawson to buy books and that wasn't always easy. I had to wait until someone went with the truck and they had to have the room and the patience to put up with me.

Spring arrived again and Pa bought a sow pig. He said that she would soon have little pigs. The men all worked and built a pig house and a little fence to keep them in. Pa had been hauling grain for some people and he bought some to feed the pigs. Pa and Alf were saying that they needed to grind this grain and they needed some sort of a grinder. Pa said that he knew where there was a grinder but they would need some sort of a motor to run it. They remembered that Bud Brunning had a model T Ford in a barn and he hadn't used it for years. They went over to see Bud and they bought the front half of the old car.

They brought home the front wheels and the motor and built a power unit out of it. They had to make a governor for it to control the speed of the engine. They made a wooden pulley and hooked the engine to the grinder with a wide belt that they found someplace and they tried it out. It worked great! So, we are going to have pigs.

A couple of weeks passed and Frankie, (that's what we named the sow pig) gave birth to a litter of baby pigs. Lord, but those little pigs were cute. Frankie was quite protective of them and she got mad if you made one squeal. Pa told me to be real careful around her because sow pigs could be dangerous. I looked but I didn't touch them. Pa said that we'd be able to make our own bacon and ham as soon as those little pigs were big enough.

Correspondence schoolwork was working out really fine. If I worked hard enough I was able to get all the lessons finished a whole month early. This way I got three months holidays instead of two. I'd been getting high marks on my lessons and I passed into grade four with honors. I didn't know what that meant and I was the only one who knew it but it made me feel good.

Ma was still taking her turn at having her ladies meetings but I always made sure not to show up at the cabin when those ladies were there. After the last couple of episodes it just wasn't worth the trouble I got into. I stayed out in the bush and cooked squirrel legs and smoked my pipe and wished that I had a friend like Huck Finn. *It would sure be nice to have someone to play with and talk to.* I decided that I had better stop talking to Tim that maybe it sounded a little nuts to anyone that heard me talking to a cat. If Pa heard me he might want to send me to that funny farm he talks about when he thinks that I'm acting crazy.

I was a little ticked off with Alf. I'd been asking him for days what would happen if you shot a bear in the eye and he wouldn't give me an answer. I asked him again today and he got a goofy look on his face and told me that he supposed it would put his eye out. *Crap anyway! I already knew that, I wanted to know if it would kill him right away or just make him mad. I wonder why I ask these guys anything at all.*

Alf and Francis cut some wood and sold it to a Chinese café in Pouce Coupe. I wondered how they found out about all of these things. They sawed it with a Swede saw and split it and put it in piles. After it dried for a couple of weeks they loaded it on the old truck and hauled it to Pouce. One day I was helping them throw a load in the truck and it was nearly full. A few sticks fell off the back and Alf bent down to pick them up. I threw a little round stick up on the truck and just as I threw it, Alf stood up and it hit him right behind the ear. He fell down like he was shot.

This scared me really bad. He didn't move. He just lay there with his eyes rolled back in his head so far that all we could see was the whites. Francis went over and knelt beside him and told him to wake up. *Oh God, I hope that I didn't kill him, and if I didn't kill him he's gonna kill me when he wakes up.*

Finally his eyes came into focus and he sat up and looked around. "What the hell was all that about, one minute I'm loading wood and the next minute I'm zonked right out?"

I figured I should tell him that I hit him on the head with a stick but he just might not take too kindly to that. Just when I was trying to figure out what to tell him my big mouth brother said "Lewie hit you with a stick of wood."

"Well, I sure didn't try to hit you with a stick, I threw it and you stood up right in line with it."

Alf didn't say anything but he walked around and rubbed the back of his head. "Holy hell, I've got a lump as big as a egg back there, here feel it."

Oh no, I'm not going to get that close until I find out if he's going to be mad.

"Oh I'm not mad," he said "you didn't do it on purpose." Well, I really was glad to hear that because I was feeling bad enough about it as it was. He said he felt all right so we threw on the last few sticks and got in the truck and headed for home.

The hill that we live on runs east and west and goes for miles. The width of the hill is about a mile wide and we live right in the middle. A half a mile to the south the hill goes very steep down to a beautiful valley with a nice creek running through it. The valley is about a half a mile wide and then it slopes gently up into a pine ridge. The top of the hill has big sandstone boulders that one can sit on and enjoy the view of the valley below. There are a lot of skunks that live among the rocks so we call this place, Skunkville.

The valley to the north is also a lovely little valley. It also has big sandstone rocks at the edge of the hill. This is the way that we go when we go to town and to the road that all our neighbors live on. Across this valley is another hill. They call this hill "Old Baldy." It's a barren hill with a little clump of five or six trees on the east side of it. I like to sit on these big rocks and look over at that clump of trees. It's quite a long way over to that hill and I plan on going over there and looking back this way when I get big enough.

Last summer they made a new garden on the south side hill. The soil was a beautiful sandy loam and it sloped gently to the south so it would get the full benefit of the sun. Just below the garden was a huge rock outcropping and they figured that the heat from that would extend the growing season by a bit. They were right. They planted it this spring and the plants were growing like crazy. We were growing all kinds of vegetables that we couldn't grow in our old garden. We had corn and cucumbers and vegetable marrows and I wondered why they planted those things. I hated them worse than turnips.

Francis and I went to get the cows one evening and when we got to the edge of the hill we stopped to look in the valley to see if we could see them. There was a big flat rock about three feet high right at the edge of the hill and Francis told me to jump up on it to see if I could see the cows. So I jumped up on the rock and landed feet first on a big snake that was sleeping there, soaking up the heat from the rock. I let out a yell and jumped straight up in the air and the snake had wrapped himself around my foot and was going up my pant leg.

Well, there was some fancy jumping and dancing going on for a couple of minutes and I finally leapt off the rock and the snake went flying in the dirt. Francis was having himself a fit laughing over these proceedings. After I gained my composure and got my heart back in my chest I suddenly realized that the big dummy saw that snake up there and had me jump on it just for fun. I told him so, in no uncertain words but he swore up and down that he never saw the snake. I didn't believe him for a minute and I told him that too and that I was mad as hell. He just laughed and I had to figure out some way to get even with him.

The men took a couple of days and built a new outhouse. They hewed the logs and fit them all together. It was a nicer outhouse than the one that had the accident with fire. Pa had cooled off so I could be around him again. He told me that I was not to smoke in there ever again. I promised him that I'd never do it again. He really meant it and told me that if I ever burnt the shithouse down again that he'd knock some very important parts right off of me.

I don't think that Pa ever paid any attention to what I say to him. I was with him when he fed the pigs and I asked him if it was all right if I smoked but don't burn anything down. Pa said that he didn't care but I'd have to buy my own tobacco. I figured that was a good deal for me because I don't smoke tobacco, only moss. I got my pipe and a can of moss and took it into the house and put it by the storage box near the door. That box was also right in front of Pa as he sat in his rocker and relaxed after supper.

We had our supper and as he always did, Pa rolled himself a smoke, went over to the stove and lit his cigarette with a long sliver of wood that he took from the kindling and lit in the fire. Pa went back to his chair and sat down and enjoyed his smoke as he slowly rocked. He nearly fell asleep but not quite, he just rocked and smoked and had his eyes nearly closed. I took out my pipe and tobacco can and filled my pipe. Then I did just what Pa had done. I got up and went over to the stove and lit my pipe with a long sliver of wood.

I went back to my seat, sat down and started to have my smoke. Ma hadn't seen me yet but I knew that when I told her that Pa said it was all right for me to smoke that she wouldn't mind. I saw Pa's eyes starting to open and then they opened really wide. He sat up with this look of disbelief on his face and then he blew his cool. "What in bloody hell do you think that you're doing?"

"I'm just having a smoke."

"Well, you ain't going to be having a smoke for very long," he said.

"But Pa, you told me today that I could smoke if I bought my own tobacco." That was all the reasoning that I was going to try with him for the moment because he was heading for me and I was heading for the door.

Boy, there is just no pleasing that guy sometimes. I could hear Ma ask him what all the hollering was about and I could sure hear him explain it to her. The only thing that he left out was the fact that he told me, just this afternoon, that it was okay for me to smoke. It looked like I'd be smoking behind the icehouse for quite some time yet. I'd stay out of his way again until he forgot about it.

I waited until he came out and went to the barn and then I slipped into the cabin and into the bedroom. Ma came in and asked me just what I thought that I was doing, smoking like that when I was not supposed to be smoking at all. I told her about Pa and my conversation that afternoon and she kind of gave her shoulders a shrug and told me not to do it anymore. At bedtime I had another big talk with Jesus and asked him if he could help me not to get into so much trouble with Pa. I hoped that he heard me.

Chapter 23
Shotguns and Soapbox Racers

Pa came home one day and he had a shotgun that he had made a deal for. Ma asked him what he planned on doing with it and he told her that he would like to shoot some ducks down on the creek with it. She asked him if he tried it out and he said no but shotguns always work so he felt there was no need to try it. He must have given it some thought because he decided to take it out and try it, just to show her that it worked. Pa took the gun and went over toward the icehouse. In a minute we heard a loud bang and soon Pa came walking in the door. "How does it work?" she asked him from beside the stove where she was cooking supper.

"The son of a bitch kicks like a damn army mule." Ma looked at him and his cheek was bleeding and all skinned up and his eye was a little black.

"What happened?" she asked.

"Like I said, the damn thing kicks something ferocious. It woulda liked to have knocked my head off." Pa took the gun and put it in the corner behind the bed in my room. "Don't you touch the bloody thing," he said and he was looking right at me.

I wished that he hadn't said that, now I wanted to look at it more than ever. Alf came home and took one look at Pa's face and asked him what happened. Pa told him about the shotgun and Alf wanted to see it. Pa told him where it was and Alf brought it into the kitchen to have a look. Alf looked it over and read the printing that was stamped into the barrel. "No wonder that it kicks, its full choke, pinched down like a rifle." I asked him what choke meant, the only choke that I knew was when somebody grabbed you by the neck and squeezed until your eyes popped out.

Alf said that choke on a shotgun meant that the barrel is made smaller at the end than where the shells go in and that full choke is as tight as they can make them. I asked him what good that did and he said that it makes the pellets go further and keeps the pattern smaller. I was not too sure that I understood it all but I let on that I did. Alf told Pa that it looked like a pretty good gun if you could stand the kick. Pa said that he didn't plan on standing it very much. Alf asked Pa if he got any shells with it and Pa told him that there was nearly a full box in the cupboard. Alf looked and grinned, "Small wonder that it kicks, these are two and three quarter inch shells and number two shot." Pa said that whatever the reason the bloody thing kicks real bad.

I had to wait until there was no one in the cabin and then I took out the gun and had a good look at it. It felt smooth and hard in my hands and I put it up to my shoulder and it felt good. I read the printing on the barrel and it said *Richardson Greener* and below it had *12 gauge. Full choke. Max 2 ¾ shells.* I liked the color of the barrel, it was kind of mottled, blue and brown and the stock was a nice reddish brown shiny wood. I liked this gun and knew that someday I'd shoot it but I just put it away before Pa caught me with it. I used the twenty-two all the time and so I wondered why he didn't want me to look at this gun.

I got to go to Dawson Creek with Ma and Pa and when we were there I looked for a magazine that had some stuff that I might be interested in. I found a little book that showed kids making and racing soapbox racers. I had never heard of that before but it sounded like a great thing to me. In the back of the magazine there was even more great stuff. They showed kids making airplanes that take off by going down a long ramp on a big hill. They called them gliders. I had to have that magazine and I begged Ma for ten cents so that I could buy it. She gave in and so I wound up with the blueprint for a lot of fun.

Seeing as how we lived on a big hill and everything in the magazine worked by rolling down a hill I figured that I really had it made. All that I had to do was build these things and I would have more fun than anyone could ever imagine. It didn't really show how to make these wonderful things but there were a lot of pictures and I thought that I should be able to figure it out from that. It was getting late in the fall so I decided to leave the airplane until spring and build the car first.

I wondered where they got the nice wheels that they had on their racers. I didn't have any like that so I figured I would have to make some. I took the

Swede saw out to the logs by the woodpile and found the roundest, smoothest log that I could. It was about eight inches across and it wasn't cracked too bad so all I had to do was to saw off four wheels. It was hard work and I had trouble sawing straight but after a long while I had four wheels that were somewhat the same thickness.

I took them to the cabin, got Pa's brace and one inch bit and did my best to drill a hole in the middle of each wheel. That was not easy either. Then I needed two axles, so I found a little sapling that seemed the right size and was not too crooked. I cut it off to the right length and whittled the ends to fit the wheels. *Boy, this thing is really shaping up. I can already picture myself speeding down the big hill.*

I cut a couple more saplings for the frame and nailed the axles to them. I got an old apple box and nailed it on upside down for a hood and nailed on a stick of wood for a seat. It was a thing of beauty! I could hardly wait to try it out. I would have to do it soon as winter was going to be blowing in any day. It was already so cold that I had some trouble building my car. I had to wait until Saturday to try it out because by the time that I got my schoolwork and my chores finished, it was too late and it started getting dark.

Saturday arrived and it looked like snow so I decided to head for the hill as soon as I could. I tied a rope on the front of my racer and pulled it the half-mile to the top of the big hill. The road down the hill is steep and there is a curve where the road is cut into the side of the hill. It is about fifteen or twenty feet over the bank to the brush and trees. I seemed to have forgotten to make some way to steer this car but I hoped that somehow I'd make it down the hill.

I positioned it right at the top of the hill and got on the seat and hung on. It started to roll very slowly and I noticed that the wheels didn't seem to be as round as I had thought they were. It started to go a little faster as the hill got a little steeper and all of a sudden it really took off. Oh Lordy, I hung on like a burr on a dog and we were just bouncing down the hill.

I thought that this was the most exciting thing that I had ever done and then we came to the curve. The past excitement was nothing compared to the curve. I could see that we were not going to make the curve but I couldn't get off so I rode it over the bank. Me and that racer went flying over the bank and didn't hit the ground at all. We landed in the trees about ten feet off the ground and the whole thing flew to pieces and I went tumbling in the brush and rose briars. Oh boy, the ride was wild but the landing was a killer.

I lay in the bushes for a little while, afraid to move in case I'd broken something important. The pain was all over and I finally checked myself out.

There didn't seem to be anything broken but there was a lot of skin missing and rearranged. I got up and to my amazement I could still walk. I checked my car over and there was nothing left of it worth mentioning. Even the apple box was smashed. It was back to the drawing board for me!

I walked back home and Ma took one look at me and wanted to know what happened. She didn't know about my racer because I knew that she'd have a fit if she thought that I was going to ride it down the hill. She made me change my clothes as they were ripped quite badly and she put some iodine on my cuts and scrapes. I also got a good bawling out about what a stupid thing that I had done.

It was too late in the year to build a new car but I tried to work out a blueprint for a new car next year, one that I would be able to steer. Winter had arrived and I had to turn my attention to my schoolwork and a little trap line. Next summer was going to be a blast, I had racers to build and the glider airplane that I would try to build. I planned to watch all winter for material that I'd be able to use for these projects.

I went out to the barn one day and I found a little purple finch that had flown into the barn and broken a wing. He looked like he was nearly dead but when I picked him up he had a lot of life left in him still. He pecked my fingers hard enough that it hurt but I didn't let him go. I carried him to the cabin and showed him to Ma. She said that if I kept him he probably would die. I told her that if I didn't keep him he'd die for sure. She said that it was against her better judgment but she'd let me keep him for a while if I didn't make a mess.

I named him 'Robin' and put him in a little box for the time being. As soon as Francis came home I asked him to help me make a birdcage of some kind to keep Robin in. Francis could always figure out how to make things and in no time he had fashioned a cage out of a wooden box. It had little bars in the front and an end that opened to clean the cage and get the bird out. He fastened it up on the wall and we put Robin in it. We gave him a little dish of water and some cereal to eat and Francis made a little thing for him to perch on.

I figured that Pa would make me get rid of Robin but to my surprise he said that he was a pretty little fellow. We were all surprised to find that Robin started to eat and drink and he seemed to settle right down. Ma helped me tape up his wing so that it didn't hang down and it didn't seem to bother him too much. He sat on his little perch and after a couple days he even sang a little. Tim saw him too and I thought that he would like to have him for dinner but the cage was up on the wall and he couldn't get close to it. He just sat back and watched and it seemed to me that he was waiting.

After a couple of weeks passed, Robin got really tame. We could take him out of the cage and he sat on my shoulder and seemed happy as could be. His wing healed up and he could fly but it seemed like he didn't really want to. I wanted to keep him for good but Ma said that when spring came I'd have to let him go. Everyone liked Robin. Even Pa said that he liked to hear him sing. I'd have to let him go when spring came but in the meantime I was going to enjoy him all that I could. I wondered how such a little life could brighten up the day for people.

That winter was much the same as the last. I did my schoolwork and chores and peeled ties and trapped in my spare time. The men were really busy cutting ties and looking after the stock. The cattle herd had grown to five and there were pigs and chickens and horses to look after. It was a cold winter and the dam had frozen solid which meant that they had to take the cows and the horses to Sullivan's little lake, twice a day for water. That used up a lot of time.

Ma and Pa and I went down to Fossum's for a visit after supper one night. It was cold and we took the horses and the sleigh. Ma had put some big rocks in the oven to get hot and when we were ready to go Pa put them down by our feet and we covered our legs and feet with an old quilt. It was only a mile to Fossum's and it didn't take very long to get there. I sat and listened to Pa and Mr. Fossum talk and waited until Ma Fossum made tea and put out her shortbread cookies. She made the best shortbread cookies of anyone in the whole area. A couple of them made the whole evening worthwhile.

Pa and Mr. Fossum got the horses from the barn and hooked them up to the sleigh. They had brought the rocks inside and put them in the oven to get warm again. I didn't want to sit in the sleigh on the way home so I got in the sleigh box near the back. As the horses trotted along, I sometimes got out and ran behind the sleigh. I could hardly believe how beautiful it was out. It was a very cold night and the sky was a deep purple-blue. The moon was bright and I could see nearly as well as in the daylight. Northern lights flashed with all the colors of the spectrum and the stars seemed so big and close. With the northern lights, the moon and the stars all reflecting on the snow it was a sight that I knew that I would never forget.

The sleigh runners squeaked on the frozen snow as did the horses hooves. The harness and bells made a sharp clear sound in the cold air. I was cold but I wished that this beautiful scenario could last forever. I wondered as we went along if everyone had this kind of feeling about a frozen winter night. I felt sorry for people who had never experienced a scene and night like this. They were missing one of the most wonderful feelings that no one could ever explain to them.

It didn't take us very long to get home and Ma went into the cabin and I helped Pa put the team away and give them some hay. They liked that and made that funny "Na ha ha" sound as I squeezed beside them with the hay. I liked the way they pushed their noses against me and bobbed their heads up and down. Horses are nice.

Pa and I went into the cabin and Ma had lit the fire in the stove. It was quite cold inside but it would warm up soon. Ma made us a cup of hot cocoa and I went to bed. Tim had been laying there waiting for me and there was a nice warm place where he had been. As I knelt down and said my prayers I thanked God for making such a beautiful place. I went to bed feeling as contented as a person could possibly feel.

I had never stopped trying to sell those Christmas cards since the year before. I sold some in the spring and in the summer and some more before last Christmas. I still had some left but only a few boxes. I knew that if I kept at it I could have them all gone soon and then I could get my watch. It took a lot of patience to sell that many cards and if I didn't want that watch so badly I would have sent them back the whole works. One thing for sure, this was the last time that I was going to sell cards.

They had made a kind of a blacksmith shop over by the icehouse. It was just a windbreak on the west side and a forge made in the shelter of it. Francis and Alf had found an old cream separator and they fitted a fan on it and made a blower for the forge. Alf was doing some blacksmith work and I was turning the handle on the blower. When he took the hot iron from the fire and hammered it, I looked in the air intake hole to see the fan go around. Alf told me not to put my face by the hole and be sure not to turn it backwards.

I asked him why I shouldn't turn it backwards but he didn't answer me. I decided the only way to find out was to do it and see what happens. I turned it backwards and looked in the hole. All of a sudden the thing backfired through the hole. It knocked me backwards into a snow bank. My eyelashes were burned off and my eyelids were kind of melted together. I felt my face and it was all wet feeling and I was sure that it must be blood. My neck stung and I thought that my head was ripped off of my neck and just sitting there.

My big dumb brother was looking around in the snow, "where are you Souris?" he kept saying.

"I'm here you big dummy," I hollered at him as I headed for the cabin, holding my head so that it wouldn't fall off. I didn't see what was funny but Alf was laughing his head off. I made it into the cabin and with one hand I held my head and with the other I pushed a chair over to the washstand and climbed up on it so that I could see in the mirror.

Ma heard the noise and came out of the bedroom. She looked at me and busted out laughing too. *What is wrong with these people? I'm dying and they think that it's funny.* Alf came in and then they were both laughing. I looked in the mirror and what I saw was not what I had expected to see. That pipe must have been full of coal dust and oil because my face was totally black. The only things that I could see were my eyes and my teeth.

Ma came over and said that she was sorry for laughing but by the way she kept on laughing I doubted it. She got a rag and wiped my face and it was really hard to get that stuff off. I was not hurt at all, just lost some eyelashes and my face stung a little where the stuff hit me. Alf said that I was lucky that I didn't get burned badly and that the next time that he told me not to do something that maybe I should listen. I had to agree, but I told him that it was his fault for not telling me what would happen. He said that if I had waited until he was finished hammering that he would have. He told me not to be so bloody impatient.

Ma was having an awful time getting that black stuff off and she got some coal oil on a rag and washed my face with that. Coal oil really smells bad when it's all over your face but it worked. Then she washed the coal oil off with soap and water. This must have been the cleanest my face had been in years. My skin was fairly raw after all of that scrubbing so Ma put some salve on my face and told me not to get it all over everything. *Well, now I know what happens when you look in that hole and turn the crank backwards. I think that if anybody ever asks me what happens if you do that I'll say that I have no idea.*

All we heard on the radio and read in the paper was about the war. The government wanted everyone with a radio to register it and buy a license for it. I wondered what that was all about and they told me that it had something to do with sabotage and radio transmissions. I still didn't know what it was all about.

Francis was still making radios and all kinds of electrical things. He had made himself a little shack that he invented things in and he even slept there in the summer time. One day he told me that he had made a transmitter and wanted to try it out. It was illegal but he wanted to see if it would work. He said that he would go in the cabin and tune in the radio and he wanted me to hit two sticks together to see if he could hear it. He told me not to say a word into the little microphone that he had made.

I always thought that it would be neat to be a radio announcer like the ones that we heard everyday. I waited the couple minutes that he told me to and I pounded the sticks together. I just couldn't contain myself any longer. I got close to the microphone and made my first announcement. "Hello skunk!"

I never got to say anymore, he came hollering from the cabin, "Shut your big mouth, you want me to be in jail for the rest of my life?"

"Would they do that?" I asked him.

"If they caught me they would."

"Did it work?" I asked. He smiled and said that I came in loud and clear. He said that he had better dismantle it and put it away for a while.

A few days later he called me over to his shack and he had something else that he was working on. I stood in the doorway and he said, "Hold this wire for a minute." I was glad to help my brother invent something so I held the wire and I asked him if I was doing it right. He said that was just fine the way that I was doing it. He went back over to his invention and turned on a switch. I made a couple of flips and my hair stood on end and I flew out the door and landed on my back in the yard.

"Holy crap, what was that?" I asked him when I was able to breathe again.

"Fence charger, it seems to work pretty well."

I walked away kind of jerky like a chicken and was not all that thrilled with Francis for the moment. At least he could have told me what might happen. Of course if he had I probably wouldn't have held the wire. That would have been even better. He kept doing those kinds of things to me. Someday I hoped to come up with something to get even with him but I didn't want him to get hurt, just shook up a little. Maybe someday.

Chapter 24
Ponies and More Cars

Spring had eased out winter once more and the water was running in little trickles all over the place. Helen came home for a visit and we took the hoe and made little rivers in the yard. This was one of my favorite times of the year. The sun was warm and the geese and ducks were once more flying north to nest. Here and there the grass tried to come up again and the cows seemed to watch for every new green shoot that came from the ground.

This was also the time of year that we had to watch the cows very closely as larkspur was one of the first shoots to appear and it was deadly poison. Within a few minutes of eating it they get down and bloat up. The only antidote that we had for it was milk. It worked well but you had to find the sick cow before she was too far gone and get some milk down her throat.

Pa had put a little lard pail and a beer bottle in several places where the cows pastured so that they would be handy if they found a cow down. Then they had to get one of the other cows and get some milk in the pail. They'd pour the milk into the beer bottle and pour it down the cow's throat. If they found the downed cow in time, the milk worked fairly quickly and she recovered. If they didn't find her in time it meant the loss of a valuable animal.

I finally sold all of my Christmas cards and sent in the money and the order for my watch. I could hardly go to sleep at night just thinking about that new silver shiny watch. The order form said to allow three to four weeks for delivery, man that was a long wait. I had already braided a string for it out of three different colors of yarn that Ma gave to me. I thought that it was going to look real fancy on that silver watch.

Ma sent me down to Fossum's with a dozen eggs, as their hens weren't laying. Ma said that it was because they were older hens and that they were all setting right now. Just as I was leaving Fossum's to go home Percy Marquise rode into the yard on his nice little saddle horse. She was a mare and she had a lovely little buckskin colt running along beside her. The colt came over and rubbed his nose on my arm. I pet him and his fur was soft like a bunny.

"Do you like him?" Percy asked me.

"Oh yes, he is beautiful."

"You can have him if you think that you could look after him," he told me.

"I couldn't pay for him, I don't have any money."

"You don't need any money, you can have him for free, I have to get rid of him as I don't have a place for him."

"Oh yes, yes, I'll take him, when can I have him?"

"You have to ask your father first and if he says 'yes' then you can come to my place and get him."

I could hardly wait to get home and tell Pa the good news. I'd have a real buckskin pony all of my own. I could see myself riding like the wind with his black mane and tail flying. This was about the best thing that had ever happened to me. I could have him for free! I just couldn't get over it.

Pa wasn't home when I got there and I had to wait until he came. It seemed to me that I'd spend my whole life waiting for something. It was just about suppertime when Pa got home and I could hardly wait for him to get into the cabin. "Pa, I was so lucky today that you won't believe it. Percy Marquise gave me that beautiful buckskin colt that he has, he said that all I have to do is ask you and then I can go and get him."

"You can't have him," Pa said.

"Why not Pa, he's really nice and he's free, Percy said that all I have to do is look after him real good."

"Forget it, we don't need another horse to feed and besides that, buckskins are ornery little bastards."

"Aw Pa, he won't be any trouble, I'll look after him and I'll even break him. Percy says that if I spend a lot of time with him and crawl around on him that he'll be so used to me that I won't have to break him."

Pa looked at me with a look that said 'shut up'. "I said that you can't have him and that is all there is to it, now shut up about it and don't bring it up any more."

I was really surprised by Pa's attitude, he loved horses and he had a buckskin pony himself when he was young. Maybe if I talked to Ma about it she could get him to give in a little. I asked her what she thought and she said that he sounded pretty adamant about it but that she'd try. I didn't say anymore about it and the next day I asked Ma if she talked to Pa and she said that she had and he was just plain miserable about it. He said that was his decision and it was final. I couldn't help but wonder why.

I felt so bad about that little colt and kept on hoping that he might change his mind but he never mentioned it and I didn't dare to. We went into town to get the mail and on the way we saw Percy on the road. He was riding his horse but there was no colt. I asked him where the colt was and he told us that when he never heard from me after a couple of weeks he gave him to Bucky Paynter. Lord, now I was really ticked off, especially the fact that he gave it to Bucky.

We went on into town and got the mail. There was a package for me from Regal Card Co. I could hardly wait to open it but Pa said to wait until we got home so that I didn't lose something that might be in the package. I was feeling good about having my watch, at least I thought that it was my watch, but I was still feeling sick about losing that little pony.

It didn't take too long to get home and I hurried in and opened my little parcel. Sure enough, there was my new shiny watch. It was a real beauty, probably worth about three dollars. I put the strap that I made on it and put it in my pocket. I was feeling pretty darn good, walking around and taking out my watch and looking at the time. I'd seen Uncle Fred do that so many times and finally I could do it too.

The next morning, Pa told me to come with him to check out the fence on the west side of the homestead. He said that it had a break in it over by the detour hill. He had to carry a saw and axe and some other things and he needed me to help carry it all. We repaired the fence in a couple places where the rails were broken. Every once in a while, Pa asked me what time it was and I got out my watch and told him. The third time that he asked me for the time was when I went into a panic. I reached for my watch and it wasn't there. Somehow the strap came off and it must have slipped out of my pocket.

Man, this made me sick to my stomach. I hadn't had it for a whole day and already I'd lost it. Pa said not to freak out completely until we had at least walked back the way we came to see if we could find it. We walked back and watched carefully for it. We kicked the grass and brush from side to side but my new shiny watch was nowhere to be seen. Finally Pa said that we had to go home and it looked like it was lost for good.

As we walked home I was feeling lower than a snake's belly in a wagon rut. I spent two years selling cards and I lose my watch in less than twenty-four hours. I was thinking that maybe the Lord was getting even with me for lying about that little tractor. I didn't know if that was the case but I swore that I would never cheat about anything ever again. I told that to Jesus as I said my prayers and I asked him if he could help me find my watch. I never did.

My poor Ma gets migraine headaches all the time. Sometimes she has three of them in one week. They make her really sick and she lay on the bed and I put a cold cloth on her forehead. I change the cloth frequently so that it's cold. The headaches make her sick to her stomach and she throws up. I feel so sorry for her and I also feel so helpless. I have made up my mind that when I grow up I'll be a doctor and I'll be able to cure her headaches. It's hard for her to do the work that she has to do when she is so sick and I try to help her. I wish that I were bigger so that I could do more.

It was time to start working on a new car to see if I could make it down the hill without going over the bank. This time I had to rig up some sort of steering. I made more wheels and I thought that this car was much more sophisticated than the last one. I spent a lot more time and care with this one and as I sat on it I could see myself flying down that hill and rolling all the way to the schoolhouse. This time I'd made better wheels and axles and I'd pivoted the front axle in the middle so that I would be able to steer it. *This one should work really well!*

It was right after dinner and I was really excited about this trip. I didn't tell Ma what I was going to do because she'd have a fit and maybe another headache. I pulled my new car the half-mile to the top of the hill and got on. I took a deep breath and started it rolling down the hill. It started out slowly and kept on going faster and faster. *Oh, this is wonderful.* By the time I got to the curve we were really rolling. This time I thought I was going to make it and the feeling was a real high.

Just as I was going full speed the road got quite rough with those rocks that stick out of the ground. We were flying and bouncing and I was hanging on for dear life when disaster struck again. One front wheel hit a rock and split in half. The axle dug into the ground and the car and I once more flew over the bank and down into the trees and brush. This time as I lay there I thought that I might have killed myself.

I crashed head first into a tree and it felt like I'd broken lots of stuff. I looked up at the sky and felt sorry for myself that I'd die here, all alone and no one would even know where I was. I lay and waited for death to come but it didn't seem to so I tried to move. I hurt all over but when I got up I found that there was nothing broken, just skinned a lot. I crawled up the bank and lay on the side of the road for a few minutes and sort of got myself together.

I could see my car down in the brush and it was all smashed to bits. I got up and walked home and as I did I tried to figure out what to tell Ma this time. I was already in trouble with Jesus for lying about being a cripple so I knew that I had to tell the truth and face the music. Ma looked at me with a startled look and gave a little gasp. I didn't know it but I had cut my head and there was a quite a bit of blood on my face.

She came over and asked me what happened this time and I told her that I crashed my car again. She washed my face and patched me up, bawling me out all the while. "You're going to kill yourself if you keep it up, don't you be messing around with anymore cars." I didn't say anything because I knew that I'd make another one just as soon as I got some better wheels. There had to be someplace to get some good wheels, I just didn't know where yet.

It was too late in the fall to start any new outside projects so I had to come up with some other plans. This winter was much the same as the last winter. I did my schoolwork, some trapping and peeled some ties. Of course, I still had my chores to do and all in all I was pretty busy. Father Goetz came to see us quite often and he and I went hunting as much as we could. He had me training to be an altar boy and I had just about got that down pat.

Father Goetz had a parish at Tate Creek and he started a Boy Scout group there. It was too far for me to go so he told me that I could be a Lone Scout. He got me a book and I studied it in my spare time. When he came for a visit, he had me do all of the tests that a scout has to do and I was supposed to get badges for all of these things. I couldn't afford to buy any of the uniform and he never got me the badges. After a while I sort of lost interest in it.

I had a new idea that I thought was so good that I wondered how come no one had thought of it before. There were quite a few people with dog teams but no one had a cat team. I set to making a small sleigh and two little harnesses made out of braided binder twine. I made two small collars for the harnesses out of a small willow that I bent into a loop and wrapped it with a strip from an old rag. I was thinking how everyone would look at me when I went by with my team of cats. The one thing that I forgot is the fact that our two cats hate each other with a passion. I figured that if I put a bag over their heads until I got them hooked up that would solve the problem.

The time came to give this team a tryout and just as I had planned I put the bags on their heads. That wasn't all that easy either because cats don't like bags on their heads. Getting them hooked up was no easy feat and involved a lot of scratching and loud meowing. I sure hoped that getting scratched up like that was worth it and I'd find out as soon as I took off the bags.

Those suckers really did hate each other! Tim let out a yowl and headed for the cabin. Pug did the same thing only he headed for the barn. They were still both hooked to the sleigh and each tried to go a different direction. There was a lot of tearing up the ground as they tugged and scratched to get away when suddenly the harness broke and away they went. Tim had broken free and was streaking for the cabin and pug still had the sleigh and was careening for the barn with the sleigh bouncing behind him.

He didn't even slow down when he got to the barn, he went straight up the log wall with the sleigh still dragging behind him. I had to catch him and get that harness and sleigh off before he hung himself on something. There was a lean-to on the east side of the barn and it had a straw roof. Where the straw met the roof there was kind of a tunnel and that's where Pug headed with the sleigh. I crawled in behind him and he was not in a good mood. Every time that I reached for him he had a little fit, complete with snarling and biting.

I finally grabbed the sleigh and pulled it out, Pug and all. He really hated it but after a lot of struggling with him I got him out of the harness. He took off like he was shot from a cannon and jumped right off of the barn and disappeared. I was so disappointed that my cat team was such a failure that I hardly noticed the blood and scratches all over my hands and arms. Ma had heard Tim meowing at the door and she let him in the cabin and took his harness off. I forgot that she knew nothing about my cat team and I had a lot of explaining to do when I walked through the door. I went to pet Tim a little bit only to find out that he wasn't too happy with me either, he didn't want anything to do with me.

Well, that was one more great idea that wasn't worth poop. By bedtime, Tim was over his little snit and seemed to have forgotten all about it and he got under the covers like he did every night. I knelt by my bed and said my prayers and I asked Jesus to help me to either get better ideas or to help me make the ones that I get, work a little better. So far this year, most of my ideas have been a disaster. I went to bed and fell asleep wondering where I go wrong.

Chapter 25
Will This Winter Never End

It was another long and cold winter. I really don't mind winter because I trap and hunt and do all those winter things but winter cuts into my building activities more than I like.

This winter kept me from working on my cars and I couldn't wait until spring to start on my airplane. I didn't have to have as good wheels for an airplane as I did for a car as I'd be flying and only needing the wheels for take off and landing. *This plane is probably my best idea yet.*

Our neighbor, Mrs. Gammon, came over for a visit once in a while and Ma usually asked her to stay for supper, which she graciously accepted. Mrs. Gammon loved bread and canned fruit and it was always fun to watch her eat. She could never get the bread and fruit to balance out. "I have too much fruit. I guess that I'll have to have another slice of bread." She had another slice of bread. "Now I have too much bread, I'll have to have a little more fruit." She did this until all of the fruit was gone and then by some miracle it balanced out just right. Ma loved it when she did that she said that it was nice to see someone enjoy their food.

There is one thing that I like to do and that is to cook sliced potatoes right on top of the stove. It makes quite a mess of Ma's stove but she has patience and lets me do it. I slice the spuds real thin and lay them out on the stove. The fire has to be going good as the stovetop has to be real hot. They bubble up and down as the steam from them tries to escape. I cook them on one side for a while and then I turn them over. I get a bowl and put them in it with a gob of butter and some salt and then I go and sit back and enjoy them. They are absolutely delicious. Tim thinks so too. He always comes and meows around until I give him some.

When I'm all finished with my messing around, Ma gets an old piece of wax paper that she keeps and uses it to polish the top of the stove again. I guess that I must have the best Ma in the whole wide world. I really love her a lot but for some reason the older that I get the harder it is to tell her. I wonder why that is and I wonder if other people are like that. It seems kind of silly that it's hard to tell someone that you love them.

I loved those long winter nights when everyone was home. We sat around and listened to the radio and sometimes Ma, Pa, Alf and Uncle Fred all sat around the table and played five-hundred rummy. I didn't know how to play it but they laughed and had a great time and it made me feel good. I liked to lay by the stove with a piece of moose steak left over from supper and chew away on it and pet old Tim. I didn't think that it could get any better than this.

Sometimes I managed to get Pa to take me with him in the old truck when he went to Pouce Coupe or Dawson Creek. I wonder why I did that, as it was always an ordeal before the day was over. It was cold in that old Chev truck because the heater hardly had any heat in it but it did help a little bit. The real freezing began when we got to Pouce. The first place that Pa stopped was the liquor store and he got a bottle of some kind of booze. Then we drove over to the grain elevator and he parked the truck by the little office.

The guy that runs the elevator is Harry Rattery and he is Pa's drinking buddy. Harry Foster who is the town butcher is also one of their buddies and as soon as Pa went in to the office, they called him up and he came over and they sat around the big old barrel heater and finished the bottle. Pa said that I was too young to be in there and that I had to stay in the truck and wait for him. Sometimes he was in there for a couple of hours and I nearly turned blue with the cold.

I wanted to go to a store and warm up but it was six or seven blocks to the nearest one and if he came out and found me gone I'd be in big trouble for sure. So I sat there and pounded my hands together and tried to think warm thoughts. The windows froze over and I couldn't see out. I held my hand on the glass and melted a little hole so I could watch and see if Pa was coming. My hand was so cold that it would hardly thaw out a little space to see through. It seemed like he was never coming back and just as I wondered if I should go inside and risk getting in trouble or just stay there and freeze to death, Pa finally came out to the truck.

He never said anything but I could tell that he was feeling no pain and I hoped that he could drive all right. He got the old Chevy fired up and we went rumbling down the road towards home. The windshield was frozen over and he scraped at it with a scraper and tried to see where he was going. Some times he had a little cloth bag with salt in it and he poured a little alcohol on it and rubbed it on the windshield. It melted the ice for a few minutes and then the glass got a blue blur on it and he had to rub it again.

We slipped and slid around in the snow and ice and finally we got to the big hill. Pa couldn't ever make it up that hill without chains on but he always tried. We got part way up the hill and then the truck spun out and we went sliding and spinning backwards down to the bottom again. Sometimes we slid off of the road and into the bush. Pa got mad and swore and got out and put the chains on. He got back in and tried the hill one more time. The old engine was roaring and the wheels were spinning and then a cross chain broke and started to pound on the box. All in all, it was a pretty scary experience for me. Sometimes we still couldn't make it and Pa got really mad but that didn't help and we would have to leave the truck there and walk home to get a horse to pull the truck up the hill.

I never told Ma about what happened when I went to town with Pa. She didn't like it when he drank and if I told her and she said anything to him, he wouldn't ever take me along again, although I wondered why I wanted to go in the first place. I was still shivering when we got home and I told Ma that the heater in the truck wasn't working very well, and that was no lie. When summer came it would be a lot better going with him and I didn't want to ruin that.

Girls seemed to be a lot of trouble to me. They always seemed to do something that frustrated me to no end. Mrs. LaForge came over one day and brought her daughter Lorna, with her. Lorna was younger than I was and I didn't know if I should try to play with her or not. One thing for sure, I was not going to play horse with her. As I was sitting there pondering what I should do, she came over to me and took me by the ears and stared into my eyes. Just as I was wondering what to do about that she really ticked me off. "Mama" she said in a little girl voice "he's got eyes just like old Ruff!" This wasn't too much of a compliment considering that old Ruff was their German shepherd dog. *Lordy, Lordy, I'm gonna swear off girls for life, and that's for sure.*

Why, it was only the summer before last, just before she got polio that Daphne Rule just about drowned me in the dugout. She came over with her folks one Sunday afternoon and as we were playing I mentioned that I had an old horse trough that I used for a boat in the dugout. Of course she had to see it and then she wanted a ride in it. It was only a log that was hollowed out and was about eight feet long and it really tipped over easy.

She sat in the back and I stood in the middle and pushed us out with a pole. Just as things were going nicely she shifted to one side and of course the trough took in water on that side. That scared her and she shifted really fast to the other side and that tipped the dang thing completely over. I fell in headfirst and since I didn't know how to swim very good I had to crawl along the bottom until I got to shore. It was either that or drown. She hung on to the trough and hollered bloody murder for me to come and get her.

It was not too far from shore and I got a long stick and pushed it out for her to hang on to. She finally grabbed it and I pulled her to shore. We were like a pair of drowned rats and I'd got a belly full of muddy water and I thought that I had swallowed a couple of tadpoles as well. Then we had to go to the cabin, all wet and dirty and face the music. I knew that I was going to get it real good for taking her out in that horse trough but it was her idea to go. I told her that it was dangerous and to sit real still but *oh no! She's a girl after all and they are nothing but trouble.*

Ma found some of Helen's old clothes and they got her dried off and I had to go get cleaned up as well. After Lorna gave me the eye compliment, I went and reminisced about Daphne, and the girl that I played horse with, and a girl named Sylvia that beat the heck out of me once. Now that was about all the girls that I had ever had anything to do with and it seemed to me that every one of them got me in trouble with out even trying. I had even got into all kinds of trouble with my sister, whom I love dearly. I thought that my best bet was to steer clear of girls in the future.

The weather had been cold and it sort of took its toll on people after a while. We got up one morning and the snow was melting and the water was dripping from the eaves. A Chinook had blown in, the first one that we'd had that winter and it was a dandy. Overnight the temperature had risen from thirty below zero to sixty above. I loved these Chinooks. I could go outside without a coat or mitts and the warm breeze blowing from the west felt like it was coming out of an oven.

The cattle loved it too, they ran around the corral and the horses rolled in the snow. Pa let the chickens out and they ran around, pecking at the snow like it was something special. By evening the wind started to die down and it started to cool off. Chinooks don't last very long and in a couple of days it was thirty below again but those couple of days really took the bite out of winter and made it easier to tough it out until spring.

The United States was in the war by this time and huge bombers accompanied by several fighter planes started flying right over our place. Pa said that they were going to Alaska and that we were right in their flight path. There were lots of them and they flew quite low. I'd never seen any planes bigger than a two wing two passenger one. Those babies were big and noisy! Pa said that it made him feel better that the States were involved. He said that we had a lot better chance of winning. I hoped that he was right.

Once more spring managed to struggle out from the grip of winter and slowly change the landscape from white to green. Like every spring, I was amazed and thrilled by the events that unfold every year. *Nature is truly wonderful!* It wasn't long after the leaves came out that the baby birds were out, trying out their new wings and seeing if they could really fly. Ma and I walked down to the side hill garden to see if it was dry enough to plow. There was a mother Partridge with a bunch of chicks along the way and like an idiot I picked up a chick. He let out a little "Cheep" and the mother came at me, flying about two feet off the ground and when I saw her coming I put the chick down real fast but it was too late.

She hit me square in the chest and knocked me flat on my back and then she proceeded to beat me up with her wings. *Man, those old hens are mean!* When she thought that I'd had enough, she went to find all of her chicks and walked kind of indignantly into the bush. Ma just stood there laughing at me. *I sometimes think that I could get killed and somebody would laugh about it.* There I was, all pounded and scratched by this partridge and she was laughing, but why not, after all, she was a girl too.

I had a tooth with a bad cavity and it ached a lot. The only thing that I could do for it was to stuff the cavity full of cloves and after a while the pain stopped but I looked like I'd been chewing tobacco. Cloves make your saliva run like a mountain stream and it's hard to keep from drooling. One day that tooth was aching real bad and the cloves weren't working. Ma told Pa that he had to take me somewhere to get it pulled out. Pa said that Dr. Glas up at Tate Creek should be able to do it.

We got ready to go and Ma went along with us for moral support. I was a little scared but I didn't dare let Pa know. The old truck rumbled along and the shaking made the tooth ache even more. It hurt so much that I was not as afraid as I was to start with. After all I knew that they freeze your mouth before they pull the tooth. At least that's what Ma said and she should know. Anyhow, I was sure that it couldn't hurt more than the tooth did.

We got to the Doctor's house just before noon. It was a little two-room place and he seemed to be doing his doctor stuff outside. He had a little table and a chair on the front step and a small black bag on the table. His wife was there and she was a beautiful young redhead with her long hair done up in a long braid down her back. He told her something in a language that I didn't understand and she took a big pitcher and went down to the creek and filled it with water. She brought it back and set it on the table.

Dr. Glas could speak some very poor English and Pa told him about my tooth and asked him if he could pull it out. He nodded and motioned for me to sit on the chair. He looked at the tooth and made some little sounds in his throat. He got out some kind of funny looking pliers and a couple of sharp looking things from his bag along with a bottle of reddish colored stuff. I figured that must be the stuff that he freezes your mouth with. I didn't know for sure because I had never been to a dentist before.

He had his wife pour some water over his hands and then he dried them on a towel hanging by the door. He told me to open my mouth and he dipped a swab in the bottle of red stuff and put it all around my tooth. I couldn't feel it freezing but thought maybe it was. He got those funny pliers and holding my bottom jaw with one hand he grabbed the tooth with the pliers and the fun began. That tooth wasn't frozen at all and the pain of this was worse than the toothache itself.

I was squirming all over the chair and trying to get away but he had a death grip on my jaw and he was kneeling on my chest. He twisted and pulled and all of a sudden I nearly went into orbit and I heard a loud crack. He took the pliers out and looked in my mouth again, twisting my head so that the sun shone in and he could see better. He told Pa that the tooth had broken into three pieces.

By then my mouth was bleeding and he gave me some water and told me to rinse my mouth and spit it out. I did as he said and spit on the ground by the step. He went back in with those ugly pliers and pulled out the three pieces. I thought that I was going to faint or die or something but somehow I managed to hang on until he got all the pieces out. I breathed a sigh of relief when he got the last piece and I thought that the pain was over. Big mistake! He got that bottle of red stuff again and swabbed all over where the tooth came out. This time that stuff hurt like the dickens. Pa paid him a dollar and we got in the truck and headed for home.

My face was swollen and my neck was sore. I told Ma that that freezing stuff wasn't any good and she told me that it wasn't freezing stuff, just iodine. Pa said that the Doctor wasn't licensed yet in Canada and he couldn't get any freezing stuff. I thought, *now is a fine time to tell me that*. My face was sore but the tooth was gone so I guess that was about all that I could hope for. If I ever needed a tooth out again I hoped that I could go to a real dentist with freezing stuff and all.

Chapter 26
Mayday—Mayday

I had been working on my plane for three weeks and it was ready for the test flight. I spent most of the winter gathering up parts whenever I came across something that I thought that I could use. I found a 1x8 board about eight feet long for the wings and a 2x6 for the fuselage and a good apple box for the front. I made the best pair of wheels that I have ever made and I found some thin boards to make the tail.

I built the whole thing on the ground but I made it so that it would come apart with a couple of bolts so that I could get it up on the barn. Oh, it looked so good I could hardly believe that I made it. The front sat up so nice on its struts and wheels and it looked like it was ready to take off just sitting there. I made a propeller that I turned with a crank. The glider in the book didn't have a propeller but I figured that it should help. I made the tail so that I could turn it back and forth to steer and the bottom part of the tail went up and down so that I could go up or down. It was time for me to get it up on the barn and make my first flight. *Ma will be so surprised when I call down to her as I fly over the cabin.*

Right after breakfast I started to get things under way. I dismantled my plane and struggled to get the pieces up on the roof. It didn't take me too long to reassemble it and I tacked down a little stick in front of the wheels to keep it from rolling off the roof. I was so excited that I could hardly wait to try it out but I had to do everything right. I put my scarf around my neck and I had Pa's goggles that he wears when he's threshing to keep the dust out of his eyes. I put on my winter leather helmet and then the goggles and *I was a pilot*. It was off into the wild blue yonder for me.

I got myself seated in my plane and did one more check to be sure that everything was operating properly. I took a deep breath and pulled the stick out from in front of the wheels. Oh man, I was rolling down the roof and turning the crank like crazy and then I ran out of roof. The next thing that I knew I was head first in the soft manure clean to my shoulders. I was pretty sure the stuff that was running up my nose was cow pee.

I pulled my head out off the poop and it made a sucking sound as it came free. I wiped the poop out of my eyes and looked at the wreck. I must have done something wrong because that plane didn't even glide ten feet. It just rolled down the roof and fell over the edge. It was sitting nose first in the manure and it didn't look near as good as it did a little while ago.

As I took stock of myself I found that I was covered with sloppy cow poop all over my body and I didn't smell very good. Pa's goggles had slipped down on my neck and so I scraped the poop out of my eyes. Ma was not going to be pleased with this mess. I had to get some of this stuff off of me so I went over to the dug out and took all my clothes off. I washed myself as good as I could and tried to wash the poop off of my clothes. I did the best that I could but the clothes were a pretty sorry looking mess.

Just as I thought that I might pull this thing off without getting in too much trouble I heard a voice behind me. Ma went to the chicken coop and she just had to look over here and see me. "What are you doing to your clothes and why are you naked?"

"I fell in the cow poop, Ma, and made an awful mess of myself." Oh no, she looked over at the barn and saw my plane sticking out of the manure pile.

"Did you take off the barn with that contraption?"

What could I say? I had to tell her the whole story before she was satisfied and after I did she was quite upset with me.

There was a lot more of that, "What's going to become of you…You'll kill yourself before you're ten years old…What's the matter with you anyhow…?"stuff.

I thought that I was in deep doo-doo after the crash but that was nothing! Ma made me come to the cabin and she got down the washtub and told me to carry some water and put in it. She added some hot water from the kettle and put me in the tub. She nearly scrubbed my skin off with some lye soap. She got me some clean clothes and put my dirty ones in the tub. I didn't have to be a genius to know that she wasn't pleased with me.

I still had to get my plane out of the poop and out of the way before Pa got home. I might just as well take it apart because Ma threatened to do me some bodily injury if she ever caught me trying to fly off the barn again. I thought that if I could have a longer runway that it should fly and I would like to try it on the same hill that I tried my cars on but the wings would be in the way. I decided to sideline it for a while and work on my cars some more.

The U.S. army had set up a base camp in Dawson Creek and started making a road up to Alaska. There were American soldiers all over the place and the main highway was lined up with army convoys hauling supplies for the road they were building. One day there was a big roar and a U.S. Army 6x6 truck drove into our yard. Helen worked in Dawson and was dating a soldier whose job was to haul water to the camp. He had taken a little side trip and brought Helen home for a little visit.

Pa was not very happy about these events and took Helen to one side to tell her so. He said to watch out for those guys because they were only after one thing. I wondered what it was that they were after but I didn't dare ask him. I'd ask Ma later. Pa listened to him talk and when they left he told Ma that he was a damn Yankee bullshitter. I thought that he was kind of neat in his uniform and all and besides that he let me play in the army truck.

Helen's soldier boyfriend's name was Clarence Wayne and he was from Indiana. He knew that Pa didn't like him and he tried to get on his good side by bringing him cartons of cigarettes and Ma chocolates that he said he got from the PX. I also found out that her boyfriends were a little goldmine. If I hung around them when they wanted to be alone, her boyfriends found out that I would disappear if they slipped me a couple of cigarettes and a dollar bill. Helen told me that I was a dirty little blackmailer but I really didn't care. *Just show me the money!*

Helen went with Clarence for a while and he told us that his Father owned a big auto garage and he worked there before he got in the army. Helen found out that he had a sister and told him that she would like to write to her so he gave her the address. Helen wrote to his sister and asked her about her family and what kind of work her Father did. A couple of weeks later she got a reply to her letter and Clarence's sister had a whole different story than he did. She said that her dad was still managing to keep things going by mowing lawns. Needless to say Clarence got the axe and Pa said, "I told you so!"

I was not too happy with this turn of events as it was not too good for my income. However Helen was young and pretty and it wasn't long before she had another guy on the string. One guy that she dated was a guy named Del and I didn't like him much. When I hung around, he didn't want to pay me off, he just gave me a look and told me to piss off. The big dumb jerk wouldn't even let me play in his truck.

Then one day she hit the jackpot and found a guy named Howard Spencer. I liked him and he slipped me a little money and a few cigarettes and told me to play in his truck. He was driving a three-ton special Fargo and hauled fuel up the Alaska Highway. He was a good trucker and he was also a fast driver. He made trips faster than anyone else on the road. I played that I was driving up the highway and I made thousands of miles without moving an inch. I loved that Fargo truck.

I thought that Helen really liked Howard because she seemed different now that she was going with him. He seemed to like her an awful lot too because he came to see her every chance that he got. She was staying at home for a while and I was really happy about that. I missed her when she was away. She seemed to be able to tolerate me a little more than she could before, maybe I'd grown up a bit and didn't bother her as much as I used to. I thought that she was in love and maybe that had mellowed her out a little too.

It was a beautiful Sunday morning and after breakfast, Alf and Francis got talking and decided that it would be a nice day to go fishing. As soon as they mentioned it, I was right there begging to go with them. They said that would be fine and we got our bit of gear together and climbed into the old truck.

We went over to Bill Cundiff's place and borrowed his boat. He said that it was good fishing in the little bay on the north end of the lake so that was where we headed. We cut a couple of fishing poles from the willows that grew on the lakeshore and tied our lines to them. Alf rowed the boat and Francis and I got our hooks in the water.

It was only a matter of minutes until we started to catch fish. They were all good-sized ones and they were biting like crazy. Alf and Francis took turns rowing and fishing. They said that they had never seen the fish biting like this before. We fished for maybe an hour and the front part of the boat was getting full of fish. Francis said that we had better count them to see how many we have. He counted them and said that there were twenty-two. Alf said that was probably all the fish that we could handle and we had better head for home.

We stopped at Bill's place and asked him if he wanted a feed of fish and he said that would be nice and took two nice ones. We put the rest in the truck and went home. Ma said that we would have a good feed for supper and that she would can the rest. We cleaned them all and Ma took what she wanted for supper and we put the rest in the icehouse. Ma would do the canning the next day. They tasted very nice canned, nearly like canned salmon. Ma said that if she put a spoonful of vinegar in each jar it would make the bones soft so that you could eat them without them sticking in your throat.

This had really been a wonderful day for me, getting to go fishing with my two brothers. They did things together all the time and it was not very often that I got to do things with them. It was bedtime and as I said my prayers, I thanked Jesus for letting me have such a great day and such a great pair of brothers. I lay in my bed and old Tim came and crawled in beside me and purred like a truck. I felt so contented and I thought that I must be the luckiest kid in the world to have been born into a family like this.

I loved my Pa dearly but I had trouble figuring him out. He was rough and tough and I didn't think that he was afraid of anything and I was a little afraid of him. Then sometimes he would show a side that was tender as can be and it kind of confused me. We'd be out walking in the bush and he'd stop and show me the little flowers that were growing on a hair-like stem in the moss. They were so small that I could hardly see them but they were beautiful. He showed me the little lady slippers that grew in damp areas in the woods.

He gently held their little faces up so he could get a better look at them and he told me not to pick them because they will die.

One day we were walking along the edge of the hill and he stopped and sat on a fallen log and looked down into the valley. "Isn't it a really beautiful thing to look at?" he asked me. I told him that I thought that it was and he put his hand on my shoulder, something that he rarely ever did. He had a kind of pained look on his face and he said, "Remember this moment son, because it won't last long." I was not quite sure just what he meant but it somehow made me feel sad. At that moment I felt very close to my Pa.

Maybe I learned to feel close to nature from my Pa without knowing it because there are so many things about it that I love. I love to see the sun shine down through the trees and make a dappled look where it touches the ground. I love the gentle spring breezes as they sigh through the tops of the pine trees and I also love the dark thunderclouds and the rain pouring down. I find the fierce and savage blizzards of winter beautiful in their own way. I learned early that we can't change nature. That it is much stronger than we are and that we must learn to live with it not fight it. I wonder if everyone sees nature the way that I do.

Uncle Fred stayed at the old place when he was not working and sometimes I went and spent a few days with him. Uncle was a good cook and he cooked different stuff than Ma. I went with him one day and we went home by Gilchrist's old homestead. No one had lived there for years. Where the old manure pile used to be was just covered with pigweeds. Uncle and I both liked pigweed greens so on the way, we stopped and picked a sack full. For supper, Uncle fried up some side pork and cooked up a big pot of greens. We stuffed ourselves full and then sat out in the sun and relaxed.

Uncle lit up his pipe and sat back and looked up at the clouds slowly drifting by overhead. He didn't care if I smoked so I lit up a pipe full of moss and sat back and enjoyed the quiet of the evening with Uncle. We smoked and talked and Uncle told me about when he worked on the Great Lakes and when he worked for a logging outfit in Montana. He told me about a well-boring machine that he had in Saskatchewan and how he would witch for water and then bore the well. *I could sit and listen to Uncle's stories all night.*

When it started to get dark and the mosquitoes got bad Uncle would light up a smudge pot. That kept them away and we sat in the ever-deepening darkness and continued talking and smoking. Finally, Uncle said that we had better go to bed and we went inside and Uncle lit the lamp. He made us a cup of cocoa and then it was off to bed. Uncle and I knelt down by the bed and said our prayers. I was so tired that I could hardly stay awake long enough to finish. Sleep came easily and the next thing that I heard was Uncle calling me for breakfast.

Alf and Francis and Pa and Uncle pooled their resources and decided to buy a little sawmill. They knew of a fellow up by Pouce Coupe who had a homemade one for sale and they went to have a look at it. It looked quite good so they bought it and hauled it home in the old truck. Now they had a mill but no power to run it. Alf and Uncle went to Hythe to see if they could buy a tractor. They looked around and finally they bought an eighteen-thirty-two cross-mounted Case tractor from Henry Reich who was the Case dealer there.

They had to drive it the forty some miles home and that old steel wheel beast didn't go very fast. They had to buy four 2x12 planks for when they crossed the wooden bridges. Uncle was mad because they had to pay a dollar for each of them. He said that was an outrageous price to have to pay for a plank.

They finally got home with it and the next day they hooked it up to the mill and sawed a few boards. It took a little while to get the mill set so that it sawed properly but before long it was running like a charm. The old Case tractor had a good engine and it powered the mill with no trouble at all. With this they could saw ties a lot faster and easier than they could hew them and they could saw lumber as well. Francis seemed to take to sawing like a fish to water so he became the official sawyer.

There was quite a lot of timber on the homestead and on the adjoining quarters of land. They approached the Alberta Forestry department about cutting the timber on those quarters and all the legal paper work was filled in. A few days later the Ranger came out and finished the legalities so they could start sawing ties.

At about the same time as the timber became available, they got a contract from the U.S. army for a lot of railroad ties to build a spur line into the army base. It was a good deal because the army didn't care what the ties were made from as it was only a temporary line and it didn't have to last very long. They got really busy and sawed those ties up in record time and hauled them to Dawson. They got paid right away and the money was a welcome sight as it was the first that they had gotten since they had bought the mill. It was just enough to get them off the ground. As winter arrived, they got a contract to sell some ties to the N.A.R. railroad. They had enough pine on the homestead to do them for the winter and when spring came, they would have to look around for some more timber.

There was a funny sound one night and the house shook and the dishes rattled in the cupboard. Everyone seemed to think that it was an earthquake. *After all, what else could it be?* The next day Alf and Francis went to town and they came home with the news that a big ammunition storage building in Dawson had exploded. As well as ammunition there were explosives for the building of the Alaska Highway, tons of it. The explosion had just about leveled the town and the damage was extensive. No one seemed to know if it was an accident or if it was sabotage.

Chapter 27
A New Ford Truck

The old Chev truck was a sturdy little fellow but it was just too small and slow to haul the lumber and railroad ties. With the war on there were hardly any vehicles of any kind to be had and the ones that were available were really old beaters. Alf and Francis were in Dawson and stumbled on a deal for a 1935 Ford two- ton truck. It seemed the fellow who owned it was conscripted into the army and he decided that he might just as well sell it.

Well, it wasn't a new truck but it had been in storage for quite some time and had very few miles on it. It was just about like new. They made a deal with the garage that was selling it to trade in the old Chevy and they had to go back the next day to get it. They came home all excited about the new truck and sounded glad to get rid of the poor old Chev. I felt really bad about this deal, I wanted them to get the new truck but it seemed cruel to get rid of the old one that had been so faithful. I sat in it and remembered how excited we had been when we first got it. I felt like crying.

In the morning they headed for Dawson and the new truck and with tears in my eyes, I watched the poor old Chevy rumble out of the yard and around the corner for the last time. It was late that night when they came home with the Ford. They were really pleased with it as it had a V8 engine and had all kinds of power. It also could do 85 miles an hour instead of 30. They didn't drive it that fast but it was nice that it could really move.

The new truck didn't have a box or anything so the first thing that they did was build a flat deck on it. They sawed some timbers and it didn't take them long to build a deck.

I really wanted to have a ride in this new truck but it seemed that I had to be patient. Finally my chance came and I got to go to town with Alf. Man, but this truck was different from the old Chevy. It rode smooth and the first thing that I noticed was the absence of rattles. It had a heater and an electric defroster on the windshield. It really went. Alf grinned as he pushed down on the gas pedal and the truck jumped ahead. This Ford truck was really something.

They were sawing railroad ties again and in my spare time, I peeled them again. I wanted to save my money to buy a bicycle but somehow I never seemed to save any. I bought a few clothes and books and a lot of shells for my twenty-two rifle. I liked to shoot and I did a lot of target shooting. Pa said that it was an awful waste of bullets but I did it anyway. I liked to throw tin cans up in the air and try to shoot holes in them. The more I practiced the better I got and I was getting so I could hit them most of the time. If I kept on practicing, I hoped that I could hit them every time.

Spring came one more time and like every year the miracle of life repeated itself. Howard was still driving a truck up the Alaska Highway and one day he brought home the greatest things that I had ever seen. He brought four cast iron wheels. They were about a foot across and had a hole for a two-inch axle. The only problem with them was that they had a flange like they should run on a track and the other problem was that they weighed about fifty pounds each. The good thing about them was that if I could build a car and use those wheels, it was for sure that they would never break.

In my spare time, I worked on my new car. This one was going to be the absolute best one that I had ever built. I cut a nice straight sapling that was just about the right size for the axles and cut it to length. I only had to pare it down a little to get a nice fit in the wheels. Those wheels were heavy so I built the rest of the car as sturdy as I could. I was feeling really good about it because I thought that it looked great.

Then I made a little mistake and got myself in big trouble with Pa. There was an old board that I needed for my car. It was over by the barn and it had several nails in it and that made it hard to carry so I took Pa's hammer and pulled the nails out. I left the hammer lying on the ground and carried my board over to where I was building my car. I saw Pa coming with the team and wagon and as he drove by the barn I heard this awful crack. He ran over the hammer and broke the handle. He stopped and got down from the wagon to see what the noise was and found his hammer broken. He was mad! He wanted to know just what idiot left his hammer lying on the ground. The trouble is he already knew what idiot left it there and for sure he was gonna kick my arse when he caught me.

I did my best to stay out of his sight for a few days to give him a chance to cool off. I heard him tell Ma that he just had no idea what to do with me because I was always in trouble. I felt sad that my Pa felt like that about me. I'd like to tell him that I didn't have time to go back and pick up the hammer but he wouldn't listen to me anyhow. I'd like to tell him that I was sorry about the handle but I couldn't do that either. I just stayed away from him for a few days.

I got my car all put together and ready for the trial run down the big hill. The only problem was that the wheels were so heavy that I couldn't pull it the half-mile to the hill. My only chance was Howard. I took the wheels off and when he headed out to haul another load, I got him to help me load the wheels and the car on the back of his truck and haul it to the hill. He said that he shouldn't do it because I'd probably kill myself and he shouldn't be part of it. I told him that I wouldn't bother him anymore when he was with Helen and he agreed to do it.

We got to the top of the hill and he helped me unload it and he left. I put the wheels on being careful to grease them well with some grease I had gotten from the grease can at the sawmill. I was so excited! I just knew that this time would be the time. I'd roll down that hill all the way to the schoolhouse. I started off slowly as the wheels were so heavy that they would hardly roll. Then it started to pick up speed and those heavy wheels really started to gain momentum.

We were really going and bouncing over the rocks that were lying in layers on the road. I could feel the wind whistling past my face and I was hanging on for dear life. I tried to steer it around that corner that always wiped me out but the wheels were so heavy that I couldn't turn them. "Oh, help me Lord," I prayed as I knew that I was about to crash again but this time it was going to be a humdinger of a wreck. I was probably going to kill myself this time.

I closed my eyes and hung on as we went flying over the bank and into the trees. I hit the first tree about eight feet off the ground. Me and part of the car stopped there. The wheels just kept on going and I heard them crashing and bouncing through the brush. I figured that if I could still hear I must still be alive but I was not quite sure. I hit that tree really hard and then fell through the branches to the ground.

When I could breathe again, I tried to get up and to my amazement I found that I really hadn't hurt myself too badly. There seemed to be quite a bit of skin missing and my shirt was all torn to shreds but there didn't seem to be any broken bones. I had no idea where the wheels went and I really didn't care. *This is the last time that I'm going to try to build a car and absolutely the last time that I will ever try to go down this hill.*

I took my time hobbling home, partly because I hurt and partly because I had to tell Ma how I ripped my shirt to pieces. As I walked along, I tried to think up something to tell her. Maybe I could tell her that a bear beat me up or maybe that I just fainted and fell down the hill. I knew that I had to tell her the truth because she knew when I lied. I didn't know how she did but she always did.

It was just like always. Ma looked alarmed and looked me over and fixed up the cuts and scrapes. She bawled me out for doing such a stupid thing and told me never to do it again. I told her that I wouldn't and she said that she didn't know what would become of me. I asked her not to tell Pa and she said that she should but to save my skin, she wouldn't tell him. I'd been treading pretty lightly around him lately and I sure didn't want to set him off again.

Ma wanted to know why I was always in so much trouble. Did I do all these things without thinking? "Lord no Ma, I'm thinking all the time." Ma said that maybe that was my problem.

There seemed to be no end to the trouble that I could get into without even trying. We had quite a few pigs by then and there was a litter that was just old enough to have the little boars castrated. Alf and Pa got their stuff ready to go to the pigpen to take care of that little chore and I wanted to go along and watch to see how it was done. Pa said no that I couldn't go and not to be bothering them while they were doing it.

I wanted to see this real badly and a plan popped into my head as to how I could watch and they would never know. I hurried to the pigpen before they got there and climbed up on the roof. The roof was quite flat and was made of small poles covered with straw. My plan was to move enough straw away so that I could see through the cracks between the poles. I got the straw moved away just as they came into the pigpen.

They got the little boar pigs and put them into a stall and put the old sow outside so she couldn't attack them when the little pigs squealed. It was pretty dark in there and I couldn't see very well so I tried to move over just a little and held my hands by my face as I peered through the crack. I didn't know that the poles were rotten and just as I got where I could see, the worst happened.

There was a crack and the roof caved in and I fell right on top of Pa and Alf and a little pig. There were pieces of wood, straw and dirt all over and once Pa got himself up out of the pig poop there was hell to pay. To say that he was mad would be the understatement of the year. I was trying to get out of there and he was trying to get a hold of me and he was hollering some pretty violent statements and using some language that I knew Ma would not approve of.

I was sure by what he was saying that if I didn't get my butt out of there before he got me that I'd be the one to be castrated. I got over the trough and the stall and out the door and I was really moving. I didn't know where to go or what to do because he was going to be mad for a long time over this. I stayed out of his sight for days. I told Ma what happened and she just shook her head and looked up at the ceiling again. She was not all that pleased with me either.

Francis had got himself a girlfriend and it seemed that whenever he wanted to go see her, Pa or Alf wanted to have the truck for something. Francis was getting a little ticked off with this arrangement and so he bought himself an old Star car. It was not the greatest car in the world but with a little fixing and a lot of luck it got him where he was going. Sometimes we went to town with him in his old Star car and when we came home and got to the big hill, we all had to get out and walk up the hill. We laughed and teased him about his one-man car. It didn't have enough power to pull two.

Just about when things were cooling off and I could show my face disaster struck again. I was out in the truck with Alf and he was backing the truck around some trees to get to some logs. He was standing on the running board so he could see where he was backing and I was playing that I was driving too. Unknown to Alf, I also had my door open and I didn't see the tree until it was too late. There was this awful screech of tortured metal as the door remodeled itself around the tree and jammed into the fender.

Alf heard the noise and got in the truck and got it stopped, but it was too late, the damage was done. He said some things that I didn't think a young boy like me should hear, and seeing as how the truck door was already open I thought that there was someplace else that I should be, and I didn't waste anytime getting there. I felt so bad about that door and I didn't want Alf to be mad at me but I was sure that he was.

He took the truck over by the blacksmith forge and as I watched from a distance I saw him working on the door. He took the door off and took the hinges off. Then he got the forge going and straightened the hinges out. He put the door back on and it seemed to fit. Somehow with all the noise there was, the only thing that seemed to get hurt was the hinges. The door and the fender hardly had a mark on them.

I was not too afraid of Alf, so in a couple days I went over to where he was working and told him how sorry I was about what happened. To my surprise he told me to forget it, that accidents happened. Sometimes he amazed me. I wished that Pa had as much patience as Alf.

Howard was a real goldmine for me. He and Helen were engaged to be married in the fall so Howard was bringing some of his stuff out to our place. He hauled out what I guessed was once a little travel trailer. It was about six feet wide and eight feet long and was shaped like a teardrop. It was made out of plywood and heaven only knows where the wheels were. He told me that I could have it. It made the most beautiful shack that I had ever seen!

I'd already decided that I would be a doctor or a veterinarian or a scientist and that little trailer would be just right for my laboratory. I'd been saving Carters little liver pill bottles for a long time and I decided to use them for my test tubes. I made a rack out of a board and drilled holes in it for the bottles to fit into. Oh but it looked good! Helen found me a piece of litmus paper somewhere and now I was ready to do some experiments.

I had a good new scribbler to write my notes in and Ma gave me a new pencil so I was all set. Pa had a neighbor come over to help him castrate a bull and this time they did it outside by the barn and he let me watch. I wrote down all the details and made drawings of the whole operation. If I ever had to do that little job on a bull, I would know just how to do it.

Along with the little trailer, Howard brought home a stray dog. Pa wasn't too happy about that but the little white dog and I were instant companions. His name was Bum and he was a nice round, shorthaired little fellow. Howard rescued him as he was not owned by anyone and was a nuisance around town and was going to be put down by the police. He loved riding in trucks and if there was a truck door left open, Bum went in it. He rode with dozens of trucks up and down the Alaska Highway and bummed his meals wherever he could, thus the name of Bum.

Bum and I had lots of fun, he liked to play all the time and he also loved to chase groundhogs. If he caught one, it would be a goner for sure. Bum grabbed them by the neck and gave them such a flip that it broke their necks. One evening as we were going for the cows, Bum mistook a skunk for a groundhog and got a bad load of skunk. He smelled really bad and as soon as we got to the creek, he jumped in and swam around like crazy. He got out and rubbed himself in the grass and then he smelled himself. I guess that it was no good because he jumped back into the creek and went through the whole routine all over again. It took him three tries before he was satisfied with himself.

LIVING ON A HILL

Bum and I were playing out by the icehouse and Francis came out with the water pail to get some ice. I liked to irritate him so as soon as he got inside, I took a long stick and rubbed it on the roof. "Get off the roof," he hollered. I did it again. "If you do that again, I'm gonna smuck you with one of these rotten vegetable marrows that are in here." I knew that there were some old marrows in there that had to be thrown away but I didn't think that he would actually throw one at me. I rubbed the stick on the roof one more time and all of a sudden the dirty sneak broke one of those rotten things right on my head.

"What did you do that for, you big dummy" I asked him as I wiped the rotten stuff off of my head.

"I told you that I would, if you went up there again and you did so you got what you had coming."

"But I wasn't on the roof. I just made a noise up there with this stick."

"Too bad," he said as he walked away. Those rotten things were just like cow crap and smelled just as bad. Now I had to figure out a way to get even with the big turkey.

He still had his old Star car and it really wasn't the greatest car in the world. One time he and I were going to his girlfriend's place and the road was muddy. We could only go about fifty yards and the engine stopped. It didn't have a fuel pump but something he called a vacuum tank and the old engine didn't have enough vacuum to function when it was working hard. Every time that it stopped he had to get out and blow in the gas tank. He blew so hard that it looked like his eyes were going to pop out. I tried to blow in the tank but I could hardly blow hard enough to do any good. He said that as soon as he had enough money together, he was going to trade the old crock off.

Chapter 28
A Wedding and Another Truck

When the men didn't have a contract to saw railroad ties they had to look around for other things to do. There were not many trucks around and that made for quite a lot of hauling for people who had them. Somehow Francis seemed to have been squeezed out of the Ford truck and Pa and Alf were busy hauling things for people. They moved a family named Gould from Demmit to Grande Prairie and another family named Underwood to Pouce Coupe. Francis seemed to be left out of this and I thought that it kind of bothered him.

He came home from town one day and told me that he made a deal with a guy named Chapman. Chapman lived on a homestead at the bottom of Canyon Hill and was always dealing in old cars and trucks. Francis said that he had traded his old Star car on an International truck. The next day he took his old car and made the deal. I heard a loud engine sort of moaning up the big hill and soon I saw this long nosed old truck come rumbling into the yard.

I thought that this was quite an impressive looking truck. It was a 1931 ton and a half International and it had a square cab and a long nose. Francis showed me the engine and it was a whopper of a thing. It looked like it weighed a ton. It had big fenders with big lights sitting on top of them and a big bumper. The tires were really bad. With the war going on, everything was rationed and that included tires. A couple of tires had belting bolted to them and you could see the inner tubes on some of the others.

Francis was really proud of this truck and he spent all his spare time painting and polishing on it. He got some jobs with it and he and Alf both got jobs hauling rocks to dam up the Pouce Coupe River where it ran out of Swan

Lake. Ducks Unlimited wanted to raise the water level in the lake by a couple feet so they hired them to do the job. There were a lot of rocks along the fence lines up by Tate Creek and that's where they hauled the rocks from.

That old International looked like a truck and sounded like one but it was really slow and that big engine didn't have much power. That kind of irritated Francis but there wasn't much that he could do about it. I knew that he had in mind to get a better truck when he could afford one and when one became available to buy.

They hauled the rocks and then they got a job hauling ties for the Czechs, who had a sawmill out on the Cutbank River. The road was terrible, not really a road but a wagon trail through the bush. There were muskegs and big hills and it put a strain on those trucks. Francis had a hard time keeping up with Alf because his truck was so slow. Sometimes it broke down and Alf didn't wait for him. I wondered why he didn't.

I was still mad at him for smashing that rotten marrow on my head and I was always looking for a way to get even with him. We were at a dance one night and I saw a couple of guys shove a potato up the exhaust pipe of an old car. I heard one tell the other that if you did that, the car wouldn't run. He said that it would start and then quit. I thought that I just found my way to get even.

In the morning and I got outside before Francis. I had a big potato in my pocket and I crawled under his truck and pushed that spud in the exhaust pipe. It wedged in real tight and I was sure that I'd got him this time. I hid behind a tree right behind his truck so that I could get a first hand look. Francis came out and climbed up in the cab and stepped on the starter. I grinned to myself as I watched. *Boy, is he going to be surprised.* The old engine caught and with a mighty roar, blew that potato right out of the pipe. It came out like a ball out of a cannon and before I could move, the bloody thing hit me right square between the eyes.

It just about knocked my head off, man but those spuds are hard! The only redeeming thing about it was that Francis hadn't seen it. It really bugged me that he had gotten the last laugh and didn't even know it. I would have liked to shove that spud someplace on that guy that said what a great idea it was. Boy was he wrong!

I got a good-sized egg on my forehead and a headache. I went in for my breakfast and Ma asked me what happened to my head and I really didn't want to tell her the truth, it sounded too stupid. I told her that I fell down and hit my head on a log. I didn't think that she believed me but she just gave me a look and let it go at that. Some days it just didn't pay to get out of bed.

Helen and Howard's wedding date was set for November 21 and that day finally arrived. Howard's dad came up from Didsbury for the wedding and he stayed at our place too. It was awfully crowded in our little cabin, with the extra people and it was hard to find places for them all to sleep. Ma was beside herself.

We all got up early so that everyone could get ready and the chores still had to be done as well. Pa milked the cows and Alf took them and the horses to the little lake for water. It was dark when I got up and I went out to the outhouse. I could hardly see where I was going but I knew where it was so I sort of felt my way there in the dark. It was cold out and when I finished I headed for the cabin as fast as I could run. I could see the light from the windows so I knew just where to run.

I could see the outline of the truck parked in the yard and I ran around the back of it. Just as I got behind it, something hit me right across the bridge of my nose and knocked me right on my back. I had no idea what happened and I stood up and hit my head on something that I couldn't see in the dark. I felt to see what it was and I found out there were a few planks on the truck and they were sticking out about four feet past the deck.

I hobbled to the cabin and went inside. My nose was bleeding all over the place and my eyes were getting kind of black. Ma had a fit about it and wanted to know how I managed to do this to myself. I told her, "I guess that I'm just lucky." I had to be altar boy for the wedding and I thought that I was not going to look too good.

It was kind of disorganized confusion around the cabin and I just tried to stay out of the way. After my nose stopped bleeding I washed myself and brushed my teeth. I put my best clothes on and Ma put some makeup on my nose and around my eyes. I hated that but she said that it looked better than it did before.

Francis and his girlfriend, Mavis, were standing up for them and he had to leave early to go get her. It was time to go and we all got into the truck. Well, Ma and Pa and Helen got into the cab and the rest of us got on the back. Helen didn't have her wedding dress on yet. She had planned to put it on at the church. We got to the church and someone already had the fire going. There was no snow yet but it was pretty cold outside. It felt good to stand by the stove after riding on the back of the truck.

Everything was ready and we were all in our places. It was time for Helen to come down the aisle. I looked up and saw her and I got a very strange feeling. It was like I saw her for the very first time. She looked small and beautiful in her white dress and I wondered why I never noticed before that she was beautiful. She didn't look like the sister that I'd lived and played with all of my life. She looked angelic and I wondered how that had happened.

The priest spoke and jolted me out of my daydream and I commenced my altar boy duties. What a lovely couple they made! Howard looked so handsome in his new suit. Francis and Mavis were all dressed up too and I thought that it was a beautiful wedding. Ma was wiping tears from her eyes and Pa looked like he was holding some back.

The wedding was over and the rice and confetti were thrown and everyone lined up for the pictures. When the pictures and the congratulations were over we got back in the truck and went home. A few neighbors came over and there was a kind of reception. The little cabin was bulging at the seams. I took my good clothes off and got outside away from the noise.

Later in the day a fellow from Tupper came out with his car and took Helen, Howard and his dad to Hythe where they spent the night. The next day they got on the train and went to Didsbury to spend some time with Howard's folks. I wondered how long they would stay there because I didn't think that Howard got along with his dad very well.

It seemed very quiet now that the wedding was over and they had gone. Everyone else was back at work and the cabin that had been so crowded was empty all day until they came home from work. Ma had another bout with migraines and I felt so sorry for her and so helpless to do anything about them. Pa took her to see Dr. Glas and he told her to drink weak tea and eat dry toast and in the summer to eat raw rhubarb. I wondered if that was what other doctors would tell her to do. Somehow I doubted it.

Christmas came and went and somehow I just didn't get as excited about it as I used to. Somewhere along the way it seemed to have lost something and it made me feel bad because I liked the way it used to make me feel. This year Ma got me a nice little hunting knife and that was something that I wanted. I wished that I still believed in Santa Claus. It was more fun that way.

In the middle of January Helen and Howard came back from Didsbury. There wasn't much room but they didn't have any other place to go so they stayed with us. Howard got a job driving a truck for Mr. Jorgensen hauling ties. The snow was really deep and they couldn't get up the hill with the trucks so they parked them at the bottom of the hill and walked home at night. They each had a gas barrel at the bottom of the hill and a gas pump that fit in the barrel so that they could gas up.

The pump belonged to Alf. One morning Howard used the pump to gas his truck up and instead of putting it back in Alf's barrel, he put it in his truck and left with it. When Alf got there to gas up there was no pump. Needless to say he was not happy. That night Alf and Howard had a big fight about it and Helen and Howard said that they were moving out. Ma was crying and Helen was crying and it made me feel like crying too.

Morning came and Helen and Howard took off to find a place to stay. They went to Tupper and found that Mr. Taylor had a little house for rent so they rented it. They came home and got their few belongings and moved. There were more tears and Helen and Ma hugged and all this stuff made me feel bad. It was quiet again in the little cabin and it took a few days before the tension wore off. Ma hoped that it would all blow over and Pa said that it eventually would.

In the meantime, Francis's girlfriend's cousin, Marie came to stay with them for a little while. She was from Saskatchewan and she had joined the army and was just waiting for her time to go. She was to be stationed in Red Deer. Alf had taken her out a couple times and for some reason the big goof seemed to be really hooked on her. I had a hard time understanding how come the big guy had fallen for a girl, but it seemed to have happened.

Marie's time to go to the army had finally arrived and she had to leave. For days Alf went around like the world had ended. They wrote letters to each other all the time and it seemed she must have fallen in love with him as well. He couldn't wait to go to town to get the mail and he read her letters over and over. I sure hope that I never fall for a girl like he had. He didn't want to go hunting or fishing or any of that fun stuff that we used to do. I just could not understand it. This love thing must be powerful.

Howard had been working on the railroad when they lived in Tupper but he was really a truck driver and that was all that he was happy doing. He got a job driving for George Schmidt, hauling fuel up the Alaska Highway and he and Helen moved to Pouce Coupe. They rented a little house in the north end of town, right next to Carl Malmberg's garage. The row over the pump had cooled off and things seemed to be getting back to normal.

Marie's basic training was over and she got to come home for a few days leave. By this time, Alf had figured out that he couldn't live without her and he proposed to her and she accepted. The wedding was to be on the sixth of August. She had to go back to the army base and he had to carry on working and both of them could hardly wait for the big day to arrive.

Amidst all of these goings on, I was still trying to be a scientist of some kind and doing as many experiments as I could find out how to do. I read in a book about making coal gas with a little piece of coal in a test tube with a Bunsen burner under it. I didn't have a Bunsen burner but I found that a candle worked just as well. With a cork in the test tube and a little piece of pipe in the cork I found that when it heated up the gas came out of the pipe and I could light that as well. What a great experiment!

I wondered what would happen if I sealed the test tube up tight? I tried it and lit the candle under the tube. Just as before, the coal got hot and a little white smoke started to curl up in the tube. Soon the tube filled with white smoke and just as I was about to blow the candle out there was a loud bang and a flash of light and the whole thing blew up. I was splattered with broken glass and hot wax and my eyebrows were all singed. I got my book out and made a note not to ever do that again.

I wanted to do a lot more experiments and I was after Ma and Pa to get me a chemistry set that was in the Eaton's catalog. They were both adamant about me not getting one. Pa said that I'd probably blow myself up and Ma said that I'd burn the cabin down. Man, this really bugged me. *Other kids must get those sets. How am I ever going to learn anything if they won't let me do this stuff?*

Chapter 29
Big Brother Gets Wed

On a lovely day in June everyone had gone to town except Uncle Fred and me. Uncle was making something over by the blacksmith forge and I played with Tim as we sat in the sun by the barn. I heard the swish of wings and I looked up just in time to see two big mallard ducks circle and then land on the dam. They looked like supper to me and they would be if I had my way.

I crawled around the corner of the barn so that I didn't frighten them and once I was out of their sight, I ran to the cabin for a gun. Seeing as how there were two ducks, I figured that my best chance to get them both would be with Pa's shotgun. He told me not to touch it but if I got those ducks surely he wouldn't be mad about that. I got the gun from the corner behind the bed and the shells from the drawer in the cupboard.

I loaded the gun and walked quietly back to the barn and then I crawled behind the bushes until I figured that I was close enough to shoot. I carefully peered over a bush and had a look. Both of them were still swimming around totally unaware that I was there. Now, Pa had said that that gun would probably break my shoulder, so in my wisdom I decided to put the stock under my arm and save my shoulder.

I slowly raised myself up on my knees and put the stock under my arm. I waited until both ducks were close together and with the front sight between them I squeezed the trigger. With a loud bang my whole world seemed to come apart. I was knocked backward on the ground and the gun went flying over my head and landed somewhere in the brush behind me. My glasses were knocked off and I had this terrible pain under my right eye. I could feel something running down my face and dripping off my chin. I wiped my chin with my hand and it was covered with blood.

I staggered to my feet and looked to see if I hit anything. Both ducks were lying still in the water. I had to get them out but I had to do something about this bleeding first. I picked up my glasses and they were all bent out of shape. Uncle had heard the shot and came over to see what was going on. He took a look at me, "What in hell have you done now?" I showed him the ducks and told him that I just shot them.

"Holy balls!" Uncle said, "You just about lost your eye, how did you do that?" I explained to him that I put the stock under my arm to save my shoulder. "You dumb little dork, the gun kicked back and the hammer slammed into your cheek, it's cut to the bone and the piece is just hanging there." Uncle said that he'd try to patch it up and he took me to the cabin.

I looked at myself in the mirror while Uncle looked for something to fix me up. There was a piece just the shape of the gun's hammer cut to the bone in my cheek, just below my right eye. My eye was already turned black and my nose was swollen. Uncle found some tape and a piece of cloth and put it on my wound. "Your Pa is gonna give me hell for this cause I'm s'pose to be watching you."

"It ain't your fault Uncle."

"I know that, but you know that your Pa is gonna be real mad about you shooting that gun when he told you to leave it alone."

I told uncle that I'd just have to face the music but right now we had better go get those ducks and get them cleaned. We went to the dam and I got my dugout and went out to get them while Uncle watched. I couldn't see very well, partly because of my swollen eye and partly because of my twisted glasses. Uncle tried to fix them but they were still bent pretty bad. I picked up the ducks and took them to shore. Uncle took them and told me that at least I made a good shot and that they were a nice pair of ducks. He said that they'd make a nice change of diet.

Uncle and I cleaned the ducks and he put them in a dish of salt water. We had just finished when I heard the truck coming down the road. It was just as I thought it would be. Ma was all upset as soon as she saw me and Pa asked Uncle what I had done this time. Uncle tried to smooth things over for me and told Pa that I made a really good shot and got two nice big mallards for supper. Pa laid down the law to me once more and asked me what I had to say for myself. I told him that this time there was nothing that I could say. I did what he told me not to do and that I would just have to face the consequences. Pa kind of grinned and said that it looked like I had already paid and as he walked away he turned he head and said, "That damn gun really does kick hard, doesn't it?"

I couldn't believe it! He let me go without a switching or anything. I still had to go get the gun and put it away. I went and got it and wiped the mud and dirt from it and put it around the corner of the cabin. I decided that I'd wait to put it inside until Pa went to the barn after supper. Ma rolled the duck in a flour mixture that she made and fried it up for supper. It was really good and Pa even commented about them. He said that I could shoot some more if I could do it without killing myself.

I had to go around with a black eye for a couple of weeks and I felt like a real idiot when someone asked me what happened. Ma said that the scar under my eye would take years to go away. If I ever planned on shooting that gun again, I would have to come up with a better plan than the last one. In the meantime I thought that I'd just hang around home so nobody saw me.

Howard was driving a truck again and was gone a good part of the time so sometimes I went and stayed with Helen to keep her company. I liked to stay with her, she was a lot of fun to be with and she took me to the movies and places like that. I also liked to be around Pouce Coupe. I hung around the county shop and got to know the guys who repair the machinery and fix the old trucks. It was a good town for a kid to make money as well. There was a lot of work splitting and piling wood and doing odd jobs for people.

I met a kid named Raymond Furling and he was a nice fellow. He was a couple years older than me and I really liked him. He lived on a farm not too far from town and he came to town on a nice little saddle horse. He let me take his horse for little rides and it made me think about that little buckskin pony that I could have had. We rode double down by the river and we lay back on the sunny bank and smoked and talked.

Raymond told me that the rodeo in Dawson Creek started the next day and that they had calf riding for kids under twelve and that they paid two dollars if you could stay on one for eight seconds. That didn't seem like a very long time and I'd been riding all the cows and calves at home so this seemed like a good idea. He told me that he had ridden for a couple of years but this time he was a year too old. I decided that I would do it.

I didn't think that Helen would let me go so I thought I had better do it without telling her. I told her that I was going to the county shop. There's a bus between Pouce and Dawson and it costs ten cents to ride on it. I had a little money that I made piling wood for Mrs. Harris so I was all set. I caught the bus to Dawson and asked the driver to let me off as close to the fair grounds as he could. He did and he told me how to get there.

It was not very far to where the rodeo was going on and I heard it long before I saw it. Because I was a kid, they let me in for free and I asked the man at the gate where I should go to find out about the calf riding. He told me to go over by the grandstand where a guy was talking over a loudspeaker. I walked over and found a fellow with a nametag on his shirt and I asked him about it. He told me that it wouldn't be for another hour and showed me another man over by the chute and told me to go sign up with him.

I finally found the right guy and he asked how old I was. I told him that I was ten and would be eleven in November. He wrote my name down on a paper and said to listen for my name when the calf riding was announced. I got out of the way and watched the bronc riding. There were a lot of American soldiers riding and some of them were real good. The last rider up had a bad bucker. It was bucking and sunfishing and rearing up on its hind legs. His ride was nearly over when the horse reared up and went over backward and fell on the guy. The horse kicked and struggled to get up and the guy had his foot stuck in the stirrup. The horse made a couple more jumps and the guy's foot came loose and he fell to the ground. He lay there holding his leg and some other cowboys ran out to see how he was. His leg was broken and they took him away in an ambulance. I'd never seen a man get his leg broken before and it kind of made me sick.

There were a couple more bronc rides and the man at the grandstand announced the calf riding. I walked over to the chute and there were about a dozen farm kids wearing overalls and most of them in their bare feet. I got in the group and waited for my name to be called. Four of five kids make their ride and then the man called my name.

I was a little nervous feeling going out in front of a bunch of people but I didn't have time to think about it. Most of the calves seemed to be Herefords and were not too big. A fellow held mine and I got on and they opened the chute. He didn't buck very much, just sort of ran out in the ring and the horn blew and I jumped off. I walked back to the chute and the man gave me a little ticket and told me to go to the grandstand and get my money.

It was getting late and as soon as I got my two dollars I headed for the bus stop. I was feeling good about making two dollars in eight seconds but I couldn't tell anybody about it. If I told my sister, she would give me hell for doing it and when I got home I wouldn't be able to tell Ma because she'd tell Helen that she should not have let me do it. If I told Pa, he would tell Ma and I'd really be in deep doo-doo.

Helen gave me what for because I was late and I made up a story about being down at the river fishing with some other kids and didn't realize it was so late. I told her that I was sorry and that I wouldn't do it again. I hung my head and got a sad look on my face and Helen said that it was all right and gave me some supper. I love my sister. She's a real pushover for a sad face.

I stayed with Helen for a couple more days before Ma and Pa came to get me. It was getting close to the day of Alf and Marie's wedding and there was a lot of preparation to do. Marie had come home on leave and everyone was busy getting things ready. Francis and Mavis were standing up for them and I was going to be the altar boy.

On the Sunday before the wedding we went to mass in Tupper. As usual, I was the altar boy and I was in the little vestibule behind the altar, putting on my little gown and getting some wine for mass. As I poured the wine into the crucible, I wondered what it tasted like. I thought that Father Goetz must like it because when I poured the wine and water over his fingers he always whispered, "Not too much water, a little more wine."

The only way that I'd ever know what it was like was to taste it. I tipped up the bottle and had a little sip, it didn't taste too bad but it was hard to judge with one little sip so I had another. Just as I was judging the taste, Father walked in. "How is it?" he asked me with a look on his face that told me that he was not too pleased. I told him that it was not bad. He gave me the lecture that I knew he would and we went out and prepared for mass.

The day for the wedding finally arrived and everyone was hurrying around getting things ready. It was a beautiful sunny day and Ma said that sure would make it nice. We got to the little chapel and I hurried inside to get the altar ready. Everyone looked so nice, all dressed up in their Sunday best. My big brother and his new bride made a lovely couple and after the ceremony, all their friends and neighbors shook hands and congratulated them. I was not sure if I'd lost a brother or gained a sister, only time would tell.

Alf and Marie only had a couple of days before they headed off to Red Deer as she had to get back to the army. The day that they left was kind of sad. I hate those kinds of days. Ma was in tears and Pa seemed awfully quiet. I hated to see them go but as usual there was nothing that I could do about it. My whole life seemed to be a series of events that I couldn't change. I asked Ma why life was like that and she told me "That's just the way that it is."

When all the goodbyes were said, Francis took them to Tupper to catch the train. Again, it seemed awfully quiet in the little cabin. As I thought about it I couldn't help but wonder how long it would be before everybody would be gone. The more that I thought about it, the sadder I became and I had to get outside and go for a walk in the woods to make me feel better. Somehow the woods made me feel better. It is like the trees have spirits and the whole woods is a living thing. I don't feel alone when I 'm there.

As I got ready for bed I knelt by my bed and said my prayers and asked Jesus why good things never seemed to last. Just as things seemed to be going so well and everyone was happy, something always seemed to happen to change it. I missed my sister and already I missed my brother. I wondered what would happen next.

Chapter 30
More Than I Wanted To Know

Pa came home from town and as Ma and I helped him bring in the groceries he told us that some people they knew invited us to go pick raspberries with them. They told him that the picking was really good. Pa said that he had made arrangements with them to go picking the next day. We left home early in the morning and headed for their place. It was about twelve miles and it didn't take us to long to get there. I'd heard of these people but I had never met them. Ma and Pa knew them and when we got there they shook hands and seemed glad to see each other. I found out that they had a daughter, she was a couple years older than me and a lot bigger.

The berries were in an old logging slash and to get there we had to go with a team and wagon for five or six miles. The day was warm and sunny and the ride in the wagon was very pleasant. The girl and I sat in the back of the wagon and we talked a little. I didn't know what to talk to girls about. I didn't imagine that she wanted to talk about fishing or trapping and as we rode along I wondered what boys and girls usually talk about. Somehow she kind of made me nervous.

After a nice wagon ride we got to the berry patch. It was still about an hour till lunchtime so we picked berries for a while. The berries were big and plentiful and by the time the ladies called us to eat, I was already full of berries. The lunch was nice and the grown ups seemed to be having a good time talking and visiting. The girl got up from the log she had been sitting on and asked me to go for a walk with her down an old logging trail.

We walked for a little ways and talked a little but I still had no idea what she wanted to talk about. We came into a little open place and the grass was long and soft. She lay down in the grass and motioned to me to come lay down beside her. I didn't know if that was a good idea or not but I decided it couldn't hurt. It felt nice lying in the soft grass, the sun was warm and it would have been easy for me to fall asleep. I lay there enjoying the sun and my mind drifted off into daydreams. *This is nice.*

I suddenly came back to reality with some strange sounds. I looked over at her and she had her eyes shut and was sort of moaning. She seemed to be in pain. She was rubbing her chest and stomach and way down low by her crotch. My god, maybe something she ate made her sick or she had appendicitis or something serious like that. I sat up and asked her if she was sick and she opened her eyes and told me no. Now I didn't know what to do because she took me by the arm and pulled me over to her and told me to hold her. This was getting downright scary.

She told me to put my hand inside of her blouse. I didn't want to do that and as I hesitated she grabbed my hand and shoved it in her blouse, right on one of those things! Oh boy, I didn't want to touch that, it felt hot and wet and sweaty and I could feel a little hard end sticking up, yuck.

"Move your hand around and rub it," she told me.

"What for?" I asked her.

"You don't know a damn thing, do you?" she said in a cranky sounding voice.

"What am I supposed to know, I'm only ten years old and I know how to fish and skin squirrels, what else should I know?"

She told me that I was dumb as dirt and pulled my hand out of her blouse. That was a relief for me. She seemed mad at me though and she got up and went behind a tree. She told me to stay right there, that she was going to take a pee. I didn't want to know that, what's with girls anyway. I decided to ask Ma about girls tomorrow to see if I could make some sense out of all of this. We walked back to where the rest were picking berries without saying a word. There was a little stream close to where we had lunch and I went down to the water and washed my hands.

The sun was getting low when we all got in the wagon and headed for home. They asked us to stay for supper but it was getting late so we just got in the old truck and went home. I was glad because I wanted to get away from that girl. When we got home, Ma made supper and I helped Pa with the chores. I fed the cows and got in some wood while he did the milking. I was tired and right after supper I said my prayers and went to bed. I wanted to ask Jesus about girls but thought maybe what I wanted to know was a sin so I decided to wait and ask Ma.

In mid-morning I knew that Ma would have a little break and a cup of tea so I hung around and waited. When she sat down I went over and asked her about this girl. Ma was great, I could ask her anything and she tried to explain things to me without making me feel like a dummy. I told her about my escapade and asked her what was going on. Was this something to do with love or something?

Ma told me that boys and girls go through a thing called puberty and sometimes they act strange. She told me that their bodies were going through changes and they got urges to do love things. I asked her if I had to go through that puberty thing because I didn't think that I wanted to do that stuff. She said not to worry about it that it would all work out. *That's what I'm afraid of.*

Autumn arrived and the leaves turned color and fell from the trees. I loved this time of year. There were still a few raspberries around and lots of low bush blue berries. I liked to sit in the warm autumn sun and eat berries and listen to the sounds of fall. The wind blew steady to get the leaves from the trees and the squirrels hurried around gathering food for winter. The geese and ducks made their fall flight back to a warmer place and the rabbits were already getting white spots on them.

When we got up one morning the rain was coming down quite hard. It looked like a good day to stay inside. My schoolwork had started so that was the first thing that I had to do. I finished my lessons early in the afternoon and it was still raining so I decided to spend the rest of the day inside. I'd been working on a balsa wood airplane and so I finished it. I wanted to see how good it would glide so I gave it a little toss in the air. It flew good and soared over and landed on top of the wardrobe in Ma's bedroom.

The wardrobe was quite high and I had to get a chair to get up there to get my plane. I had never seen on top of there before and as I got my plane I saw a box up there. It was a blue box and it said Kotex on it in big white letters. I wondered what was in it but it hadn't been opened so I couldn't look. Maybe it was something to eat and they didn't want me to know about it. Well, I decided to ask Ma and find out.

"Ma, what's in this box that says Kotex on it?"

"It's nothing for you so don't worry about it."

"I want to know, Ma, is it something to eat?"

"Never mind, just leave it alone and get out of there," Ma told me. Well, if she didn't want to tell me then it must be something important and I wanted to know what it was so I asked her again.

"All right," she said, "come in here and sit down and I'll tell you about it if you just have to know."

I went into the kitchen and sat down and Ma started to tell me about this stuff. I didn't want to hear it but she said that I just had to know so I had to sit and listen. Oh my lord, she was talking about blood and I thought that maybe I would faint. I told her that I'd heard all that I had to about this stuff but she kept on telling me anyways. I tried holding my hands over my ears but I could still hear her. By the time she finished telling me I didn't feel very good, I thought that I might be sick.

Ma went about her work and I went to lie on the bed for a while and think about this stuff. I thought that girls were complicated before, well this clinched it for me, I was really sure. I was so glad that god made me a boy instead of a girl. I didn't know anything about girls and every time that I learned something about them I wondered why they were so complex and confusing. I decided the best thing for me to do was not have anything to do with them and maybe I'd be all right. I wondered if Alf knew about that messy stuff before he got married. If he didn't, boy was he in for a big surprise! I thought about that girl in the berry patch. I was sure lucky that she didn't shove my hand down inside of her pants! *There is way more to girls than I want to know.*

The more I think about it the more confused I become. Why are girls so different from boys? Girls hug one another, you never see boys doing that. At the dances sometimes the girls dance together and they always go to the washroom together, you never see boys do that either. Most of them don't want to hunt or fish and they all seem to go crazy over babies. They whisper things to one another and then they giggle, what's that about? It's just downright confusing.

I saw an ad in a magazine for a book on nature. It said that it was all about things like chlorophyll and photosynthesis and all about trees and animals. It also came with a free microscope if I ordered right away. It cost three dollars and ninety-five cents and that was a little more than I had saved up. I told Francis about it and told him that I was a little short. He said that he'd give me the money but I'd have to wash his truck a few times to earn it. That sounded like a good deal to me so he gave me the money and I sent for the book.

I had to send to New York for the book and it seemed to take forever for it to arrive. A month passed but it finally arrived, it was a beautiful big book and the wait was worth it. The microscope on the other hand was a piece of junk. It was made of cardboard and the lens was made out of some kind of plastic and it was all wrinkled and rough. You couldn't even see through it. It sort of looked like a microscope so I kept it and put a piece of glass from a broken bottle in it. It didn't magnify but I could see through it.

I really loved this book and I read it from cover to cover. I learned about the cambium layer of bark on trees and about Komodo dragons and all kinds of things. After reading this book, I was sure that I'd be a naturalist of some kind. I examined bugs and frogs and plants and wrote down my observations in a scribbler that I had just for that purpose. The book made me see things that I never seemed to see before and it gave me a whole new outlook on nature.

Winter came again and I still owed Francis a couple wash jobs on his truck that would have to wait until spring. Francis was a pretty good brother and he always seemed to help me out with a dollar or two if he thought that it was for a good reason. I'd been reading his Popular Mechanics magazine again and I found an ad for taxidermy. The ad showed one fellow showing another his stuffed animals and birds and the other fellow was all impressed about it. It also told how much money you could make and how you would be the envy of everyone who saw what you could do.

The course cost twelve dollars and could be paid for at the rate of one dollar a month. I wanted this real bad and I thought that I should be able to come up with a dollar a month but once more I went see my brother about it. He said that if I couldn't always come up with the dollar that he would help me out but I had to try hard on my own. I wrote the letter to the Northwest school of Taxidermy in Omaha, Nebraska, and got a one-dollar money order made out and put it in the mail. Then I had to wait again. It seemed like I spent all my time waiting.

All things come to those who wait and one day the first couple of lessons for my taxidermy course arrived. A letter said that after the next payment, they would send the rest of the lessons. I eagerly read these little lessons and they were very interesting. There only seemed to be a couple of problems. They used arsenic to preserve the skins and a lot of excelsior and string to make the bodies. Arsenic is a bad poison and not something that I could get or have. It went on to say that small animal skins could be preserved with borax, instead of arsenic.

I didn't have any borax so I had to wait until someone went to Pouce Coupe to see if they had any there. I only had to wait a few days before Pa went to town and he bought me a small box of it. Then came the fun part of seeing if I could stuff a squirrel. I did as the book said to do and took the skin off the squirrel and prepared it for mounting.

Then I had to make a body out of wood wool and string. Luckily Ma had some wood wool that had been used for packing around some dishes that she got from Eaton's catalog. It was pretty tricky to make a body out of that stuff. I had to put a stiff wire in the legs and tail. I finally got it done and tried to stretch the skin over it. This was not easy! Once the skin was stretched over the body it had to be sewn up so that it didn't show.

Sewing was not one of my better skills so I sweet-talked Ma into doing it for me. She was kind of reluctant about it but after a while she agreed to sew it and when it was finished it looked pretty good. I felt quite proud of my efforts even if I didn't sew it myself. *This taxidermy stuff is all right after all!* I hoped that some day I'd be able to mount some big things like deer heads but I would have to have arsenic for that.

Ma and Pa came home from town and Ma was all excited and happy sounding. I asked her what was going on and she said that she got a letter from Alf and Marie and Marie was expecting a baby sometime in June. She said that Marie would be discharged from the army soon and that they would be coming home. That made me happy because I sure missed my big brother and on top of that, I was going to be an uncle. Ma told me that she had some more news. Helen was also expecting a baby at about the same time. I was happy to hear that, it looked like I was going to be an uncle twice. I wondered what it would feel like to be an uncle.

I went to spend a weekend with Helen and when I was there I heard about an old guy who was a retired taxidermist. I asked Helen if it would be all right for me to go over to see him. She said that she didn't suppose he would mind so I went over to his place. His name was Mr. Chase and he was quite a big man. He answered the door and asked what he can do for me. I told him my name and that I wanted to learn about taxidermy and he asked me to come in.

He seemed like a nice man and took me into his living room. It was full of all kinds of stuffed animals and birds and in one corner was a display in a glass case. It looked just like a coyote den, complete with the mother and father and two baby coyotes. I was really impressed and he seemed pleased by that. He made some tea and we had tea and cookies that he had baked himself. He was a pretty good cook.

Mr. Chase was nearly ninety years old and was born in the States. He could remember the Civil war and told me stories about it. He told me about old black powder rifles and how the woodsmen would have shooting contests. I could have stayed and listen to him all day but I had to get back to Helen's for supper. He invited me to come back any time. He said that he liked the company and that he would teach me more about taxidermy. I thanked him and headed off to my sister's place.

Alf sent a letter to say they would be coming home the next Wednesday and to ask someone to meet them at the train. Ma was all excited and started baking cookies and bread for when they arrived. The day that they arrived was a terrible day. The snow was coming down like it wanted to bury everything in white, and it was doing a pretty good job of it. They had trouble getting up the hill and they got stuck in a drift not far from the cabin.

They waded through the snow to the cabin and there was a lot of hugging and handshaking going on. Ma made some tea and lunch. Pa and Alf got the horses harnessed and pulled the truck up into the yard. They had their tea and they all seemed to be talking at the same time. I had some cookies and shared them with Tim and wondered about this baby that was supposed to be on the way. When Marie stood up I noticed that there was quite a bump on her belly and I guessed that must be the baby. Somehow I felt a little embarrassed about it and I didn't know why. The only one that I could talk to about that stuff was Ma and I had to wait until she was alone.

It was crowded in the little cabin again but it was nice to have everyone home again. As I thought about it I realized that we were a very close family and it gave me a good feeling. I was glad to have my big brother home but somehow he seemed to have changed. I imagined that the idea of him becoming a father had changed his way of thinking a little. I didn't know Marie much before but now that they were living here I found out that she was like a big sister.

Winter really hated to give up its icy grip but as it did every other year it lost out to spring. The snow slowly disappeared. This was a time of year that I loved. As soon as the sun pushed the snow back, the little green shoots started to appear. I wondered how they could lay under that frozen ground all winter long and still be alive. It was like they played a trick on winter and now winter couldn't do anything about it.

Chapter 31
Babies and Wolves

The snow had gone and it was a beautiful spring day. Everyone had gone to town except Marie and me. The road was rough and she was big with child so the best plan was to stay home. It was such a nice day that I decided to go do some naturalist stuff. I got my little packsack and put my notebook and pencil in it and I walked up to the sawmill. I thought that I'd study some big carpenter ants that spent time in the sawdust pile.

The road to the mill was full of ruts and the ruts were full of water and I picked my way carefully to avoid getting my feet all wet. I got to the mill and looked around for some ants and tried to follow them to their home. The day was so warm and I took off my coat and just sat back in the sawdust and enjoyed spring. The birds were singing and busy building nests and the sounds of spring just made me feel plumb lazy. I was nearly falling asleep when I heard some rustling noise in the bush to the east of me. I looked down the trail just in time to see a wolf jump out of the woods and right behind that one, a much bigger one. They looked hungry to me.

They were about fifty yards away and coming my way. I didn't think that they had seen me yet but I thought that I had better be making tracks for home. I jumped up and took off running as fast as I could go all the while thinking, "Legs, don't fail me now!" I ran right down the middle of the road, over those ruts full of water and went so fast that my feet didn't even get wet. I looked over my shoulder and the wolves were running along behind me like a pair of big dogs. I thought that this was not a good time to feel like I was getting diarrhea but when I looked over my shoulder and saw them coming after me, I was feeling a little loose!

As I ran, thoughts surged through my mind, if they caught me, they would have me for lunch but if I made it home and got the rifle and shot them, I would be able to buy a bicycle. There was a twenty-five dollar bounty on wolves and if I got them both, there would be more than enough for a bike! I kept hoping not to slip and fall or I'd be a goner for sure. I looked back again and saw that they were getting really close. I guess that I could run faster scared than they could hungry because I found that I could run even faster than I had been.

I made it to the cabin and hurried inside and closed the door behind me. I ran to the bedroom to get the rifle when Marie grabbed me and asked me what I was doing. I told her that two wolves were running around the cabin and I was going to open the window and shoot them. She looked out of the window and saw them sniffing around the cabin and she freaked out. She started to cry and said that I couldn't shoot at them because if I did they would kill us. I told her that they couldn't kill us if I shot them but it was no use she made me put the rifle down.

She was really scared and she started worrying that all the excitement might make her have the baby. *Oh my lord, I sure hoped that doesn't happen. That would be worse than being killed by the wolves!* They hung around the yard for nearly half an hour and they didn't seem to be afraid of anything. It was a good thing that the dog was in the cabin or they might have killed him. Old Ranger was tied up over by the pigpen but they didn't go there and he luckily didn't bark.

The wolves hadn't been gone very long when everyone came home from town. I told them about the wolves and Marie was still half crying. I was upset that she wouldn't let me shoot them and Alf told her that she should have let me do it. She got even more upset and cried some more. I took the gun and went out to see if they were anywhere around. I looked around in the direction that they had left but they were gone. Ma was worried every time that I went outside. I told her not to worry about it but she kept saying, "What is ever going to become of you? Something is going to eat you for sure if you keep playing out in the bush." I decided that if I went very far from home I'd take the twenty-two rifle with me. That might ease her mind a little.

The time was getting close for Marie to have her baby so she went to stay with Helen in Pouce Coupe closer to a hospital. I stayed with Helen and Marie for a few days and spent more time with Mr. Chase. He was a great old gentleman to be with and I could listen to his stories forever. He showed me some things about taxidermy and how to tan small hides. I was happy that I'd met this fascinating man.

One nice afternoon we all decided to walk down to the café for pie and coffee. Marie was as big as a house and as we walked down the side of the gravel road, she stubbed her toe and fell right on her belly. Boy, that must really hurt! She sort of teetered back and forth on her belly and Helen and I helped her to her feet. She was crying and had lost a lot of skin from her hands and knees. Helen was worried that the fall might bring the baby on and I prayed as fast as I could that it didn't happen there on the side of the road. I didn't think that I could handle that.

We went back to the house and Helen doctored Marie's knees and hands and they went into the bedroom to have a look at her belly. Helen came out to get the salve and bandages and went back to the bedroom and fixed her belly up. I was really worried about the baby but she seemed to be fine except for the missing skin. Helen told her that she had better spend the rest of the day laying down.

Pa and Alf came to Pouce with a load of wood and so I went back home with them. I didn't want to be around when those babies started coming. Ma was all excited about being a grandma and seeing as how I was going to be an uncle, I felt a little more grown up. I wondered if these babies would be girls or boys, girls would be nice but boys would be nicer. We'd just have to wait and see.

We didn't have to wait long though, on June twenty-eighth Marie gave birth to a baby boy. Alf came home from town with the news and everyone was happy and excited. They named him Joseph Maurice, after his two grandfathers. Alf was so proud he nearly popped the buttons off of his shirt. It was only a few days later Marie came home with her new boy. Everyone took turns holding him and somehow it made me feel a little jealous. Pa took a new one-dollar bill from his wallet and put it in the baby's tiny little hand. Pa told him "That's a start on life for you." I felt kind of left out because Pa had never given me any money at all.

July first came and as always we went to the park at Tupper for the festivities. It was a pretty normal day with ball games and races for the kids. The C.W.L., of which Ma was a member, looked after the concession booths and ice cream stand. I turned the ice cream freezer for them and for every one that I turned I got a cone of that delicious homemade ice cream.

I'd just finished turning a freezer and I took my cone and headed over to a booth that had a ring toss game. There was a nice little plastic airplane in one of the boxes and I tried to get the hoop over that box. I tried a couple times with no luck and I was just feeling in my pocket for another nickel when, "Get out of the way kid, and let me play."

I looked up and there stood this kid from Dawson with a couple of his buddies. He looked like that 'Sluggo' in the funny papers. He was quite fat and had a little beanie on his head and he looked like a real bully. I ignored him and found my nickel and gave it to the girl in the booth. She gave me three more rings and I started to toss them at the boxes. "Hey kid, didn't you hear me, I told you to get out of the way and let me play."

I started to get a little irritated with this kid but I still ignored him. He was getting really upset with me not paying any attention to him and he told me that he would beat some respect into me. I turned to him and told him to go ahead.

"Take those glasses off."

"What for?" I asked him, "You couldn't knock them off anyhow."

He was getting really mad, "Get them off," he hollered.

I took them off and handed them to the girl in the booth. I was getting pretty upset with this loud mouth little jerk. He stood there with a smart-ass look and I took my ice cream cone and shoved it in his face.

"I don't have to take this crap from some dumb kid in a one-horse town like this," he hollered as he swung at me. He had a swing like a rusty gate and I ducked. *This is going to be fun!*

He was a lot heavier than me so I had to be careful. Pa always told me that the right-cross worked good if you did it fast enough. He was right, I feinted a left and gave him a good right in his left eye. He staggered back and took another swing at me. I ducked again and gave him another right cross in the other eye. This kid never learned! He was bawling like a suck and still swinging and this time he connected with my left shoulder. He could really hit hard I had to watch that he didn't hit me in the jaw like that or I'd be a goner.

He stuck his face out and I gave him yet another right cross on the chin. He grabbed his face and I drove him one in the guts as hard as I could. He gasped for air and fell on his back and I pounced on him as fast as I could. He was bawling and I was sitting on his chest beating hell out of his face and ears when suddenly I found myself four feet from the ground. Some big guy was holding me up by my belt and telling me that he was going to kick my ass.

I told him that his smart-ass kid started it and I finished it. He threw me on the ground and got down where his kid was still sucking.

"You're a tough little bugger," he told his kid.

Oh right, I'm thinking, if he's so tough, how come his eyes are black and his nose is bleeding and he's bawling like a baby! I got my glasses from the girl in the booth and walked back to where the ice cream freezers were. I was feeling good about the fight but bad that I ruined my cone. Now I had to crank the freezer again to earn another one.

It was going on three in the morning and the dance was over and we were heading home. The sky started to get light in the east as I lay on my back in the truck box and we rumbled towards home. I thought about the day and how it had to be the best first of July ever. I finally got that little airplane and I had a lot of fun with that kid from Dawson. My shoulder was still sore where he hit me but I'd bet that his face hurts a lot worse.

Ma was mad about me fighting but everybody told her that the other kid started it so she got over that. She said that I should always walk away from a fight but Pa said, "No, you have to fight when you have to." I thought that Pa was right. Besides, it was fun to fight when you were the winner.

A couple of weeks passed and on July thirteenth, Helen gave birth to her and Howard's first child. It was also a boy and they named him Donald. Since I was no longer the youngest one in the family I felt a lot more grown up, even more that I thought that I would. It was a lot different in the cabin with a new baby. I didn't know much about babies but I learned fast. They seemed to be little containers full of puke, pee, and poop. Every time that I held one of them, I got one or more of those things all over me. I didn't like to hold them very much.

Every day Marie and Ma washed diapers and that kid seemed like all he did was get them dirty. I wondered how come females seemed to like babies so much. It had to be some kind of a *girl thing*. They changed those poopy pants and tickled the babies' tummies and made all sorts of cooing sounds. I was kind of afraid to hold them. Their heads seemed to flop around and I was always afraid that it would fall right off. Then what would you do?

I heard the men talking at suppertime and they seemed to be quite excited over some deal that they had made. As I listened I found out that they had purchased a timber limit from the Sudetens, somewhere out on the Cutbank River. It was the same place that Francis and Alf hauled ties from last year. It seemed that, Francis, Alf and Uncle Fred would all be going out there and that they would be moving the sawmill out there. Of course Marie and little Joe would be going there as well.

As I thought about it I realized that there would only be Ma, Pa and I left on the homestead. The more I thought about it the more excited I became. With everyone else gone, I'd be able to help Pa and get to do some of the things that Alf and Francis did. Maybe if I worked real hard, Pa would realize that I could be good for something too. The way it was it seemed like I was more of a nuisance to him than anything else. As I said my prayers I thanked Jesus for giving me this chance and asked him to help me not to blow it.

They decided that they should overhaul the mill before they moved so they sawed some nice new timbers for the track and the carriage. Then they took the mill apart and replaced all the old wood. They painted it red and set it aside as they got all the other things ready to move. All of this work took up most of the summer and it was early fall before they moved. It seemed strange with everyone gone.

It had been quite a year and for the first time in four years the school was going to reopen. There were finally enough kids and I was real happy about that. This year Ma bought me a real lunch pail with a thermos and all. The first day of school arrived and Ma walked to the top of the hill with me. I loved my Ma dearly and I looked back and waved at her as she watched me go down the hill. I wished that I knew how to tell her how much I loved her.

Going to school was a real pleasure. Mildred Pratt was the teacher and she was really a good one. She knew how to explain things and somehow learning with her was easy. Dave Hamilton and I were in the two highest grades and we rebuilt an old desk and made one where we sat side by side. Only then did I realize how much I missed school by taking correspondence at home. Home was fine but it was sure nice to spend some time with the other kids.

I loved going home after school. Ma put hot cocoa in my thermos and I saved a cup for on the way home. There was a little blueberry patch on the way and on a warm fall afternoon I liked to go there and eat some berries and drink the last of my cocoa. The sun felt so nice and as most of the leaves had fallen from the berry bushes, it made for easy picking. The partridges thought so too and I often shared with a flock of them. Sometimes there was a lot of crashing in the bush as a bear heard me coming and decided to leave.

At the bottom of the hill there was a small raspberry patch and I ate a few of those to give me strength to climb the big hill. When I got to the top of the hill I liked to sit on one of the big sandstone rocks that jutted out of the ground and looked north across the valley. I could see the school from there and a few miles to the north was another big hill that they called old Baldy. I wanted to go there some day to look back across the valley to where I am now. I figured that in a couple more years I'd be big enough to go there. It was high on my 'When I Get Big Enough' list.

I worked hard helping Pa now that we were alone. I got up at six, when he did and helped with the milking. By the time we finished the milking, Ma had breakfast ready. Oh, but that hot oatmeal porridge was good and the pancakes were even better. After we ate I turned the cream separator and then got ready and headed off for school. The snow had come early and as nice as the fall had been, winter had moved in with a vengeance.

As the snow got deeper, more timber wolves moved into the area and Pa thought that I better start taking the rifle to school with me just in case. I couldn't take it right to the school so Pa took a couple of boards and we made a place to hide it behind a tree not far from school. The boards kept the snow off and kept it dry. I felt a lot safer carrying it but it was heavy and sometimes I felt like dragging it along by the barrel. Of course I didn't do it but I felt like it.

Saturdays were always spent hauling hay from the old homestead or the hay meadow. We had twenty-seven head of cattle and the horses and they ate an awful lot of hay. Pa pitched the hay up on the rack and I spread it around and tramped it down so we could get as big a load as possible on the sleigh.

We were going home with the last load of hay and about half way up the big hill, Jim fell down on the ice and got all tangled up in the harness. The sleigh slid backwards down the hill until finally the hayrack jammed itself into the bank and we stopped. Jim was fighting like crazy, trying to get up and old Brian was getting spooked with all the thrashing around. Pa tried to get the tugs undone but Jim was kicking so hard that Pa was having a hard time.

Pa finally got Jim unhooked from the sleigh but he still couldn't get up on the ice so Pa said that we had to roll him over and let him roll down the bank. Between the two of us we managed to get him rolled over and he tumbled down the bank in the deep snow. When he got to the bottom, he got up on his feet but he was covered with snow. He had been sweating, trying to get up and now with all the snow on him, Pa was afraid that he'd catch pneumonia if we didn't get him dried off and in a warm place really quickly.

Pa led Jim back up the hill and wiped off as much snow as he could and then he put me on his back and told me to ride him home as fast as I could and get him in the barn and dry him off with some old gunny sacks. It was cold and as night started to fall so did the temperature. I rode him home at a full gallop and he was so wet and slippery that I could barely stay on his back. I got him home and into the barn and ran to the cabin to tell Ma to bring a pail of warm water for Jim to drink and then I ran back and dried him off.

He was shivering with cold but Ma brought a pail of warm water and he drank it down. I rubbed him down as hard as I could and that seemed to help warm him up. Pa came along a little later with old Brian and he took over rubbing Jim and I took the cows to the lake for water. I got back with the cows and put the milk cows in the barn. The more animals that we got into the barn the warmer it was and Pa said that Jim would probably be fine.

It was still dark when Pa and I took the team back to the hill to get the load of hay that we had to leave the day before. We got the horses hooked up but they couldn't move the sleigh. It was frozen down to the ice. Pa got a pole from the bush and we pried each runner loose. Pa tried again and the horses pulled hard and the sleigh started to move. The runners squeaked on the ice and we were on our way. It was cold and I ran behind the sleigh to keep warm. Pa always seems tough, his hands and feet never seem to get cold. Mine seem to be frozen all the time. Sometimes when my hands are really cold, Pa takes his mitts off and tells me to put my hands in them and warm them up. His mitts feel warm as toast and it helps for a while.

It was Sunday and after we got home with the hay Pa said that I had better take a run around the trapline to see if we'd caught anything. This made me feel so good, for the first time in my life I went with Pa when he set the traps and now I even got to check the traps. The snow was deep and the snowshoes were a lot too big but as I didn't weigh much I could walk right on top of the snow with them. It was about five miles around the line and it would take me nearly that many hours to check it.

I warmed up good and Ma gave me a cup of hot cocoa and a slice of bread and butter before I left. She didn't like it when I went that far alone but Pa told her that I'd be fine. I took the old Winchester rifle and set off. I loved that old rifle but I hated to carry it, it felt like it weighed a ton. It was a dull day and the snow was falling lightly as I went down the trap trail. It was so quiet that when I stopped and stood still all that I could hear were the trees cracking with the cold. The stillness was almost eerie and as I stopped and looked across the valley it was almost like a dream.

I came back to reality when I reached the next coyote snare and found myself face to face with a big coyote that must have just been caught because he was very much alive. I was not too sure what I should do with him. When I got too close he bared his teeth and growled so I decided that hitting him on the head with a stick was not an option. I hated to shoot him with this rifle because it would make a big hole in him and the skin would not be worth as much. I wondered if Pa would give me hell if I shot him and as I was thinking about it he gave a jump and I saw that the willow that the snare was hooked to had cracked and was about to break off. That revelation made for a sudden decision and I shot him in the head.

The rifle shot echoed and re-echoed back and forth across the valley and then the silence returned. As I took the coyote from the snare, I felt a feeling that I couldn't explain but it didn't make me feel good. Somehow I wished that I could have let him go and I felt bad that I had to shoot him. I took the snare from the willow and tied it around his hind feet and put him on my shoulder. He was big and heavy and I decided that I had better take him home and finish the rest of the line another day.

Pa was happy when I got home and he said that he should get at least twenty bucks for that coyote. I watched as he skinned it out and stretched the hide. I'd grown up with trapping and hunting but this was the first time that I'd had to shoot something that big so close that I could see the look in the eyes and I wondered what was wrong with me that I felt so bad about it. I decided I'd talk to Jesus about it when I said my prayers.

The one thing that I wanted more than anything was a bike and as bad as I felt about trapping, it was the only way that I could make any money. The fur that we caught on the line that Pa and I set was all his and I didn't get any money from it. If I wanted money I had to set my own traps and have my own line.

Chapter 32
Deer and Foxes

It was a Friday afternoon and I was nearly home from school. Dusk was already settling over the forest and I could see the moon waiting to spread its blue glow on the landscape. As I turned the last corner from the main road, I saw that Ma already had the light lit in the cabin. The road either turned to the cabin or went straight on to where we took the cows to drink at Sullivan's lake. As I looked down toward the lake I saw a nice little deer nibbling on some branches. I knew that we were low on meat and that deer would help out nicely.

I had the rifle with me and if I could get this deer it would be my first one. I stayed close to the side of the trail so the deer couldn't see me and stole along as quietly as I could. When I thought that I was close enough, I slowly moved toward the center of the trail to see if he was still there. He hadn't a clue that I was there and was still eating. I slowly raised the rifle and took aim at his shoulder. That old rifle was so heavy that I could hardly hold it up like that and the barrel seemed to be wobbling all over the place. When it wobbled by his shoulder, I squeezed the trigger.

The crack of the rifle nearly deafened me and the kick just about knocked me down. I got myself together and looked to see if I had hit the deer. I had and I saw him lying in the trail. I felt pretty proud of myself as I ran up for a better look. It was a little buck and he just lay there. There was a trickle of blood running from his neck and making a little red pool in the snow. As I looked at him lying there, somehow I didn't feel as elated as I had a few minutes ago.

I came back to reality and I knew that I had to get it dressed out and that I had to hurry before it was too dark to see at all. It was not far to the cabin and I ran there as fast as I could. Ma had heard the shot and wanted to know what I had shot at. I told her that I shot a deer and that I needed my hunting knife to dress it out. She said that Pa wasn't home but that she would come and help me. I told her that I could do it by myself, I'd helped Pa before and I'd watched him butcher pigs so I knew that I could do it. Besides, what grown guy had his mother help him dress out a deer?

I hurried back to where the deer was and rolled it on its back. It was not too big so I knew I would be able to handle it. It was really cold out and when I cut through the skin and the stomach lining the steam hit me right in the face. The steam and the smell of the insides nearly made me sick. I thought for a minute that I might pass out but a few breaths of cold air brought me around and I got at it and finished the job. I wiped the insides out with snow and got the liver and the heart and headed back to the cabin. My hands felt frozen and I was cold all over.

Pa was late coming home and I still had to get the cows to the lake for water. I warmed up by the stove for a few minutes and washed my hands in some hot water and took the cows for a drink. It took an hour to water the cows and by the time I got home Pa was there. Ma had already told him about the deer and he said that it would sure help out with the meat supply. After supper Pa went with me and we dragged the deer home and put it in the icehouse. Pa said that it was in good shape and that it would be good eating. I hoped so because I really had mixed feelings about shooting that deer. I hoped that God was not upset about it.

On Saturday morning I took the cows to the lake for water again and as I did I noticed some really big rabbit runs in the snow. One in particular was wide and well packed down and in the new skiff of snow I saw some fox tracks. There were lots of rabbits and the foxes and coyotes were eating well. I thought that if I could catch a fox or two I could get that bike I wanted so badly. I felt bad about catching a fox but that was the only way that I would ever get enough money to buy one.

Pa and I had to haul another load of hay and I could hardly wait until we got home so that I could go and set a snare on that rabbit run. As soon as we got home and got the hay unloaded I found a snare and headed over to that run to set it. The run was hard and it held me up easily. I followed it a little ways until I found a spot where the run went between two willows. The space between the willows was quite small and it looked to me like a perfect spot to set my snare.

I fastened the snare to one of the willows and with a little string I tied the other side to the other willow. I got a few small sticks and pushed them into the snow on the sides of the trail and angled a couple more over the snare. That way the fox would be funneled right into it. The snare was big enough that the rabbits would go right through it and I hoped that it was the right size for a fox.

By then it was time to take the cows and horses to the lake again and to hurry home to get in the wood supply for the night. I didn't tell Pa about the snare, if I caught a fox I'd have a good surprise for him and maybe he would be proud of me. He didn't say too much about the deer that I shot. He said that it was good and that was about the most praise that I'd ever gotten from him.

The nights were bitterly cold and with the moonlight on the snow looking sort of blue and the darkness of the shadows it sort of mesmerized me. I liked it out at night and after the chores were done I often went out and looked at the stars and listened to the sounds of the night. Over across the valley to the south I heard the coyotes howling and further over by the meadow I heard another one howling back. To the east I heard an owl hooting as he looked for rabbits close to the pine grove where he lived. All of this gave me a feeling that I cannot explain. All that I knew was that I loved this place with all my being.

The cold got to me and I went into the cabin where Ma and Pa were sitting and talking. It was warm and cozy and it gave me a good feeling. Ma made me a cup of cocoa and Pa a cup of tea. I sat on the floor by the stove and drank my cocoa and old Tim came and lay down beside me and I pet him. He purred like a truck and I leaned back against the wall and closed my eyes. If there were a picture for 'content' in the dictionary this would be it. I didn't know how life could get any better. As I said my prayers I thanked Jesus for this wonderful place and these times that seemed so perfect to me.

I thought about the bike that I wanted so badly and how hard it was to make enough money to buy it. I thought about my venture with the tame rabbits that was supposed to make me a lot of money and smiled to myself.

A fellow in Pouce once told me that there was good money in raising tame rabbits and selling the skins. He said that a pair of rabbits would have about forty little ones in a year and that the skins were worth nearly a dollar each.

He offered to sell me a pair for two dollars and I would be in business. I had a hard time scraping up the two dollars but I did and he gave me two nice rabbits. I took the old box that Pa made to catch rabbits and remodeled it. I put a divider in it so they would have a place in the back to sleep and I took one end out and put some chicken wire on it. All in all it was a pretty good-looking pen. I put them in it with a dish of water and some lettuce and alfalfa leaves that I got from the bottom of the haystack.

After a few months with no baby rabbits I discovered that Adam and Eve were really Adam and Steve and that they would never have any baby rabbits. This made me feel pretty foolish but no matter how many times that I checked them out I could never figure out how to tell which sex they were. Just another venture that didn't work out. Maybe I'd get a couple female rabbits next spring and see how it worked out.

On Sunday morning I woke up to the sound of Pa making the fire in the cook stove. I hurried out of bed to help him milk the cows and when we came in Ma had breakfast on the table. Breakfast was so good, oatmeal porridge with brown sugar and pancakes with Rogers golden syrup. There was bacon and some little fried deer steaks to go with the pancakes. What more could you want?

After breakfast I took the stock to the lake for a drink and on the way back I checked my trap. I didn't think that I'd have caught anything in one night but I wanted to look anyhow. As I came in sight of my snare I couldn't believe my eyes. I had caught the most beautiful cross fox that I had ever seen. I had to hurry to catch up with the cattle so that they didn't get in the hay. I could hardly wait to get them home so that I could come back and get my fox.

As soon as I got the horses in the barn and the cattle in the corral I ran to the cabin and told Pa. Pa said that he'd come with me and he put on his coat and boots. We hurried up the trail and I showed him where the fox was. It was not quite dead and he hit it on the head with a stick. Pa took it from the snare and we headed for home. Pa said that I had really caught a dandy this time. I asked him how much it was worth and he told me that it should bring thirty to forty dollars. That was plenty to buy my bike. I was overjoyed.

We got home and Pa skinned the fox and put the skin on a stretcher to dry. I looked in the Eaton's catalog at the bikes and the one that I wanted was a red C.C.M. There were lots of accessories that you could get and already I was dreaming about tire kits and pumps and if you had enough money you could get a Sturmey Archer three speed rear wheel complete with gearshift and everything.

It took a few days for the skin to dry out and when it did Pa turned it fur side out and brushed it until it shone. He told me that next Saturday he had to go to Pouce and that I could go with him and we would sell our fur to Mitchell's. Mitchell's had a store and they also bought fur and Pa said that they pay quite well. It seemed like Saturday would never come but it finally did and after the chores were finished, Pa and I headed to Pouce.

We stopped in Tupper to get some gas and while we were in the store I saw a new gun up on the rack. I asked Mr. Shaftner if I could look at it and he handed it over the counter to me. It was a beautiful single shot Winchester. The stock was a rich walnut color and the barrel was a deep, deep blue. It had to be the nicest little twenty-two rifle that I had ever seen. Mr. Shaftner asked me if I liked it and I told him that I really did. He said that it was nine dollars and that he would like for me to have it. I told him that I would like that too only I didn't have nine dollars.

All the way to Pouce I kept thinking that maybe I'd get enough money for my fox to buy a bike and the gun. I asked Pa if he liked the little rifle and he said that it was all right. He didn't seem to be as excited about it as I was. We got to Pouce and Pa parked by Mitchell's store. He told me that he'd do the talking and to keep my mouth shut. When Pa tells me something like that, I know that I had better listen or there'd be hell to pay.

We went into the store and Pa showed the fox to Mr. Mitchell. He looked it over and said that it was one of the nicest furs that he had seen and that he'd pay thirty-five dollars for it. I could hardly contain myself but I managed to keep quiet. He paid Pa the money and we went back to the truck. As soon as we got in the truck I expected Pa to give me the money but he didn't and I knew better than to ask for it. I decided I'd just have to be patient.

Pa drove around town and picked up a few supplies that he needed and then he drove over to the liquor store and went in. He was in there for quite a while and when he came out he had a bag full of bottles. He drove by the butcher shop and went in for a minute and then he drove over to the grain elevator. He told me to stay in the truck and that he wouldn't be long. I knew about this deal and I hated it because I knew that he'd be in there for a long time and that I was going to nearly freeze to death.

In a little while the butcher came walking over and went into the elevator office. It was already starting to get cold in the truck and I thought about the nice coal heater that was keeping the office toasty warm. I pounded my hands together and pounded my feet on the floor trying to keep warm. It was dark by the time that Pa came out and got into the truck. I could tell by the way he walked that he had more to drink than he needed.

Pa got the truck running and we started off for home. After a little while some heat started to come from the heater and I held my hands close to warm up. Pa didn't say much and after a little while I mustered up enough guts to ask him if I could have my money. He said some swear words and reached into his coat pocket and pulled out some money and threw it on the seat. Some of it fell on the floor and I hurried to pick it up in the dark.

There were only a few bills and after I found them all I tried to see by the lights in the dash how much there was. I counted it twice and there was only nine dollars. I didn't say anything but I knew where the rest of it went. I felt really crestfallen. My bike was down the drain and my chances of ever catching another fox like that were next to nil. Well, maybe I still could buy that nice little gun at the store in Tupper. At that point Pa was not my most favorite person.

The store in Tupper stayed open late and it was nearly nine o'clock when we stopped in to see if there was any mail. While Pa was getting the mail I went over to where the little gun had been that morning. It wasn't there anymore. I asked the storekeeper about it and he told me that he sold it that afternoon. Then I really felt down, I lost my bike and my gun before I even got them.

We got in the truck and went home. We got stuck halfway up the big hill and Pa told me to go home and get the horse to pull him the rest of the way up. I ran the half-mile home and stopped at the cabin for a minute to tell Ma what was going on. She had been worried sick that we were so late but I told her that everything was fine and I had to hurry with old Brian.

Ma lit the lantern and I hurried to the barn and struggled to put the harness on the horse. It was heavy and it was a good thing that Brian was gentle because I had to take him next to where the harness was hanging and get on his back and pull the harness from the peg and onto him. He stood still while I crawled around and got it in place and buckled it up. The collar was heavy and I had to buckle it up and then get him to put his head through it. He did and I finally got the harness on him and rode him to where Pa was waiting.

Pa had already put the chain on the truck and I handed him the single tree that I'd been carrying. I grabbed hold of the halter shank and we started up the hill. I hated this so badly. The horse was running and the truck was roaring close behind and I was having a hard time avoiding falling down as I ran beside the horse. If I fell down I knew for sure that I'd get run over. I wanted to ride the horse when we did this but for some reason Pa wouldn't let me.

We got to the top of the hill and unhooked the horse from the truck. Pa went home and I tried to climb up on Brian's back but my hands were so cold that I couldn't hang on to the harness to climb up. I got about halfway up and he decided to go home. I hung on as long as I could and fell off in the snow.

I called him a few choice words but he just kept on going. I ran home and found him eating hay from the haystack. I put him in the barn and went into the cabin.

Ma had supper on the table and I could tell that she was not too pleased with Pa. I didn't mention a thing about him spending my fox money on booze. She was mad enough at him as it was. I asked her about the chores and she said that she took the stock to the lake for water and all the chores were done except the milking.

After some supper and getting warmed up Pa and I went out and milked the cows. It was really late and they were in agony waiting to be milked. We took the milk in and separated it and I took the skim milk out and fed the calves. They were hungry and nearly knocked the pail from my hands. I gave some milk to Pug and he walked around with his tail straight up like he was important or something.

Eagle, our old white horse was not doing too well. His teeth were worn out and he had trouble eating. I scraped up the alfalfa leaves from the bottom of the haystack and gave it to him. He seemed to be able to gum that down. I got a pail of warm water from the cabin for him and he seemed to enjoy that too. That should warm him up. By the time I went in Pa had gone to bed and Ma was sitting in her rocker by the stove.

Pa was snoring in the bedroom and I sat by the fire to warm up. Ma made me a cup of cocoa and asked me how much I got for the fox. I didn't want to tell her because she would want to know where it was. I told her that I didn't think that Pa got too much for it and I took the nine dollars out of my pocket and put it on the table. "Is that all that you got?" she asked me. I nodded and she shook her head.

"It's ok Ma, don't say anything to Pa about it, it'll just make him mad."

She smiled and put her hand on mine, "It's time to go to bed son," and we did. It had been a long day.

I knelt by my bed and said my prayers but I had trouble saying anything extra to Jesus. I just felt down and thought that trying to do things was useless. I crawled into bed and lay there feeling dejected when old Tim came and lay down by my side and started to purr. Somehow that made me feel a lot better. I smiled to myself as I remembered how I used to talk to him and tell him all of my problems. He is a great old cat and I love him.

I thought about the bike on page 297 of the Eaton's catalog. I visualized myself riding that maroon bike they called the Rambler. It had wide handlebars and chrome wheels. I could just see it, rolling silently along the road. There was a headlight that you could get for it and if you had enough money, there was even a three speed Sturmey Archer rear wheel, complete with a gearshift that mounted on the bar. I went to sleep wondering if I would ever have enough money to buy one.

Chapter 33
Heartbreak

It was nearly Christmas and we had already had our concert at the school and were on holidays until after New Years. Ma and Pa said that we had to go to town early the next day to take care of some things. I told them that I didn't want to go and that I'd stay home and saw some wood and do the chores. Ma said that they might be late and maybe I should come with them. I really didn't want to go and I told them so. They agreed for me to stay home.

Morning came and as soon as the milking was finished they got ready to go to town. It was cold and hard to get the old truck running. Pa drained the radiator the night before and heated the antifreeze up on the stove. When he poured it in the engine warmed up and he managed to get it started. Ma told me to be careful and Pa told me to be sure and listen for him blowing the horn if they couldn't get up the hill and to come with the horse.

After they went I banked up the fire and took the cows and horses to the lake for their drink. I watched for more fox tracks but there didn't seem to be any new ones. Maybe that was the only fox around. I got the stock back to the barn and put them in and gave them some feed. I was cold so I went to the cabin and put more wood in the stove. As soon as I warmed up I took some warm water to old Ranger and gave him the left over porridge and pancakes. He barked and wagged his tail and nearly knocked me down. I gave him his feed and as he ate I pet him. He was a good dog and I felt sorry that he had to be tied up.

By the time I got the pigs and chickens fed it was time for lunch. There were some deer steaks cut in the icehouse and I got one to fry for my lunch.

The steaks were frozen so I brought in enough for supper as well. I put my frozen steak in the frying pan and let it cook for a while. I filled the kettle and moved it up on the stove to make some tea. Ma said that cooking frozen steaks made it tough but I didn't care, they tasted good anyway. When my steak was almost ready I put a couple of slices of bread on the stove and made some toast.

As I ate my lunch, I listened to the radio and shared my steak with Tim. He loves steak as much as I do and he let me know it. With everyone gone I sat back and drank my tea and had a smoke. I put some of Pa's tobacco in my pipe and enjoyed myself. I couldn't help but think how good life could be. I nearly fell asleep thinking about when I get a little bigger. I daydreamed about building myself a cabin down by the spring below the hill. I thought about how I'd take Tim with me, and maybe even Ranger. They would be good company for me.

When I finished my daydreaming session, I cleaned up my dishes and went out and sawed some wood. I wanted to get a little supply ahead so when we came home late or something, there would be some cut. I sawed wood until it started to get dusk and then it was time to take the stock to the lake again. It was dark by the time we got back and I got them in the barn and fed. I fed the pigs and chickens and gave Ranger some supper.

I filled the gas lamp and got it lit and stoked up the fire. I went to the barn and put the harness on Brian because I just knew that Pa would need a pull up the hill again. I listened for Ranger to bark so that I would know when to go give Pa a pull. I knew they would be home soon so I started supper because I knew that Ma would be tired and would probably have a headache. I peeled some potatoes and carrots and put them on to cook. The deer steaks were thawed out and I rolled them in flour and put them in the pan on the back of the stove so they would cook slowly.

Supper was cooked and they still weren't home. I was beginning to worry about them when I heard Ranger barking. I hurried outside and listened and I heard Pa blow the horn. I hurried to get my clothes on and get Brian from the barn and with the singletree in my hand we headed off for the hill. Pa nearly made it to the top of the hill before he spun out. I gave him a little pull and we were to the top. As we unhooked the chain, I told Ma that supper was cooked and in the warming oven and she seemed glad. They went home and Brian and I followed along behind. They went inside when we got home and I put the horse in the barn and went in for supper.

As we had our supper, they told me that they had sold all the stock and that we were moving to Tupper and I would go to school there. I couldn't believe what I was hearing. Pa told me that they had sold the cows and pigs to a buyer named Miller Patterson. He said that the horses would go out to the bush where the sawmill was and that he would be going there as well.

I just could not comprehend what they were telling me. What about old Eagle? He was too old to work anymore. Pa said that we'd have to put him down. How about Ranger? He would have to be put down as well. Why were they doing this, I wanted to know? Ma said that Pa was sick with stomach trouble and would have to go to Edmonton in the spring and that the work here was just too much for him. I told them that I could do it but they said that I was too little and too young.

Pa and I went and milked the cows and as I milked I thought how this would soon be the last time that I would ever milk these cows or be in this little barn. I got some alfalfa leaves for old Eagle and a pail of water and the tears flowed freely as I knew that Pa had to shoot him in the next day or so. Why were they doing this, why were they messing up our lives so badly?

Pa told me that the trucks would come to pick up the cows two days after Christmas. He said that he had sold the pigs and chickens to a farmer at Tomslake and that we had to load them in the truck so that he could deliver them. He told me that after we got them loaded tomorrow that I had to go over the trap line and pick up all the traps.

I had a hard time saying my prayers. Somehow it seemed like God had abandoned me. How could he let a thing like this happen? I lay in bed and tried to sleep but thoughts kept running through my head and the luxury of sleep had a hard time coming. The lump in my throat had been there ever since they came home and told me the news. My throat was so sore I could hardly swallow. Sleep finally came and all the dreams were bad.

I awoke to the familiar sound of Pa lighting the fire and I got up to go help with the chores. Pa talked a bit but I had nothing to say back. It was only two days until Christmas and Pa said that he had to haul the pigs today. I took the cattle to the lake and when I got back Pa had the truck backed up to the pigpen and he and Ma were loading the pigs. I put the stock in the barn and went to help them.

Pa had knocked my two rabbits on the head and put their pen in the truck for the chickens. I was nearly sick as I helped load our friendly old hens in the truck. Pa said that I had better skin those rabbits before they freeze. He left with the animals and I skinned the rabbits and stretched the skins. I felt sick to my stomach. I felt like I might not survive this ordeal.

Ma and I had lunch and I drank some tea but I didn't feel like eating. Ma tried to explain to me why we had to do this. I knew that Pa had been sick with his stomach for a long time but I didn't know that it was getting worse. I tried to tell her how I felt but I got all choked up and couldn't say anything. I tried not to cry because Pa said that only sucks cry.

Lunch is over and I take the rifle and put on the snowshoes and go to pick up the traps. There are not many animals in the traps, a couple weasels is all. I trip the traps and unhook them from their anchors. I put them over my shoulder and go on to the next set. It is a strange day, dull and quiet, the ravens and whisky jacks aren't even squawking. It is like the whole of nature is depressed.

I sit on a log and look into the snow-covered valley below. It is so beautiful to me. That's where I had planned to build my cabin some day. As I look around I see all the things that are so important to me and I wonder if anyone knows how I feel about this place.

It's getting dark and I come to my senses and realize that I had better get home and do the chores and water the stock. Pa will probably be stuck on the hill again and he'll be real mad if I'm not there to give him a pull. I hurry home and Ma is upset that I have been so long. She was worried that something must have happened to me. I take the cows for water and hope that Pa doesn't come home until I get back.

I'm lucky and I get back and get the harness on Brian before I hear the horn blowing. I wish that he could get up that hill without a pull. As we have our supper I ask Pa how those other trucks will get up the hill. Alf and Uncle Fred are coming to get the horses and we won't have anything to pull them with. Pa says that if we're lucky and it doesn't snow that we will get a truckload of sawdust from the old sawmill site and put it on the wheel tracks so that they won't spin out.

Christmas day comes and goes just like any other day. I'm not even interested in it. Ma gives me a set comprising of a necktie and a matching handkerchief. It's nice but I have a hard time to show any enthusiasm about it. We don't have a tree this year. Ma asked me if I wanted to cut one but somehow it didn't seem to matter. Ma cooks up a nice chicken that she saved for the day along with all the other good things that she can cook, but I don't feel like eating.

The day after Christmas, Francis brings Uncle Fred and Alf so that they can take the team and sleigh back to camp. It's nice to see them again as it's been a couple months since they have been here. They take the wheels off the wagon and put it in the sleigh box and take it as well. They don't stay long as it's a long trip to camp with the horses. Uncle and Alf leave and Francis stays a little longer and visits. Pa asks him how things are going and tells him that he will be there with them as soon as he can.

As soon as they are gone, Pa and I go and get that load of sawdust and put it on the hill. Pa turns the truck around by the school and we go up the hill like there is nothing to it. That sawdust works really well. Pa says that as long as it doesn't snow and cover it up it will be fine. It's getting quite late when we're finished and its time to take the cows to the lake again. As I walk along behind them, I think about how tomorrow morning will be the last time that I will do this. I think about how they walk along, not having any idea what tomorrow will bring.

As I wait for the cows to take their turn drinking, I hear a rifle shot. It sounds like it came from home. My heart sinks as I wonder what old friend of mine has left this world. I get back with the cows and put them in the barn. It's nearly dark when I give them some hay. Old Eagle is still in the barn so I think that it must be Ranger that got shot. I don't want to know but I have to.

I walk slowly in the growing darkness over to where Ranger is tied. As I get close enough I can see his lifeless body lying in the snow. There is a rush of tears as I can see where he was coming to meet Pa when the bullet hit him. I bend down and hug his still warm body, somehow hoping that he would lift his head and look at me one more time. He doesn't, he is dead. I wipe my eyes and walk slowly to the cabin, knowing that I'll never play with my buddy anymore.

I eat very little supper and Pa and I go out and milk the cows. We go in and separate the milk and I go and lie on my bed. I think about all that's been happening in the last two weeks. I wonder what it will be like living in Tupper in the little house that Pa has rented for Ma and me. I wonder what the new school and the kids will be like. I sort of doze off when Ma comes in and says that it's time to say the rosary and go to bed. I kneel by the chair in the kitchen and as Ma leads the rosary, Pa and I answer. I have a hard time concentrating and find myself mumbling something that even I don't know what it is. When the rosary is finished I go to bed and sleep finally takes me from my misery.

Pa is up early and I get up as soon as I hear him stirring. We get the cows milked and I take them to the lake for the last time. I'm not back from the lake for very long when I hear the trucks coming. Pa shows them where to back up to the manure pile and one by one they load the cows in the trucks. I watch as they load old Snow, she was our first cow and she has been a great old cow. She has had many calves and has always been so gentle. I wonder what will happen to her now.

It doesn't take very long until the cows are all loaded and a big man gives Pa some money and they leave. The only animal left is Eagle. Ma has some lunch ready when we go in. I eat a little and Ma asks me if I'm feeling all right. I tell her that I'll be fine. I don't even know myself how I feel. I guess that I feel tired and kind of numb. Pa sits back and has a cigarette and another cup of tea. He is quiet and his face looks drawn.

Pa's cigarette is finished and he gets up and puts on his coat and boots. He takes the rifle and without a word he goes out the door. I get ready and follow him out. Ma tells me not to go but I have to. Pa goes to the barn and unties Eagles halter shank and leads him out the door and down the trail that goes to the lake. He gives me a look and tells me to stay home. I can't do that.

I walk along behind and he leads the old horse slowly down the trail for a long ways. Finally he stops and ties the rope to a big poplar tree. Eagle stands there and looks at Pa like he is wondering what he did that for. Pa steps back a few steps and he raises the rifle to his shoulder. I can't be quiet any longer. "How in hell can you do this, Pa?" He lowers the rifle and turns to me with a look that I will never forget. There are tears running down his cheeks,

"Do you think that I want to do this? It's one of those things that have to be done and I'm the only one to do it. You'll find that there are lots of things that you have to do that you don't want to before you're finished."

Now I feel twice as bad as I watch Pa raise the rifle again. The sound of the shot seems to deafen me and I watch old Eagle fall straight down. There's a little round red spot in his forehead. All of this seems like it's in slow motion. Pa lowers the rifle and turns slowly and walks towards home. This time I feel sorry for Pa, maybe I understand him just a little better than I have before.

Life will never be the same for me again. I've grown up a lot in the last few days and I feel like my way of looking at things has hardened. The tenderness and innocence that comes with childhood is gone. The tears are all dried up but the lump in my throat is so big that I can hardly swallow.

I look at Pa as we walk back home. He seems to look a lot older than he did a few days ago. I reflect on the words that he told me and I wonder if I would be able to do what he has had to do. I'm not mad at him anymore but instead I feel sorry for him. I know now that this is just as hard for him as it has been for me. It doesn't make it any easier, but somehow it helps.

Ma has been packing our few belongings and the next day we load them on the truck and her and Pa take it to town and put it in the new place. Tomorrow we will take the rest and it will be all over. Ma asks if I'm going and I tell her no, I have a few things to do. She must understand because she lets it go at that. I watch as they get in the truck and leave.

After they are out of sight I put on the snowshoes and go to look one last time at all the places that I love. I want to imprint them in my memory forever. I snowshoe to the top of the hill where the garden used to be. I look down in the valley and record the view in my mind. I follow the edge of the hill and go down to where the little bridge crosses the creek.

I keep going until I come to the old cabin where I was born. I take off my snowshoes and go inside for a last look. I can barely remember living here but I remember the warm glow of the lamp and Helen doing homework at the table. I come back to the present and with one last look, I go out and put the snowshoes back on. I have to hurry as it's getting late.

When I get to the trail where Pa and I hauled hay, I take the snowshoes off. I walk along with my thoughts as dusk begins to settle in. As I come to the road to the lake I go the little ways for one last look at the old horse. I wonder why I punish myself like this. I get to the spot, somehow hoping that this is all a bad dream. It's not, he is still lying there, only now his eyes are frozen white and seem to be staring, unseeing, into space. I take one long last look at him and then walk slowly home.

Ma and Pa are there when I arrive and Ma asks me where I've been. I tell her that I was just having a last look around. She seems to understand. I ask Pa what we will do with Pug, our old barn cat. He says that we will just leave him here. He's not a house cat and likes to be alone, he's a good hunter and there are hundreds of mice so he will be fine. I feel glad about that, I didn't want him to be shot like Ranger and Eagle.

I go to bed early and look around the room for the last time. Tonight will be the last time that I will ever sleep in this little cabin. I look at the wall by the bed and for the first time I see little birds eyes in the shiny wood where the blankets have polished it over the years. Tim comes and lies beside me and I hug him. At least he is coming with us. Ma and Pa are in the kitchen, talking and I can hear the Andrew sisters singing 'Don't sit under the apple tree' on the radio.

I think about Ranger and Eagle and how quickly that life can be snuffed out. I realize for the first time how precious and fragile life is. I wonder why people are so careless with it. Maybe they just haven't seen anything to make them even think about it. I doze off and Ma wakes me to say the rosary and go to bed. I go to sleep wondering what my new life will be like.

Ma and Pa are up early and Pa makes just enough fire for Ma to make breakfast. As soon as we have eaten we start to get things ready to go. I empty the ashes out of the stove and Pa and I take down the pipes. The stove is still warm and it's all that we can do to lift it on the truck. We get all loaded and look around the cabin one last time. Pa goes to the truck and gets a bag and a hammer. He takes a hasp from the bag and fastens it to the door and puts a new padlock on it. I wonder why he is doing that. All the years we have lived here there has never been a lock on the door.

We get into the cab and I sit between Ma and Pa. A wave of sadness sweeps over me as Pa drives away for the last time. Memories seem to race though my mind. I wonder if this is what it's like when you drown. As we come to the corner to make the last turn from the place, I look out Pa's window and for a moment I can see the little cabin in the pines in the rearview mirror. And then it's gone forever.